# Making Abortion Rare

## A Healing Strategy for a Divided Nation

David C. Reardon, Ph.D.

Acorn Books
*Springfield, Illinois*

*Dedicated To Kim,*
*Because I can never fully express in words how much I love*
*and appreciate you, please accept this dedication of my work.*

Printed in Canada. Published by Acorn Books, P.O. Box 7348, Springfield, IL 62791-7348.

Although the authors and publishers have exhaustively researched all sources to ensure the accuracy and completeness of the information contained in this book, we assume no responsibility for errors, inaccuracies, omissions or any other inconsistency herein. Any slights against people or organizations are unintentional. Readers should consult with an attorney for specific information regarding their rights under the applicable law for injuries which may have resulted from induced abortion. The author and publisher shall have neither liability nor responsibility to any person or entity with respect to loss or damage caused, or alleged to be caused, directly or indirectly by the information contained in this book.

Portions of this book have been adapted from these previous works by the author:

David C. Reardon, *Abortion Malpractice* (Denton, TX: Life Dynamics, Inc., 1993).

"Identifying High Risk Abortion Patients" *The Post-Abortion Review* 1(3):3-6 (1994).

"Politically Correct vs. Politically Smart: Why Politicians Should Be Both Pro-Woman and Pro-Life" *The Post Abortion Review* 2(3):1-3 (1994).

"A Healing Strategy" *The Post-Abortion Review* 3(1):1-4 (1995).

"Despair Versus Hope" *The Post-Abortion Review* 3(2):1-2 (1995).

**Cataloging-in-Publication Data**
Reardon, David C., Ph.D.
    Making abortion rare: a healing strategy for a divided nation / David C. Reardon
    p. cm.
    Bibliography: (p. )
    Includes bibliographical references and index.
    ISBN 0-9648957-6-5 (paper)   ISBN 0-9648957-7-3 (cloth)
    1. Abortion—United States.
    2. Abortion—Law and legislation—United States.
    3. Abortion—Political aspects—United States.
    4. Abortion—United States—Psychological aspects.
    5. Abortion—Moral and ethical aspects.
    6. Abortion—United States—Handbooks, manuals, etc.
    7. Pro-life movement—United States—Handbooks, manuals, etc.
    I. Title.
    HQ767.5   1996              363.4'6            95-81057
                                                   CIP

*Attention Non-Profit Organizations, Colleges, Universities, and Professional Organizations:*
Quantity discounts are available on bulk purchases of this book for educational training, fund raising, or gift giving. Special books, booklets, or book excerpts can also be prepared to fit your specific needs. For information contact: Marketing Department, Acorn Books, PO Box 7348, Springfield, IL 62791-7348.

# CONTENTS

# ACKNOWLEDGMENTS

It is always a challenge to acknowledge all the people who have directly or indirectly contributed to one's work. This is especially true in this case, where countless people have gone before me. Their ideas and insights have given me knowledge, shaped my vision, and encouraged me to more fully articulate this pro-life strategy. Indeed, I must confess that much of what I present here is little more than the result of fourteen years of scavenging the best insights of others, including those whose names I never learned or have long forgotten. A few I have met in person; many more I have met only in their printed word.

There have been many pioneers in the area of post-abortion litigation. As far as I have been able to determine, Feminists for Life were the first to propose the idea of legislation to expand the rights to redress for women injured by abortion. Two organizations, Charlie Wysong's American Rights Coalition and Mike and Vickey Conroy's Legal Action for Women, pioneered the effort to inform women of their right to sue abortionists under existing malpractice statutes. Through their efforts, many injured women who would have "fallen through the cracks" have found the help they have needed not only to win compensation for their injuries but also to find emotional and spiritual healing.

Since 1987, I had been urging national pro-life leaders to sponsor a conference where post-abortion researchers could educate attorneys about findings which would contribute to more successful outcomes in abortion malpractice cases. I was convinced that many injured women were being denied the right to recover because most attorneys simply didn't understand post-abortion issues. In 1993, Mark Crutcher, founder of Life Dynamics, arrived at a similar conclusion and commissioned me to write *Abortion Malpractice* specifically for personal injury attorneys. That book, which had been rumbling around in my head for five years, suddenly had a market and was completed in three months. Life Dynamics mailed it, together with other materials promoting abortion malpractice as the "most lucrative field of personal injury in the 1990's," to 4,000 personal injury attorneys. In 1994, Life Dynamics continued on this course and sponsored a three-day conference on abortion malpractice for attorneys. It was sold out. At that conference, post-abortion researchers, including myself, experienced malpractice litigators, and a former abortion provider had the opportunity to educate over a hundred attorneys on abortion malpractice issues. The enthusiastic response of these attorneys encouraged me to bring these issues to the attention of the broader pro-life audience.

In the area of post-abortion research, I am especially thankful to Thomas Strahan, Dr. Vincent Rue, Dr. Wanda Franz, and Dr. Philip Ney. Together they have helped to encourage and direct my efforts, especially in those times of self-doubt when it seemed that the more we tried to do, the less anyone cared. I hope that I have been able to do the same for them.

In the area of post-abortion healing, the pioneers are even more numerous. I should begin by acknowledging that Nancyjo Mann, who founded WEBA, first prompted my interest in this area. Others who have led the drive to promote post-abortion healing, and who have shaped my vision of how post-abortion healing must occur *before* we will bring an end to this present holocaust, are: Vickie Thorn, Nola Jones-Noboa, Ken Freeman, Karen Crabtree, Patty and Jim Goodoien, Kathy Kelly, and Olivia Gans.

With regard to the technical production of this book, I want to thank Anita Kuhn, Nancy Hanlon, Jean Elmore, and C.J. Petlick who have all helped make this a readable and attractive book.

Finally, nothing I have done would have been possible without my wife, Kim. She has sacrificed the conveniences and pleasures of a "normal" life so that I might pursue our "cause." In this she has had faith both in God and in me, often when the latter has not deserved it. I dedicate this book to her as a permanent testimony of how deeply grateful I am for all that she has given me and our children. If this work accomplishes any good, it must be credited to Kim, who made the first and greatest investment in its completion.

# INTRODUCTION

I never intended to write this book. For the last twelve years, my goal has been to educate the general public about how women are seriously injured and exploited by abortion. I have discovered, however, that I am instead spending most of my time trying to explain to pro-life activists exactly *why* post-abortion issues are so important. Indeed, it is my claim that post-abortion issues are *the key* to converting hearts—*the key* to winning the battle for life.

It is my belief that every aspect of the pro-life movement will be transformed and energized by a better understanding of post-abortion issues. Everyone who works for the pro-life cause—crisis pregnancy counselors, public relations directors, fund raisers, political activists, direct action activists, pro-life politicians, doctors, lawyers, and lobbyists, and, most of all, pastors and other religious leaders—can and should use this knowledge every day in order to be more effective. And not least of all, grassroots supporters must understand post-abortion issues because they are the ones who will most directly display to friends, relatives, and fellow workers the compassion which opens minds, converts hearts, fosters healing, and ultimately, saves both lives and souls.

To many, this claim that post-abortion issues must become the centerpoint of the pro-life movement will appear quite radical. But it is not my belief alone. Many of the people with whom I have worked in post-abortion ministry have expressed the same view. We also agree that while post-abortion issues have become increasingly important to the pro-life movement during the last ten years, they are still misunderstood and treated like a distant relative of the "main" pro-life cause. They have yet to become as central to the pro-life strategy as they must be if we are ever to become a pro-life society.

So it is that I have finally realized that for the last twelve years I have been placing the cart before the horse. Before I spend any more time trying to awaken the public to a truth it doesn't know, I must first convince pro-lifers about the *pivotal importance* of a truth they already know: abortion hurts women.

The attainment of every pro-life goal hinges on this truth. If we ignore it, we are faced with an uphill battle against the cultural currents of our society and our goal of protecting the unborn will never be achieved. On the other hand, if we use this truth as the pivot point for all of our other arguments, the currents of our society will automatically work to our advantage. We will be engaged in a downhill effort, where the dynamics of human nature and these same cultural trends which now block our efforts will supply the irresistible gravity that assures us of reaching our goal with only a modest effort.

This book is not about fighting harder in defense of human life; it is about fighting smarter. It is about removing the plank from our own eyes before we tend to the wounded eyesight of our neighbors. This book is about fundamentally redefining the abortion debate, redrawing the lines of battle to reemphasize our commitment to being *both* pro-woman and pro-life. Most of all, it is about developing a comprehensive strategy which integrates post-abortion issues into political campaigns, legislative initiatives, litigation efforts, public relations efforts, and Christian ministry. This holistic approach creates a powerful synergy in which each field of activity adds impetus to the whole, effectively multiplying our resources rather than consuming them. In this approach, all things work together for the defense of human dignity and for the glory of God.

By now many readers are prepared to accuse me of shameless exaggeration. But I beg you to give me the benefit of the doubt and the chance to show you how all that I have claimed here is true. Indeed, I beg leave to claim even more: the downfall of the abortion industry has already begun. By God's providence, everything described herein has already commenced, but how soon the process is completed depends on how quickly we pro-lifers accept our duty to reshape not only the hearts of others, but our own hearts as well.

Is this promise of a quick and easy victory just more hyperbole? No. Remember how Communist Russia and the Eastern Bloc disintegrated and fell apart with startling speed? The same thing is beginning to happen with the abortion industry. What is now a trickle will soon become a deluge. Soon the abortion industry will find that it can no longer hide the fact that the only way to kill an unborn child is by maiming and traumatizing the child's mother, not to mention the father, grandparents, siblings, and society as a whole.

Thousands of grieving mothers and fathers are already beginning to speak out and organize in revolt against their "benefactors." With the right kind of assistance, millions more will join them in expressing their outrage, demanding reform, and filing lawsuits. The dangers of abortion will become so well known that even if it remains legal, no physician will dare risk the liability of performing one. Abortionists will become uninsurable.

The end is certain. It won't be the moral arguments that topple the abortion industry; it will be women's rights. Ironic, isn't it? But this time it will be the *authentic* rights of women which transform our nation. Specifically, these include the right to know about abortion's risks, the right to be screened for predisposing risk factors, the right to be offered safer alternatives, and the right to sue abortionists and hurt the only thing they care about—their bank accounts.

This strategy is already moving forward. There are hundreds of individuals already working in this direction and achieving tremendous strides. But our ultimate success will come far sooner if the pro-life movement, in general, better understands the dynamics of the post-abortion movement and becomes more active in supporting it.

Abortion in the United States, and throughout the world, has been legalized because of two basic lies. The first lie is that abortion only destroys a "bunch of cells," not a human being, much less a baby. During the last two decades the pro-life movement has concentrated its efforts on dispelling this first lie. Millions of dollars have been spent on advertising campaigns, books, brochures, and films, such as the powerful *Silent Scream*, to educate the public about the humanity of the unborn child. The result is that nearly 80 percent of the public will now admit that abortion involves the destruction of a human life, even though many in this group still believe abortion should be legal. In fact, studies show that at least 70 percent of aborting women believe that what they are doing is morally wrong or, at least, "deviant" behavior. These women are seeking abortions not because they believe it is the right thing to do, but because, given the pressures they face, they feel it is the *only* thing they can do. Indeed, all the pro-abortion rhetoric about "freedom of choice" has actually only served to conceal the truth that most aborting women feel they have *no* choice. They are choosing abortion not in accordance with their own conscience, but *against* their own conscience.

Clearly, the vast majority of citizens understand that abortion involves the taking of a human life. So, in large part, abortion advocates have now abandoned the first lie in favor of a much repeated claim: "The needs and rights of a woman are more important than those of a fetus."

There is an important lesson we should learn from this. While efforts to educate the public about the unborn's humanity may help to motivate pro-lifers, such efforts will have no effect on those who support abortion. This ambivalent majority may admit that abortion is wrong, but they believe it must be tolerated as an "evil necessity"—with an emphasis on necessity. These people have hardened their hearts to the unborn "fetus." It may be human, they admit, but it is a less important human than the woman. End of argument. Nothing we can say on behalf of the unborn will sway them from this position. Their concern is focused totally on the woman. Therefore, the only way to reach them is for us, too, to focus on the woman. We must change the abortion debate so that we are arguing with our opponents on their own turf, on the issue of defending the interests of women.

To do this, we must begin to concentrate our efforts on exposing the second lie behind legal abortion. That lie, which is the key to legalized abortion, says, "Abortion is safe."

The truth is the exact opposite. Abortion is inherently unsafe. Well over a hundred significant physical and psychological complications have been linked to abortion. This list of complications is quite diverse. One cross-sectional sample would include increased rates of breast cancer, sterility, substance abuse, and sexual dysfunctions. An equally interesting cross-section, which parallels the first, would include increased rates of liver cancer, ectopic pregnancies, suicide attempts, and broken relationships. The psychological effects of abortion can be particularly devastating, literally crippling a woman's ability to function in normal relationships with family or friends, and even at work. The frequency and severity of abortion-related complications have led some critics of abortion, including myself, to conclude that the phrase "safe abortion" is an oxymoron.

Yet most people have little or no awareness of the pervasiveness of abortion-related complications. It is the widespread belief that "legal" means "safe" that is seducing the middle majority of Americans. Even though they are uncomfortable with the fact that unborn children are being killed, they tolerate abortion because they believe the lie that "at least women are being helped." But once this lie is exposed, the middle majority's thoughts will dramatically change. At that point the middle majority will begin to ask themselves: "If abortion is causing women so much suffering, what are we doing this for?!" It is then that their moral ambivalence about abortion will tip the scales against the abortion industry. It is then that we will be able to protect *both* women and their unborn children.

Because this book involves an intertwining of theoretical and practical issues, moral and strategic issues, and legal and medical issues, there is no perfect way in which this material can be organized. Thus, a subject touched upon in one chapter may reemerge as a major theme in a later chapter. At other times, I will appear to assume that the reader is already familiar with a topic which will not actually be discussed in depth until much later. In such cases, I trust that readers will read the subsequent chapters which clarify the point. To accommodate readers who like to skip about and browse, I have tried to make each chapter somewhat self-sufficient, although, in some cases, this results in a bit of redundancy. In fact, since many readers will already be familiar with some of the ground I am covering, I encourage skipping around, even over entire chapters. After all, my goal is not that you learn everything covered in this book, because it simply doesn't cover everything you need to know in this field. Instead, my goal is really to see you totally convinced of the unbeatable power of post-abortion issues in winning the abortion debate. It is that which will motivate you to learn more. Once you are convinced, this book will show you where to find the additional knowledge you need and how to put it to effective use.

To assist both browsers and linear readers in understanding my organization, the following is a brief outline of the chapters.

In Chapter One, I examine the moral appropriateness of the woman-centered pro-woman/pro-life strategy as compared to the traditional pro-life approach, which emphasizes the sacredness of human life. I attempt to show that the former approach is not only moral, but is morally demanded of us, a theme which is revisited in Chapters Ten through Twelve.

Chapter Two turns to the practical matter of assessing this strategy's likelihood of success in the square of public opinion. It includes a look at the attitudes of the middle majority of Americans, those who believe abortion is the killing of a human life yet favor keeping it legal. This examination is useful in explaining why post-abortion issues are *the key* to the hearts of this ambivalent majority.

Chapter Three continues with a look at the political aspects of this strategy. While most politicians avoid the abortion controversy for fear of alienating voters, candidates who adopt the pro-woman/pro-life stance are empowered with the key for aggressively building common ground with the ambivalent middle majority. Instead of fearing a negative reaction at the polls, these candidates can be assured of gaining the support of voters even in pro-choice districts. Best of all, this political strategy uses post-abortion issues to expose the anti-choice and anti-woman beliefs of pro-abortion candidates in a way which is sure to weaken their support among pro-choice voters.

After these preliminaries, we turn to the three major fronts of our pro-woman/pro-life strategy: legal issues, healing issues, and research and education issues. It is notable that each of these fronts is independently capable of bringing an end to abortion on demand, but together they are an unstoppable combination. Indeed, the latter two prongs of our attack, post-abortion healing and education, are the most important parts of our strategy, and they cannot be obstructed by politicians or the courts. But since it is the legal issues surrounding abortion which most dominate the public discussion, especially among pro-lifers, the strategic analysis will begin with these.

Chapter Four examines how the Supreme Court's decisions, beginning with *Roe v. Wade,* have actually shaped the law in a way which can be used to our advantage. Indeed, it is a splendid irony that the same *Roe* decision which spawned the modern abortion industry also provides the precedent for sustaining the pro-woman laws which will eventually smother it.

Chapters Five through Eight examine how to get maximum leverage out of the Supreme Court's pro-woman decisions. We will look at how the abortion industry routinely violates the rights of women and ignores the standards of medical practice required by the Supreme Court and the common standards of medicine. These are the issues for which abortionists can and should be held liable in civil suits, and here readers will discover how abortion is always bad medicine and therefore *always* provides a good opportunity for malpractice attorneys.

Chapter Nine describes important legislative initiatives which can facilitate the right of women to recover damages for abortion-related injuries. In addition to its practical impact, the process of passing this legislation will help to advance our goal of educating the public, the legislatures, and the courts.

The second major front of our strategy, and the most important, is the task of promoting post-abortion healing for the women, men, and families who have been traumatized by abortion. This aspect doesn't require changing laws so much as changing ourselves. Chapters Ten, Eleven, and Twelve explain why we must seek to create a society which is conducive to post-abortion healing and how we must expand our understanding of these issues in order to succeed at this task. These chapters underscore my firmly held belief that we have a moral obligation to promote post-abortion healing. Until we commit ourselves to it, we, the Church, will not have learned the lesson of compassion which we are meant to learn from this great holocaust.

The third front of our strategy is post-abortion research and education. By completing more research into post-abortion sequelae, we will increase the liability for performing dangerous abortions, and by making the public more aware of post-abortion injuries, we will advance all aspects of our strategy. Chapter Thirteen describes how research and public education initiatives relating to post-abortion issues can be most effectively coordinated and funded. Specific research concepts are outlined in Appendix D.

In Chapter Fourteen, we will look at why this three-pronged pro-woman/pro-life offensive is more dynamic and self-energizing than the traditional pro-life strategy. We will also defend our claim that this approach makes more efficient use of our resources.

In Chapter Fifteen, we will return to a discussion of the political aspects of our pro-woman/pro-life initiative in light of all the information covered since Chapter Three. Here, we will look especially at ways of translating the opinions of the middle majority into concrete gains for both women and the unborn.

Finally, in Chapter Sixteen, we will look at the critical role that post-abortion issues will continue to play even after *Roe* is over-turned and a Human Life Amendment is in place.

This book is not intended to document post-abortion injuries. As a companion to this book, readers should refer to my previous book, *Aborted Women, Silent No More*, which is a comprehensive treatment of the negative effects of abortion on women. Additional resources are listed at the end of that book.

It is also assumed that readers who are not familiar with post-abortion issues will at least accept as a premise that the physical, psychological, and spiritual consequences of abortion are serious and lasting for many, and probably most, of the women who undergo abortion. If this premise is true, then the strategy described herein cannot fail. If it is false, then the pro-abortionists will win the day. But I assure you, women are hurt by abortion, and in far greater numbers than most people can imagine.

A related assumption is that readers will understand the immense pressures which constrain the majority of women who seek abortion. For most women, abortion is a marginal choice. It is an ambivalent and irresolute choice initially made without an accurate understanding of risks and alternatives. Consider the following research findings: approximately 40 percent of women who experienced post-abortion problems were still hoping to discover some alternative to abortion when they went to the abortion clinic for counseling; over 80 percent say they would have carried to term under better circumstances or with the support of loved ones; between 30 and 60 percent of all women having abortions have a positive desire to carry the pregnancy to term and keep their babies; approximately 70 percent have a negative moral view of abortion and are choosing against their consciences because of outside pressures; over 75 percent would not have sought an illegal abortion—presumably out of a concern for safety; and over 60 percent report having felt "forced" to have the abortion by others or by circumstances.[1] This data, combined with over a thousand case study reports, demonstrates that the decision to abort is often tentative, or even undertaken solely to please others. Indeed, it is our belief that the majority of women seeking abortions, if guaranteed a free and informed choice, would decide that childbirth is clearly their healthiest choice.

These are important facts which must be incorporated into pro-life thinking. All too often, pro-lifers have tended to characterize aborting women as selfish and immoral. A far more accurate generalization would be to portray aborting women as confused and driven by despair. This insight is vital to our pro-woman/pro-life strategy.

I should also point out that in placing the emphasis on women in this book, it is not my intention to ignore the negative effects on men, siblings, and parents. By its very nature, abortion injures everyone it touches. Nonetheless, next to the unborn, abortion is probably most injurious to the women who actually experience this invasive violation of their persons. In addition, as a practical matter in our attempt to influence public opinion, we must remember that since abortion is seen as a "woman's issue," its impact on women has more political weight than its impact on men. Furthermore, because so many men see it as a "woman's issue," post-abortion healing for women is a prerequisite for increasing awareness of the need for post-abortion healing of other third parties, such as post-aborted fathers, siblings, and grandparents.

Another distinction which I believe should be made at the outset has to do with our specific goal. Pro-abortionists will attempt to criticize our pro-woman strategy as merely a smear campaign intended to frighten women away from "necessary" abortions and as an attempt to encourage "harassment" suits. We must not lend credence to this assertion by making the claim that our goal is to shut down the abortion industry. Instead, we must always emphasize that our goal is simply to help and protect women. We may *predict* that our efforts will lead to the demise of the abortion industry, but that is not our direct goal—it is merely a byproduct of our legitimate concern to protect women's rights. Indeed, it is our belief that if women's rights are truly respected, the abortion industry will shut down for lack of demand. Furthermore, if we are right in our belief that abortion is inherently dangerous, it will also be shut down for lack of physicians who are willing to hurt their patients, and thereby violate their Hippocratic oath to "first, do no harm."

Another way of describing our position is this: we believe that the only reason there are so many abortions is that abortion profiteers are exploiting women who either (1) are being denied the truth about risks and alternatives, or (2) are being coerced into unwanted abortions by other people. If we are wrong, then our pro-woman/pro-life initiative will have no effect on the abortion industry. If we are right, then it is the abortion industry's own medical incompetence which will lead to its demise.

Our immediate goal, then, is simply to ensure that whenever an abortion is performed, it is done as safely as possible and with proper respect for the freedom of women, a goal which everyone should be able to agree upon. While we *predict* that abortion will never be safe, and that therefore abortionists will always be faced with liability risks so great that abortion will become very rare, we are challenging pro-abortionists to prove us wrong by accepting proper liability for protecting the health of the women whom they claim to serve. Will they voluntarily accept this challenge? Not very likely. But in refusing proper liability for their mistakes, they will expose themselves as being more concerned about abortion industry profits than women's rights.

While this issue of proper legal liability for abortions will generate the most controversy, it is not the most important aspect of our proposal. Post-abortion healing and education are far more important to achieving our ultimate goal. This is because the political goal of making abortion illegal has always been a truncated vision. Our real desire has always been to create a culture where abortion is not just illegal, but is *unthinkable*. In such a culture, the physical, psychological, and spiritual dangers of abortion will be common knowledge. In such a culture, commitment, compassion, and a sense of duty to aid and protect both the mother and the child will be universal. In practice, this ambition may never be fully realized, but it is the one toward which we should always strive. It is toward that goal that this book is directed.

# CHAPTER ONE

# REMAINING TRUE TO OURSELVES

Aᴺʸ strategy proposed for the pro-life movement must first be subjected to a moral examination. Specifically, we must ask, can we pursue a pro-woman/pro-life strategy without compromising our moral opposition to abortion? Is it right to focus our efforts on the women, men, and siblings who are being *hurt* by abortion? Or do we have an obligation to focus on the fact that children are being *killed* by abortion?

While disputes about the moral fitness of the pro-woman/pro-life strategy have never been widely discussed in an open way, private concerns have resulted in several major setbacks for the post-abortion movement. This is because many pro-life leaders believe it is both strategically and morally wrong to concentrate the public's attention on anyone other than abortion's primary victim, the unborn child.

The most significant example of the damage which has been caused by this unresolved conflict occurred in 1989, when Surgeon General C. Everett Koop gave a letter to President Reagan stating that conclusive data on the health effects of abortion on women did not exist. In a subsequent interview, Koop criticized the efforts of pro-lifers who were working to increase public awareness of abortion complications for women, saying, "I think it is wrong for the pro-life forces to get all upset about the health effects of abortion on women and get away from the health effects of abortion on the fetus. This is the marker issue there … [A]s soon as you contaminate the morality of your stand by getting worried about the health effects of abortion on women, you have weakened the whole thing…."[1]

This moral view almost certainly played an important part in Koop's handling of the report which President Reagan requested of him in 1987. On at least two occasions Koop attempted to convince the President to withdraw his request. When his petitions were rejected, Koop assigned the task to an assistant, explaining that he wanted to "distance" himself from the report. He also gave his staff the "Catch-22" instruction that only "unassailable" data could be includ-

1

ed in the report. Because there are no studies above criticism, especially in the field of behavioral science, "unassailable" data simply
doesn't exist. Koop had found his way out.[2] In the end, the "report"
he delivered to President Reagan was not a report at all. It was merely a brief letter explaining that "scientific studies do not provide conclusive data about the health effects of abortion on women," a statement which was widely construed by the media as proving that
health risks don't exist.

Some critics of Koop believe he sidestepped his assignment
because he feared that a report emphasizing abortion's risks would
result in vicious attacks from the pro-choice media and Congress.
Others have claimed that he had developed "Hollywood eyes," a
yearning for popularity, after being lifted up to national prominence
by the liberal media because of his promotion of "safe sex" in
response to the AIDS crisis. Koop's repeated complaints that the
report was forcing him to walk "a political tightrope" suggest that
there is some truth to these claims. Still, Koop has a history of taking
unpopular stands. Courage is not his short-suit. This is why I believe
it was Koop's moral view that post-abortion issues "contaminate" the
pro-life cause which was the most significant factor in his decision to
drop the ball.

President Reagan had handed Koop the opportunity to focus
national attention on abortion's health risks. Koop was aware of very
specific and scientifically defensible conclusions which could have
been made and which would have dramatically affected the ground
rules of the public debate on abortion.* But Koop did not believe the
issues of the debate should be changed. Instead, he believed it was
fundamentally wrong to move away from abortion as a moral issue

---

*In interviews given after his letter to the President was released, Koop stated that the
existing evidence was sufficient to leave "no doubt in my mind" that there are serious
physical complications and "tremendous psychological problems" resulting from
abortion. (Ibid.) But he excluded this informed "private" conclusion from his letter
because the studies upon which it was based were open to criticism. Their statistics
could not be generalized to the whole population, and they did not completely cover
all the ramifications of the issue.

What could Dr. Koop have reported? While it is true that there wasn't, and still isn't,
any solid data for determining precisely how many women suffer from post-abortion
psychological sequelae, there are three specific findings which are universally accepted upon which to build valid conclusions and specific recommendations. The following is a summary of these points, which I personally communicated to Dr. Koop in a
letter dated July 1, 1988.

First, at least *some* women are psychologically disturbed by abortion. From clinical
evidence, it is clear that some suffer severe psychological maladjustments, while others

by allowing it to become a public health issue. A report which validated concerns about abortion's health risks for women, he believed, would undercut the moral high ground of opposing abortion simply because all human life is sacred.

Other avid pro-lifers share this view. Indeed, there are not a few who have very little sympathy for women who suffer post-abortion problems. Some have even expressed their disdain for women injured by abortion with comments such as, "They deserve what they get." Less punitive pro-lifers are simply idealists. They want to believe that somehow, with just a better education program or a more articulate argument, we will be able to awaken America to the moral superiority of our position. To advance this moral argument, evidence of fetal development is relevant but scarred uteruses are not.

These views have posed a major obstacle to the development and spread of post-abortion and pro-woman initiatives. Within the overall pro-life movement, post-abortion issues remain at best just an add-on—an extra argument, an extra service. They are still not generally accepted as being an essential ingredient in our efforts.

This kind of bias inhibits the efforts of post-abortion workers every day. In my own experience, the most recent example occurred when I submitted an article on post-abortion issues to a prominent religious magazine. This publication is zealously pro-life, and the submissions editor's initial response was filled with praise for my article's "thoughtful insights" and "well argued" points. But when the article subsequently went before the review board, it was rejected because the editorial board felt it could be construed as turning abortion into a "medical-legal issue, rather than a moral issue." And no, Koop was not on the board.

---

have more moderate or mild coping problems. In short-term follow-up studies (less than six months post-abortion), researchers typically report that 15 to 20 percent of the patients experienced significant psychological problems linked to the abortion experience. These findings are confounded by the fact that approximately 50 percent of women who initially agree to participate in follow-up studies subsequently refuse to do so. This high refusal rate may itself signify post-abortion avoidance behavior which may be indicative of other psychological sequelae.

Second, in women who do experience post-abortion psychological sequelae, there are at least 14 clearly defined characteristics, such as feelings of being coerced into the abortion or strong feelings of attachment to the unborn child, which are predictive of poor post-abortion adjustment. (See Appendix A)

Third, intake information at abortion clinics shows that 60 to 85 percent of abortion patients have one or more of these predisposing risk factors.

From these three facts, we can conclude not only that some unknown number of women experience psychological problems following abortion, but that the majority of

In short, many pro-life leaders, and certainly many more grass-roots activists, are far more comfortable with the familiar "defend the baby" arguments than with our new "defend the woman" arguments. One reason is that they do not fully understand the strategic importance of the pro-woman approach. The bulk of this book addresses this concern. A second reason arises from the feeling they have that the pro-woman approach involves a shift away from the moral center of our argument. It is this second concern which is addressed in this chapter. It is my goal here to show that the pro-woman approach is not only consistent with the pro-life moral imperative, it is, in fact, a fuller and more complete expression of it.

## THE NATURAL ORDER OF THINGS

We begin with a very simple observation. In God's ordering of creation, it is only the mother who can nurture her unborn child. All that the rest of us can do, then, is to nurture the mother. To help a child, we *must* help the child's mother.

There is nothing startling about this observation. Crisis pregnancy centers have known this truth, and have been living it out, for decades. But we must explore this insight a little deeper to understand all that it can teach us.

God has created a connection between a mother and her children that is so deeply personal and intimate that the welfare of each is dependent on the other. As every mother knows from personal experience, this interdependence is for both good and ill. When a mother's children are joyful, their joy lifts her heart. When they are troubled by sorrow, their sorrows weigh on her as well. This principle can

---

women are at risk. How many of these at-risk women actually suffer post-abortion problems is not known. But the evidence is clearly sufficient to suggest that abortion *may* pose a significant public health threat. Therefore, further research must be given a high priority. In the meantime, a national effort should be undertaken to: (1) help high-risk patients avoid abortion; (2) better inform and counsel patients prior to abortion; and (3) offer better care and understanding to women who are struggling with psychological problems after their abortions.

Dr. Koop responded to my recommendations with a letter stating that he understood my line of reasoning and would keep it in mind when preparing his report. He also noted that he had a copy of my book which included the first long-term follow-up study (an average of ten years post-abortion) of women who have reported post-abortion problems. Because this study was limited to a sample of 253 WEBA members, Dr. Koop pointed out that "it is impossible to make national generalizations" from such a sample, which is true in terms of making statistical generalizations but not in

be summed up in the following truism: *One cannot help a child without helping the mother; one cannot hurt a child without hurting the mother.*

This is why, from a natural law perspective, we can know in advance that abortion is inherently harmful to women. It is simply impossible to rip a child from the womb of a mother without tearing out a part of the woman herself—a part of her heart, a part of her joy, a part of her maternity.

One does not need to be a "biased" pro-life Christian to see this truth. Consider the testimony of Dr. Julius Fogel, a psychiatrist and obstetrician who has been a long-time advocate of abortion and has personally performed over 20,000 abortions. According to Dr. Fogel:

> Every woman—whatever her age, background or sexuality—has a trauma at destroying a pregnancy. A level of humanness is touched. This is a part of her own life. When she destroys a pregnancy, she is destroying herself. There is no way it can be innocuous. One is dealing with the life force. It is totally beside the point whether or not you think a life is there. You cannot deny that something is being created and that this creation is physically happening.... Often the trauma may sink into the unconscious and never surface in the woman's lifetime. But it is not as harmless and casual an event as many in the pro-abortion crowd insist. A psychological price is paid. It may be alienation; it may be a pushing away from human warmth, perhaps a hardening of the maternal instinct. Something happens on the deeper levels of a woman's consciousness when she destroys a pregnancy. I know that as a psychiatrist.[3]

If there is a single principle, then, which lies at the heart of the pro-woman/pro-life agenda, it would have to be this: *the best interests of the child and the mother are **always** joined.* This is true even if the mother does not initially realize it, and even if she needs a tremendous amount of love and help to see it. Thus, the only way that we can help

---

terms of gaining insights into the potential size of the problem. After all, in any public health investigation, one must always study the sick population before one can even begin to measure the extent of the illness in the general population. Unless the symptoms are identified first, it is impossible to ask the right questions of the general population. Indeed, the most common methodological flaw of pro-abortion studies is that researchers have concentrated their efforts on proving that psychiatric sequelae are rare without first defining the range of emotional and behavioral problems which women report.

As one final note, it is curious that while Dr. Koop personally reported having seen my study, my research was not included in the extensive bibliography of materials which the Surgeon General's assistant claimed to have studied in preparing the "report." This omission is especially odd since all the other studies which were included in the bibliography were also dismissed as methodologically flawed.

either the mother or her child is to help both. Conversely, if we hurt either, we hurt both.

This is not an optional truth. It reflects God's ordering of creation. This principle is so important that I must repeat it again: *Only the mother can nurture her unborn child. All that the rest of us can do is to nurture and protect the mother.*

Saving the unborn, then, is a natural byproduct of helping women. Conversely, we can never hope to succeed in our efforts to protect the unborn without first and foremost protecting women. Brute-force bans on abortion will not create a pro-life society. But helping mothers through an aggressive defense of women's *legitimate* rights will. It is in this very same sense that Pope John Paul II has insisted that it is necessary for those who oppose abortion to become "courageously 'pro-woman,' promoting a choice that is truly in favor of women. It is precisely the woman, in fact, who pays the highest price, not only for her motherhood, but even more for its destruction, for the suppression of the life of the child who has been conceived. The only honest stance ... is that of *radical solidarity with the woman.*"[4] [Italics added.]

## LEARNING OUR LESSONS, TOO

Many pro-lifers scratch their heads in confusion, wondering how God can allow this holocaust of abortion to go on so long. So many millions have died, and we seem no closer to converting our nation than we were twenty years ago. When will God stop this slaughter?

This is an important question. As Christians we believe that from every evil happening God can resurrect something good—at the very least, repentance and a change of spirit, and often much more. And because the onslaught of abortion is so terrible, we must pray with hope that there is a very tremendous good which God intends to resurrect from this great evil. Greater respect for the unborn and for the sanctity of life is one lesson which our society is certainly intended to learn, but it is by no means the only lesson we are meant to learn.

I believe that at least some of us are so focused on what others need to learn that we are neglecting to see what God may be asking *us* to learn. In short, before we can help others to see, we may still need to extract a plank or two from our own eyes. I honestly believe that, short of Christ's return, God will not bring an end to the abortion holocaust until Christians learn all that *they* are meant to learn, namely, greater compassion for sinners.

## Compassion for Those Pregnant Out-of-Wedlock

Pro-lifers have clearly done a tremendous job in the last two decades promoting a more charitable understanding of women who are pregnant out-of-wedlock. But there is clearly much more that must be done. Churches, families, friends, and employers must make even greater efforts to be supportive of every pregnant woman or single parent, no matter how the child was conceived. There is no denying the fact that, in previous decades, righteous and judgmental Christians discriminated against and shamed women who were pregnant out-of-wedlock. And it is equally true that this condemning attitude shamed, and continues to shame, many women into seeking abortions. For this, we too share in the guilt of abortion.

If we are to be truly Christian, we must strive to live by and promote the principle that every pregnancy, every birth, is a gift from God. No matter how the pregnancy occurred, no matter what the physical gifts or handicaps of the child, *every child* is a blessing from God, an opportunity and challenge to follow Him in the way of love. When this gift is received by an unmarried couple, it is accompanied by the message that now is the time to become mature and responsible adults. Such couples are given children not as a punishment for fornication, but as a cure for fornication.

As a Christian community, then, we must cherish life and charitably invite others to seek God's will in their lives. To do this, we must believe that *every child* is a gift from God, and emphatically spread this message. Therefore, the birth of every child should be an *occasion of joy*, not of shame.

Similarly, without ever granting approval to fornication (which causes its own long list of social injuries), we must cultivate a society which does not view extra-marital intercourse as the greatest of sins, much less an unforgivable one. Embarrassed young girls announcing a pregnancy to their parents do not need to be reminded of their mistakes—of which they are already too pointedly aware—so much as reminded that God is now calling upon them to grow up. And they need to know that we, their families, their church, and their society, want to continue to help them along that path toward emotional and spiritual maturity, over which we too must struggle.

During the last twenty years, Christians have truly come a long way in learning this first lesson. But it is doubtful that we would have learned it if we had not been shocked into greater compassion for young pregnant women out of our concern for their unborn children, who are threatened by abortion. Nonetheless, the witnessing work of our many crisis pregnancy centers and the compassion of so many parents toward their single mother/daughters are evidence that this lesson is being learned. Let us pray that it is never forgotten.

### Compassion for the Post-Aborted

As a Christian community, however, we are not as far along in learning the lesson of compassion toward those who have actually been involved in abortion. Many good-hearted people continue to recoil in horror at anyone who could "kill her baby." They wonder, "What kind of monster could do such a thing?" For many, judgmentalism comes much easier than compassion because they lack insight into the tremendous pressures and feelings of despair which lead to abortion.

This is the second lesson which we must learn from the abortion holocaust *before* we can expect to conquer it. We must learn that abortion is an act of despair. It is not something women do with vindictive hearts. It is something they do when they feel trapped and helpless. Over *70 percent* of women undergoing abortion believe it is morally wrong. They are acting *against* their consciences because they feel they have no other choice.

This is one way in which books like *Aborted Women, Silent No More* have helped to increase the understanding of pro-lifers. By reading the stories of women who have had abortions and by seeing what drives them to choose abortion, pro-lifers are learning more and more that "there, but for the grace of God, go I." This understanding is the basis for acceptance and compassion. During the last ten years, this understanding has finally established a firm foothold within the pro-life movement, but it is still far from being universal among Christians in general.

This issue, too, will be discussed at length in Chapters Ten through Twelve. Let it suffice for now to say that Christians must refrain from condemning and judging the women and men who have been involved in abortions. Judging them will not free them from the shame and guilt they already feel. Instead, we must concentrate on sharing with them the hope of God's great mercy. To do this effectively, we must give them more than our words; we must give them our hearts.

## WHO CAN BEST SPEAK FOR THE UNBORN?

The next chapter will discuss more fully why the middle majority of Americans choose to ignore appeals on behalf of the unborn. For now, it is enough to say that they are uneasy pragmatists. While they firmly believe that abortion is the killing of a human being, they also believe it is sometimes necessary and almost always beneficial to the woman.

Because the middle majority are uncomfortable with the truth about abortion, they have a psychological need to push out of their minds any arguments or evidence on behalf of the unborn. In fact, when presented with evidence, such as pictures of the unborn, whether charmingly angelic or horridly dismembered, they are likely to resent pro-lifers for rubbing their noses into a truth which they already know but have deliberately chosen to ignore. Indeed, one drawback of such pictures is that they may actually serve to solidify the middle majority's calloused attitude by forcing them to repeatedly exercise their pattern of denial. This is why the millions of dollars spent on showing pictures of the unborn to the public have not brought about the mass conversion of hearts for which pro-lifers have frequently, and naively, hoped.

In other words, when hearts are closed, pounding heads with proofs of the unborn child's humanity is ineffective. The truth must enter in a roundabout way, through the testimony of women who grieve over their lost children. Since the middle majority are open to the concerns of women, they will empathize with the grief of post-aborted women, and, in so doing, they will be drawn into implicitly acknowledging the unborn for whom the tears are wept.

Clearly, the most powerful witnesses for the humanity of the unborn are not scientists, but mothers who mourn. All can see that these mothers weep not over the destruction of "products of conception" but over the deaths of their children. While pictures of aborted babies may increase the resentment of the middle majority, the tearful stories of women who have paid the terrible price of abortion open eyes and hearts. Wherever facts of fetal biology will not change hearts, facts of familial relationship will: "It was my innocent little daughter who died that day!"

In this very real way, the issue of the unborn child's human rights is not replaced by a focus on post-abortion issues; it is subsumed into it. In the final analysis, the humanity of the unborn child is revealed to be the only explanation for why abortion causes women so much grief and suffering.

Thus, for those of us who have not had an abortion, the best way that we can draw attention to the humanity of the unborn is by drawing attention to the testimony of those who can speak of this loss from personal experience. By our advocacy for women's rights, we draw attention to wounded mothers. By hushing the din of our own cries, we are allowing the grief-filled voices of the unborn babies' mothers and fathers to be heard by all. We are not leaving the unborn voiceless; we are offering their parents the chance to be heard. Indeed, we must demand that they be heard. After all, who is more entitled to speak for their children than they?

Looking at this same issue from another perspective, we must remember that the interests of a mother and her child are permanently intertwined. This means that the morality of abortion is built right into the psychological effects of abortion. Everyone knows that there is no psychological trauma associated with the discarding of menses. But the discarding of an unborn child's life? *That*, as Dr. Fogel reminds us, is inherently traumatic.

Therefore, when we are talking about the psychological complications of abortion, we are implicitly talking about the physical and behavioral symptoms of a moral problem. By focusing public attention on the symptoms of post-abortion trauma, we will inevitably draw the middle majority back to an understanding of the causes of the problem: the injustice of killing unborn children and the guilt of weakness and betrayal which haunts the mother's heart.

With much less ferocity, this same guilt is gnawing at the hearts of the middle majority of Americans, who know the truth but have chosen to ignore it. In helping them to recognize the psychological suffering abortion causes women, we will lead them to rediscover the horror of abortion for themselves.

## A Pro-Life Lesson Plan

The discussion above is not meant to imply that appeals on behalf of the unborn are never effective. The fact that the middle majority are uneasy with abortion can be used to our advantage. My point, however, is that we are misusing our resources when we press this advantage first. Our first order of business must be to shake their belief that abortion helps women.

The importance of maintaining this sequence cannot be overstated. It is only *after* the dangers of abortion for women are fully understood by the middle majority, not to mention pro-abortion activists, that we can even begin to open their minds and hearts to the unborn child. If women are not being helped, they will ask themselves, then why are we killing their babies?

In a very real sense, this pro-woman/pro-life agenda is nothing more than a "lesson plan" for leading our nation to an understanding of this reality. It is a process which follows the reverse path of the pro-abortion movement.

The pro-abortion movement was born from a social vision which separated the mother's interests from her unborn baby's. If their interests are separate, then there is a potential conflict between the woman's rights and her unborn child's rights, and only one of them can prevail.

We cannot accept any part of this reasoning. We must reject every ideology which frames the abortion issue in terms of a mother versus her child. We are both pro-woman and pro-child. We believe that we can and should help both the mother and her child. We believe that the legalization of abortion was not an advance for women's rights, but an advance for social engineers and others who are exploiting women in times of personal crisis.

## TEACHING MORALITY BY TEACHING SCIENCE

Believers know that God's moral law is not given to us to enslave us, or even to take the fun out of life. It is given to us as a path toward true happiness. Christians rightly anticipate, then, that any advantage gained through violation of the moral law is always temporary; it will invariably be supplanted by alienation and suffering.

This insight gives us an alternative way of evangelizing. Whenever we cannot convince others to acknowledge a moral truth for the love of God, our second-best option is to appeal to their self-interest. If an act is indeed against God's moral law, it will be found to be injurious to our happiness. Thus, if our faith is true, we would expect to find compelling evidence which demonstrates that such acts as abortion, fornication, and pornography lead, in the end, not to happiness and freedom, but to sorrow and enslavement. By finding this evidence and sharing it with others, we bear witness to the protective good of God's law in a way which even unbelievers must respect.

Research and education about the dangers of abortion, then, are not just grist for political reform. They are also leaven for spiritual reform. As people become more aware of all the hardships abortion causes to women, men, siblings, and society, they will begin to respect the wisdom of God's law. They will begin to think, "Maybe all these religious folk weren't so crazy after all. If they were right about this, when every other power in society said they were wrong, maybe they're right about other things, too."

This approach also recognizes another fundamental aspect of human nature: where there is no love of God, there is an exaggerated love of self. As a corollary to this truth, we should also recognize that wherever there is only self-love, appeals to self-sacrifice will fail, and only appeals to self-preservation can possibly succeed. Often, our warnings will be rejected. But even in these cases, by giving people the warning, we are planting the seeds for repentance and belief when they inevitably hit bottom. This is another reason why we should never be focused on condemning those who are considering or have had abortions. Instead, we should be focused on warning them and offering them mercy.

## BOTH PURE AND PRAGMATIC

Before leaving the issue of the moral imperative behind this strategy, some notice should be given to how other strategic issues have divided the pro-life movement in the past. These previous moral conflicts have led to a waste of resources and destructive infighting between allies. It is my belief that the pro-woman/pro-life strategy can help to heal the ideological divisions which have developed, restore unity, and provide a guiding vision for our movement.

In the last twenty years, the pro-life movement has been split by the very serious moral question regarding what type of laws should be sought. The key issue is whether pro-lifers can morally pursue legislation which would allow exceptions for the "hard cases," such as pregnancy resulting from rape or incest, or pregnancies where there is a suspected fetal malformation. These "hard cases" are the ones for which the middle majority of Americans most support access to abortion.

Seeking to capitalize on the opinion of the middle majority, pro-life "pragmatists" support an incremental approach to outlawing abortion by allowing abortion in these "hard cases." Such laws would save 95 percent of all the children being killed by abortion, they say. We must save as many as we can, as soon as we can, and go back to tighten the laws later.

"Purists" object that by allowing exceptions in "special circumstances," we are abandoning our claim that all human life is sacred. We are, in essence, agreeing that some lives are more sacred than others, or at least conceding that if the woman's hardship is great enough, then the sacrifice of her child is justified, or at least tolerable. But if abortion is justified under any single circumstance, why not under some other compelling circumstance? In essence, by wavering from our stand on behalf of an absolute right to life, we are lending moral credence to the claims of the other side. Instead of debating the fundamental principle—the sacredness of human life—we will end up negotiating about who can be killed and under what circumstances.

For the record, I side with the purists. But I also sympathize with the pragmatists. Pragmatists desperately want to save lives now. If we can save some by drafting laws which match the profile of public opinion polls, they think, we must do so. But this approach has many pitfalls. First, any exception will be exploited to provide for many more abortions than legitimately fit into the allowed category. Second, passing a partial ban will dissipate the drive for a ban on the remaining categories. Third, this approach really does nothing toward making abortion *unthinkable*; it only makes the remaining abortions more politically tolerable. Indeed, the incremental approach actually reinforces the public's view that abortion can sometimes be beneficial to women, at least in these "hard cases."

This is one reason why I maintain that the pro-woman/pro-life strategy is a superior approach. It is pragmatic, meaning achievable, but it is also pure, in that it does not differentiate between cases. Indeed, if anything, it would tend to place an abortionist who performs an abortion in a "hard case," such as rape or potential fetal malformation, at greater risk of punishment. Why? Because all the available research indicates that women who abort for these "hard cases" reasons are at the highest risk of suffering psychological problems post-abortion.[5] Indeed, in the pro-woman approach, the inevitable debate over the "hard cases" will provide an excellent opportunity to educate legislators and the public about post-abortion psychological sequelae in general. Rather than run from the debate over these "hard cases," we must learn how to use this debate to our advantage.

In short, the strategy outlined in this book is results-oriented. It is pragmatic. But it is also free of compromise. Because we know that every abortion hurts a woman, as well as her child, we can defend every unborn child by defending the best interests of the mother, knowing that her best interests are never served by abortion. Out of ignorance or despair, a woman may believe that abortion will help her more than it will hurt her, but we know, from both experience and theory, that it will not. Our job is to ensure that she is freed from ignorance and helped to find hope. When we succeed in this, we will have a society which is both pro-woman and pro-life.

## Summary

The pro-woman/pro-life strategy, which places defense of women's rights at the center of our national debate, is justified by the fact that in God's ordering of creation, only an unborn child's mother can nurture her child; all that we can do is to nurture and protect the mother. Focusing on women's rights is also necessary if we, who want to live as Christians, are to better learn the ways of mercy and compassion.

In focusing attention on post-aborted women, we are actually allowing their voices to be better heard. It is *their* witness on behalf of their unborn, not ours, which will soften hearts and open eyes. In this sense, by focusing on women's rights, we are not ignoring the unborn but, instead, are preparing the stage for the most compelling advocates of all for the unborn—their mothers.

Our pro-woman/pro-life strategy is actually a lesson plan for educating our nation about how the interests of a mother and her child are inextricably intertwined. One cannot hurt a child without hurting the child's mother, and this is especially true in the case of abortion. As people learn this, they will not only reopen their hearts to the unborn, they will reopen their hearts to the beauty of God's moral law.

None of what I have presented in this chapter is novel, as is demonstrated by a letter which Dr. O.E. Worcester wrote to the *Journal of the American Medical Association* over 100 years ago. Dr. Worcester wrote to complain against her male colleagues who treated women who were pregnant out-of-wedlock with great disrespect. Worst of all, she insisted, these same physicians willingly added to the guilt of these used and abandoned women by giving them abortions rather than true compassionate aid. When a colleague asked her to help perform abortions, she refused, saying, "I loved woman too well to help her add murder to her other sin. If mother love and the touch of baby fingers did not save her to God and womanhood, nothing could. That it could, I had proof in many cases where forsaken mothers had, in spite of all, carved for themselves and their fatherless children an honorable place in the world."

Dr. Worcester concluded her reprimand of her colleagues with a pointed condemnation of misogynist abortionists, an appeal to the inseparability of woman and child, and a plea for true compassion:

> I have never seen cause to hold the male element less responsible for the slaughter of the innocents than in the days of Herod. Then, as now, men seem to fear the coming of Christ born of woman....
> This is my plea: "What God hath joined together, let not man put

asunder," in the medical profession or elsewhere.

Let men and women join forces under the banner of Him who said: "He that is without sin among you, let him first cast a stone at her," and also: "Neither do I condemn thee; go and sin no more."

Let us join forces all along the line, and fight this hydraheaded monster to the death and save our nation.[6]

To this plea I can add only one word: Amen.

# CHAPTER TWO

# THE MIDDLE MAJORITY

B EFORE and after taking office, President Clinton repeatedly expressed the goal that induced abortion should be "safe, legal, and rare." The insipid hypocrisy of this slogan was immediately attacked by pro-lifers. Legal abortion is clearly not safe, especially for the unborn child, and with over 1.6 million abortions per year in the U.S. alone, it is not rare either. Furthermore, President Clinton's political agenda called for increasing federal funding of abortions, increasing the number of abortion providers in non-urban areas, increasing pro-abortion counseling at school-based clinics, providing abortions at military hospitals, renewing funding for forced abortions in China, and promoting the legalization of abortion worldwide. With all this activity designed to increase the number of abortions here and abroad, critics rightly wondered exactly how and where President Clinton intended to contribute to the goal of making abortion rare.

Clearly, Clinton's pledge to make abortion "safe, legal, and rare" had little substance, but we must recognize that it has a profound emotional appeal to the vast majority of Americans. This is exactly why Clinton's pollsters and speech writers developed this line. They know, and we must always remember, that the middle majority of Americans are deeply disturbed by abortion. They would prefer that it never had to happen at all, and would sincerely like this "ugly business" to be resorted to very rarely. On the other hand, when it does happen, they want it to be safe. And safety, they have been assured, can be guaranteed by keeping it legal.

## THE SOURCE OF AMBIVALENCE

Abortion is universally disliked because everyone knows, on one level or another, that it involves the destruction of a human life. The knowledge that the human fetus, the human embryo, or even the human zygote, is in fact a *human being* is as undeniable as the answer to the child's question, "Where do babies come from?" While a child might be temporarily diverted from the answer to this question, no child's curiosity is completely satisfied until the full truth is revealed. Life begins at conception. Babies are created by the uniting (hopefully in an act of love) of a man and woman, in the sharing of the substance of two selves who become one in the flesh—both symbolically, in the sexual act, and most truly, in the conception of a new life. Every adult remembers learning this truth, and everyone's biology bears witness to it. And it is this truth—no matter how much one tries to ignore it, forget it, or bury it beneath slogans or philosophical quibbles—it is this truth that makes *everyone* uneasy with abortion.

As I have previously shown at length, even abortionists and their staffs are filled with a great anxiety over abortion.[1] They are filled with doubts and troubled by their weak grip on a subjective morality which demands a constant shifting to accommodate the "needs" of others. In summarizing her extensive interviews with abortionists, psychologist Magda Denes reports, "There wasn't a doctor who at one time or another in the questioning did not say, 'This is murder.'"[2]

Abortionists enjoy the easy wealth of their trade, but they feel like hired executioners. This feeling that *they* are being exploited often creates calloused or resentful feelings toward the very women they are purportedly trying to help. They are especially disturbed by the fact that over 45 percent of their patients are "abusing the privilege" by coming back for second, third, or fourth abortions. With the exception of those who care only about profit, most clinic personnel view repeat abortions as a sign of failure. Somehow, they failed in their birth control counseling to help the woman avoid another abortion.

Indeed, in their nearly maniacal insistence that patients should take better "precautions" in the future, abortion counselors reveal a deep-seated uneasiness about abortion. After all, if abortion has no moral content, and if it is as safe as claimed, why should it not be used as an alternative for birth control? But only the most radical abortion advocates are even remotely comfortable with such a suggestion. Instead, most abortion defenders, though they would seldom say it this way, see abortion as an "evil necessity," an ugly thing which must be accepted as a backup for contraceptive failure, including contraceptive negligence. Even Kate Michelman, president of the National Abortion Rights and Reproductive Action League, admitted to a reporter, "We think abortion is a bad thing. No woman wants to have an abortion."[3]

Because this moral ambivalence about abortion is so pervasive, most pro-abortionists are quite sincere in their demand for more research to develop a "perfect" contraceptive. Even population control zealots, such as the top-level officials at Planned Parenthood, who may be willing to encourage abortion to achieve their social engineering goals, would much prefer a less gruesome way to their end, such as forced sterilization. The bottom line: no one, not even the abortion industry, is truly comfortable with the dismembering of human fetuses. Abortion twinges every conscience.

## THE MIXED OPINIONS OF THE MIDDLE MAJORITY

Since even those who are directly involved in the abortion industry experience pangs of conscience about abortion, it is easy to imagine why the general public is also deeply disturbed by the abortion question.

Polls have repeatedly shown that over 70 percent of Americans admit believing that abortion is immoral.[4] But of those who believe it is immoral, 40 to 50 percent would still allow it under special circumstances or simply because they do not want to "impose their morality" on others, especially loved ones.

What should we make of this apparent inconsistency between basic moral beliefs and attitudes toward public policy? In their detailed 1990 Gallup poll of over 2,000 adults, James Davison Hunter and Carl Bowman analyzed six variables regarding abortion attitudes. They found that relatively few people are consistently pro-choice (16 percent) or consistently pro-life (33 percent). The rest, who make up the middle majority, fall into four statistically significant clusters. *Excluding* the consistently pro-choice and the consistently pro-life, 16 percent of the remaining population can be categorized as "personally opposed pro-choice," 14 percent as "reticently pro-choice," 28 percent as "conveniently pro-life," and 38 percent as "secretly pro-life."[5]

The definitions of these four subgroups are very revealing. Those who are "secretly pro-life," who make up 19 percent of the general population, believe the right to life outweighs the right to choose from the moment of conception but reject calling abortion "murder." They are willing to accept abortion only in the "hard cases" (rape or incest, or serious fetal malformation) and would consider abortion for themselves only under such extreme circumstances. They tend to be pro-life in philosophy, but they view themselves as neutral or moderately pro-choice.

Those who are "conveniently pro-life," 14 percent of the general population, are also opposed to abortion on moral grounds, and even more likely than the "secretly pro-life" to describe it in terms of murder. But when asked about specific circumstances in which it would be acceptable, the "conveniently pro-life" are more likely to approve of abortion in more cases than other pro-life respondents, and are more likely to express a willingness to consider abortion for themselves, especially under the "more trying" circumstances.

The "reticently pro-choice," seven percent of the general population, have views about women's rights which strongly favor the pro-choice position, and they are likely to see personhood as attaching to the moment of viability. But they are also likely to believe that abortion involves the taking of a human life, though they would not call this act murder. This deep moral unease with abortion makes them most likely to call themselves neutral or only moderately pro-choice because they are "reticent in conceding the moral acceptability of abortion to other people.... They are pro-choice by default, rather than by conviction."

Finally, there are those who are "personally opposed pro-choice," who make up about eight percent of the general population. This group matches the philosophical profile of the consistently pro-choice, believing the fetus does not become a person until viable and that the woman's rights must prevail until viability. They also support the view that abortion is morally acceptable for others, in many if not most circumstances. But they have an "emphatic *un*willingness to consider abortion for themselves—even, for example, if their baby were shown to have serious genetic problems." In short, they are "pro-choice in philosophy but pro-life in practice."[6]

## THE ROLE OF FEELINGS FOR THE MIDDLE MAJORITY

To better understand why people answered the poll's questions in the way they did, and to learn how people would explain their apparent inconsistencies, Hunter followed up his survey with detailed interviews. In these interviews, Hunter found that the idea of "choice" was a powerful magnet for those who were otherwise confused and ambivalent about abortion. "Choice" is a safe harbor for those who simply want to escape the storm. When in doubt, leave the matter open for someone else to decide, in this case, they presume, the pregnant woman. "The labels, it would seem, express sentiment, not a conviction or even a commitment."[7]

Hunter also found that many were unable to articulate any reasoned basis for their beliefs, and some even became hostile when pressed to do so, for, as one man put it, "I know how I feel, and my feelings are valid. Look, these feelings are based on experiences that are mine alone, and you can't tell me they are wrong. Other people have other experiences and will feel differently about things."[8] This desire to "feel comfortable" about one's opinion leads many of those who form the middle majority to deliberately refuse to think about the unborn, or to focus on non-judgmentalism.[9] They desire to be and to perceive themselves as compassionate, and this is expressed through feelings of empathy "for both the woman and the fetus in varying intensity."[10]

How this empathy is divided often depends on personal experiences or the experiences of loved ones. Knowing someone who has had an abortion tends to increase one's hesitancy to take a "judgmental" pro-life stand. It is more comfortable to take refuge in popular relativism: "I would say my views are true for me, but I can't put that on someone else. I just can't force my truths on other people."[11] This same attitude is reflected in a widespread hostility toward what is seen as government intrusion into private decisions. Only individuals can decide what is right or wrong, many would say, not the government, because it is individuals who must live with their decisions.[12]

Because the middle majority are troubled by such deep feelings of ambivalence about abortion, they feel it is prudent to cling to the safe feelings of compassion and non-judgmentalism. They know with certainty that these attributes are good ones, so how can they be wrong if they simply remain compassionate and nonjudgmental?

Yet, in the public debate over abortion, nonjudgmental compassion is most closely identified with the pro-choice position. So it is the desire to be compassionate that explains the pull toward identifying oneself as pro-choice, a tendency which is exacerbated by the common portrayal of pro-lifers as accusing, judgmental, and narrow-minded. Pro-abortionists have been very skilled in using pro-choice rhetoric to appeal to this desire to see oneself as compassionate. Thus, according to Hunter and Bowman's poll, while only one percent of the moderately pro-choice were drifting toward the pro-life position, fully 12 percent of the middle majority who describe themselves as moderately pro-life said they were drifting closer to the pro-choice position.[13]

In summary, these findings show that the vast majority of Americans question the morality of abortion, and that the personal ideals of most are more consistent with the pro-life position. Yet, at the same time, the middle majority believe it is unfair to judge others, especially when you do not know their personal history. In other words, they have a moral conviction that abortion is wrong, but an offsetting moral conviction that it is wrong to judge others. Underlying these is a third component, the fear that, "maybe someday I might need an abortion, and so I shouldn't completely rule it out, nor would I want others to judge me."

## DIFFERENT GROUPS, DIFFERENT STRATEGIES

It is vitally important that the pro-life movement understand the feelings of the middle majority so that we can better discern how to develop a strategy which is in alignment with their mixed feelings.

The key to understanding is actually very simple: the middle majority is paralyzed by competing feelings of compassion for *both* the unborn and for women. They are honestly discomfited by the killing of unborn babies. It nags at their conscience. Yet this nagging is offset by their concerns for the welfare of women. They are sympathetic regarding the disruptive burdens of parenthood, and they are afraid of the dangerous "back alley" abortions. In effect, the middle majority's inability to reconcile these conflicting compassions has resulted in an uneasy acceptance of the status quo.

While this conflict of competing sympathies is generally characteristic of all those in the middle majority, there are also specific subgroups which should be considered.

First, we must recognize that within this middle majority are 20 to 40 million people who carry about unresolved guilt from actually having participated in an abortion. This group of post-aborted women and men can be divided into two classes, the "defenders" and the "concealers." The "defenders" include those who boldly speak out in support of legalized abortion as a means of defending their own actions. Since they believe that they are generally good and moral people, they are forced to conclude that abortion can be necessary for good and moral reasons, such as those that prevailed in their own circumstances. Some may even use discussions of their own abortions as a way of demanding from friends and associates an admission that good and moral people, "like me," may have legitimate reasons for choosing abortion. Less confident "defenders" generally conceal their own abortions. Instead, they focus on the political arguments for freedom of choice as a means of soliciting the nods of assent and agreement from others which they can then interpret as ratification of own choices to abort.

"Concealers," on the other hand, become uncomfortable with any conversation which touches on abortion. These are the women and men who are more consciously aware of the unresolved grief they are experiencing over their own abortions. Because they do not know how to deal with their feelings of grief, they simply wish the abortion issue would go away. They seek the passive stillness of silence. For them, silence, like denial and repression, is a coping mechanism. It is a silence imposed upon them not only by shame, but also by fear— the fear that if they even begin to talk about their own experience, the flood of their tears will overwhelm them. Compared to "defenders," who boldly assert their own basic moral goodness, "concealers" are painfully aware of their moral failings. While the former would claim to have high self-esteem, the latter would not.

Curiously, because of their experiences, "concealers" tend to become more pro-life in their personal beliefs and determined never to be involved in an abortion again. On the other hand, they are also likely to become more pro-choice in their political beliefs, but not with the bold fervor of "defenders." Instead, their support of "choice" is rooted in a deeply humble attitude of non-judgmentalism. Abortion may not be a good choice, they know from their own experience, but how can they, who have done the same and worse, condemn others who choose abortion? To do so would make them vile hypocrites. And perhaps, they graciously hope, others will fare better than they have.

The emotional conflicts of "defenders" and "concealers" can only be resolved through post-abortion healing, which is discussed further in Chapter Ten. For the purpose of the present discussion, however, it suffices to stress the importance of post-abortion healing to the conversion of this segment of the middle majority. Until "concealers" are offered the promise of compassion and the hope of being freed from shame, silence and support of "choice" are their only options. Until they are shown how to condemn abortion without condemning those who have had abortions, they will remain incapable of being anti-abortion without also feeling like hypocrites. Similarly, until "defenders" are shown how to reconcile their view of themselves as good and moral people with a condemnation of abortion, they will feel driven by the need to defend abortion. In this sense, by helping "defenders" to see how people are being deceived and exploited by abortion, we are allowing them the crutch of being "victims" on their way to assuming full responsibility for their actions.

The second important group within the middle majority is related to the first, often literally. This group is composed of the tens of mil-

lions who fear that if they condemn abortion, they are implicitly condemning their wives, daughters, sisters, mothers, and friends who
have had abortions. These kind-hearted people are simply unwilling
to condemn their loved ones. Instead, they feel obliged to stand on
the side of "choice" out of respect for their loved ones. Even while
most of these people would admit that abortion is a "terrible thing,"
they must also insist that sometimes it is the only thing a woman can
do, and we shouldn't judge her. Without access to abortion, they
believe, their loved ones' lives may have been ruined. To convert this
group, we need to show them how abortion has not helped their
loved ones, but has instead hurt them. They need to be educated
about all of the psychosocial problems associated with abortion, such
as substance abuse, increased divorce rates, and increased difficulty
maintaining jobs. Once they become aware of these associations, they
will begin to recognize for themselves how their loved ones have
actually had their lives ruined by their abortions, even if the women
themselves continue in a state of denial. In addition, as we promote
post-abortion healing, familial pressures will be reversed. Those who
are healed will begin to speak out to repudiate abortion, and their
repudiation will, in turn, motivate their loved ones to join them in
condemning abortion. Those who were once silent out of respect for
their loved ones will then be emboldened to speak in support of their
loved ones.

The third group in the middle majority which we should notice is
made up of moral relativists. These people no longer believe in an
absolute moral law, and their subjective philosophy forbids them to
judge the moral lives of others. They are conditioned by the secular
media, which defends its violent and pornographic programs with
holier-than-thou appeals for a united world built upon nonjudgmental tolerance. Relativism is also popular because it can be defended
by common wisdom and even biblical passages. "People in glass
houses... Judge not lest you be judged... Let him who is without sin
throw the first stone..."; these are the mantras of a moral relativism
which discourages moral reflection. This subjective relativism is
especially prevalent among those who feel a sense of guilt about their
own conduct, for in relativism, they have a shield for denying others
the right to judge what they have done.

While Christians must recognize that relativism is a grave problem, it does not need to be solved before we solve the abortion issue.
Rather than getting bogged down in arguments with moral agnos-
tics, we can simply capitalize on their refusal to judge. To do so, we
simply need to ask the relativists: Who are we to say that post-abort-

ed women have not suffered? Who are we to say they should not be allowed compensation for their pain? If we are to be fair and compassionate, shouldn't we allow them their day in court?

This brings us to a fourth subset of the middle majority. These are the people who have partaken of the sexual freedom of our age while continuing to view themselves as religious persons. Typical of this subgroup are young people seeking to straddle the gap between their religious upbringing and their attraction to pre-marital sex. While they have already broken one religious rule, in the name of love, they would like to think that they would never break the rule regarding death. Abortion, they sincerely believe, would be going too far. They are fairly comfortable with this self-image. It allows them to be both modern and righteous, saying, "I would never have an abortion, but I would never judge anyone else's decision." Yet, on a barely conscious level, they realize that they, too, might someday be "forced" into the "evil necessity" of abortion. Thus, for some, the refusal to formally declare abortion wrong in all cases has less to do with not judging others than with protecting their own option to change their minds. Our task with this group is to bolster their resolve to never have an abortion themselves by increasing their awareness of how abortion causes such great physical, psychological, and spiritual injuries. We must help them to truly mean the claim, "I would never have an abortion."

Fifth, there are the ambivalent feminists. Typical of this group is the student of feminist theology who once argued: "In a perfect world, abortion would be wrong. But in the real world, it's a power issue; women need this power over their bodies to control their lives." This view that abortion would be wrong in a "perfect world" is an acknowledgement that something is wrong with the killing of unborn children. But in the feminists' "real world," the right of a woman "to control her own body" has become the overarching symbol of her pursuit of bodily and social independence. Without this freedom, they believe, women would be enslaved by their biology.

Because the "freedom to choose" has become the first principle of their reasoning, this group of ambivalent feminists insists that the moral issues of abortion should be considered by each person only after the right to choose abortion has been firmly established. Many of these ambivalent feminists may already believe abortion would never be right for them, personally. But their own moral doubts are set aside because what they are chiefly concerned about is defending a symbol, the right to choose. They believe it is fine, perhaps even noble, for a woman to choose against abortion for moral reasons. It is her choice. But even if all abortions could be condemned as immoral, they argue, an emancipated woman must still be free to make her own choice. What matters to these feminists is only that women have the right to choose, for good or ill.

In this sense, ambivalent feminists are truly pro-choice, and not pro-abortion. Unlike population controllers and abortion profiteers, this subset of feminists has no vested interest in encouraging abortion.* For the purpose of developing a pro-woman/pro-life strategy, however, what is important to remember is that feminists are not a monolithic crowd. Some are pro-abortion. Some are even pro-life. But the vast majority are ambivalent about abortion's morality, just like everyone else, and are only using the issue of "choice" to avoid considering the moral issues. These feminists are potential allies if we can show them that our pro-woman/pro-life initiatives truly do expand the rights, choices, and opportunities of women in a way which frees them from being forced into *unwanted* abortions.

## BUILDING COMMON GROUND ON A SHARED CONCERN

Unless we in the pro-life movement can find a way to unravel the conflicted hearts of the middle majority, we will never be successful in our goal to create a pro-life society. Victory, then, requires a radical restructuring of our strategy. It is not enough to just identify, motivate, and coordinate the activities of pro-life Christians who share our values. In addition, we must find ways, without compromising our own values, to show the middle majority that our goals are compatible with theirs.

---

*It should be noted, however, that some feminists do have a vested interest in promoting abortion. They may be population control zealots or abortion profiteers. Or they may actively encourage abortion because in seeing others choose abortion, their own decisions to abort are ratified as reasonable and good. In short, a troubled conscience can be soothed by seeing another woman choose abortion, too. Such feminists should more properly be classified within the group of post-aborted "defenders." Still other pro-abortion feminists, especially in leadership positions, have invested so much of themselves, personally and politically, in the abortion issue that they feel it is impossible to retreat without losing face, prestige, and power. In the heat of the political battle, some of these feminist leaders have even felt compelled to push beyond the argument for choice and begin to champion abortion as a positive good, or even a liberating experience which is always morally justified.

To begin, we must always remember that the two chief concerns of the middle majority are: (1) the desire not to interfere with the autonomy of women, and (2) the desire not to condemn those women who have already had abortions. Their concerns for the unborn, which are real, though attenuated, are constrained by these concerns for women.

This insight has a direct impact on how we must package every pro-life message. Specifically, we must recognize that the middle majority will only open their hearts to concern for the unborn *after* the concerns of women have been addressed.

An example in support of this rule can be found in the lecturing experience of Dr. Jack Willke, president of Life Issues and former president of the National Right to Life Committee. Dr. Willke reports that, over the years, he and his wife Barbara have faced increasing levels of hostility during their fetal development presentations at college campuses. Their message was simply not penetrating the walls of defensive anger which they faced. But in the last two years, they have begun preceding their lectures with a five-minute talk expressing their concern, understanding, and compassion for women who have been through abortions, many of whom felt they had no other choice. Following the fetal development information, they conclude with additional information about post-abortion syndrome and post-abortion healing.

In essence, the Willkes have sandwiched fetal development between two layers of pro-woman compassion. According to Dr. Willke, "The result has been almost dramatic…. The anger and combativeness are gone. The questions are civil. We are listened to once again. The professors are surprised. They had no idea that we were compassionate to women. Now they must take a new and serious look at this issue."

We all know that pro-lifers have always shown compassion for women. This is most evident at our crisis pregnancy centers and in our post-abortion healing ministries. But this compassion has often been hidden behind the scenes in public debates which have been reduced to battles over women's rights versus the rights of the unborn. The solution to this bad publicity is to *always—ALWAYS—* place our arguments for the unborn in the middle of a pro-woman sandwich. Our compassion for the women must be voiced both first and last in all our arguments, and in a manner which shows that our concern for women is a primary and integral part of our opposition to abortion.

## ALIGNING THE MIDDLE MAJORITY'S OPINIONS WITH EFFECTIVE ACTION

Accepting the fact that the middle majority's concerns are primarily focused on the woman is a prerequisite to developing a successful pro-woman/pro-life strategy. Rather than trying to reduce public sympathy for women, we want to increase it and align it with our own outrage at how women are being victimized. By increasing public empathy for the suffering of women who have had abortions, by emphasizing the fact that women are being exploited by the abortion industry and coerced by others into unwanted abortions, and by focusing on expanding the legal rights of women to seek redress, we are aligning our interests with those of the middle majority in a way which advances our political agenda.

This work is already half done. The overwhelming public support for reforms which focus on women's rights is demonstrated by polls which show that 86 percent of the public favor improved informed consent requirements, 84 percent favor state-mandated health and safety standards for regulating abortion clinics, and 70 percent favor large fines against physicians who perform illegal abortions.[14] Even among those who describe themselves as "strongly pro-choice," 78 percent favor requirements for informing women about alternatives and fetal development prior to abortion, and 89 percent support better safety regulations on clinics.[15]

The general public is quite receptive to expanding women's rights in ways which would reduce abortion or make it safer. They are also sensitive to the issue of coerced abortions, even though this issue has hardly been raised in the public debate. In short, because they have empathy for both women and the unborn, the middle majority are quite content with regulations which might be burdensome for abortionists (for whom no one has any sympathy), as long as these requirements would not limit the rights of women. Furthermore, if the demand for such reforms is articulated in a voice of nonjudgmental concern for women, the middle majority's defensiveness will completely dissipate.

In teaching the middle majority about the necessity of protecting women from being victimized by unwanted or dangerous abortions, one of the great aids that we have is their own self-conflict over the morality of abortion. This makes them very receptive to the insight that the women who are having abortions are just like them: conflicted over the morality of abortion. Well over 70 percent of these women believe that abortion is wrong, that it is the taking of a human life, but they are choosing *against* their conscience because they feel they have no other choice. It is precisely because they believe one way and have acted another, that they suffer a sense of self-betrayal, loss of self-esteem, and so many other post-abortion psychological problems. In my experience, when this sequence of emotions and events is laid out for members of the middle majority, they immediately form a bond of empathy with the women who suffer post-abortion trauma. Their own ambivalence over abortion fires their imagination and sympathy. This empathy for post-aborted women will not be enough, at least at first, to convince the middle majority to support a complete ban on abortion, but it is enough to win their support for the types of pro-woman/pro-life legislation which we are advancing herein, which will, in the end, be even more effective than a complete ban.

Our pro-woman/pro-life strategy is also effective at capturing the middle majority's inability, or unwillingness, to come to a definitive position on abortion. By focusing on expanding women's right to redress, we are in essence saying, "Let the market decide." If abortion is already safe, then nothing will change. But if it is dangerous, women have a right to recover damages, and by making it easier for them to receive compensation for their injuries, the abortion industry will be forced to improve their screening, counseling, and abortion practices.

This approach is also appealing to anti-big-government, libertarian-minded people. All we are asking is their support in our efforts to empower the "little guy" (the woman) to take on the "big guy" (the abortion industry) in a court of law so that "the people" (the jury) can decide the truth of the matter on a case-by-case basis. We, the public, don't have to decide the truth right now. We can leave it to the jury to decide it tomorrow, with the understanding that all of our sympathies are with the woman.

To the middle majority, this is a very reasonable position. If abortion is dangerous, the market forces of liability will tend to make abortions more rare (which is appeasing to their troubled consciences). Yet, at the same time, women will continue to have the right to seek an abortion, and whenever it is considered to be "necessary," it will also be safer because physicians will be practicing medicine more carefully.

To the pro-abortionists, however, proper liability for abortion-related injuries will be absolutely devastating. As we will see in the chapters which follow, the abortion industry simply cannot provide cheap, assembly-line abortions without violating every standard of good medical practice and abusing the rights of women. The modern abortion industry can thrive only because the legal obstacles that stand in the way of women suing abortionists are too great for most women to overcome. This is why abortion profiteers will viciously fight pro-woman reforms. This is also why, in fighting against proper liability, they will expose themselves to the public as being truly pro-abortion rather than pro-choice.

## PRO-CHOICE OR PRO-ABORTION?

On numerous occasions, I have been criticized by pro-life activists for using the term "pro-choice." Their argument is that we must always expose the truth that the issue is about abortion, not choice. There are some merits to this argument, and in some cases, the broad characterization of "pro-abortion" is valid. But in general, I believe, the terms pro-choice and pro-abortion should be used with greater care to more properly identify the two different views of people who support legalized abortion.

As we have seen, the middle majority are not *for* abortion, in the sense of seeing it as a positive good, more of which would be better than a little. Most of those in the middle majority have a very unfavorable view of abortion and are quite sincere in claiming that they would never choose one for themselves. Therefore, they are rightly insulted by the characterization that they are "pro-abortion" because, in their hearts, they are really anti-abortion. Instead, they truly are "pro-choice" in that this phrase reflects a moral relativism which insists that each person should be free to choose his own way. While we may disagree with the logic of their moral theology, or absence thereof, we should respect their motivations enough to avoid calling them pro-abortion—a slur we should reserve for the next group.

Pro-abortionists include those who are financially profiting from the abortion industry, but their numbers are very insignificant. Far more significant in both numbers and influence are the pro-abortionists who see abortion as a tool for social engineering. Pro-abortionists tend to be politically minded, seeing themselves as shapers of a utopian society. They are influential in both conservative and liberal circles, in industry, the universities, government, and advocacy groups. Pro-abortionists are adamant about controlling the "population explosion," reducing the welfare rolls, and sparing the genetically "unfit" the "burden" of life—all of which demand abortion.

Pro-abortionists portray themselves as being in favor of "choice," but they are really anti-choice. To determine if a person is pro-choice or pro-abortion, simply ask his or her opinion on forced abortions in

China. Does he condemn them or excuse them? Does she favor forced abortions, or at least forced Norplant implants, for women on welfare? Should a baby with Down's Syndrome be aborted? These are the questions which identify pro-abortionists and set them apart from the middle majority, who favor *laissez-faire* choice.

Pro-abortionists, like the top officials of Planned Parenthood and Zero Population Growth, are so focused on creating the perfect society through population control that abortion-related complications are dismissed as little more than the "whining of a few disturbed women." The injuries of a "few," they believe, should not stand in the way of social progress. The imperative of controlling the quantity and quality of our population, they believe, must take precedence over a "few" torn uteruses and grieving hearts. Indeed, they accuse women who suffer post-abortion grief of only complaining now because they were already psychologically "unfit" before the abortion. "Fit" women would never complain. And even if they did, how does that compare to the common good? In this sense, pro-abortionists are truly anti-women's rights. They would prefer that women seek abortions voluntarily, but they would be quite willing to enact a program of forced abortions if it became "necessary." Unlike pro-choice advocates, pro-abortionists are not driven by the ideals of either compassion or freedom. Instead, they are driven by a desire to control and shape society into a man-made utopia.

I believe it is crucial for this distinction between those who are pro-choice and those who are pro-abortion to become better known. Pro-lifers who insist on misapplying the label of "pro-abortion" are only alienating pro-choicers with whom they at least share the common ground of compassion. In promoting pro-woman/pro-life initiatives, these people are our potential allies. Furthermore, by our indiscriminate use of the term "pro-abortion," we are helping the radical pro-abortionists to hide their true agenda by blending into the crowd of the middle majority, who are only pro-choice. For example, if Jane Smith, who is pro-choice but very opposed to the casual use of abortion, hears herself and Planned Parenthood leaders both described as pro-abortion, she will assume that Planned Parenthood leaders have the same beliefs that she does. Rather than arousing suspicions of Planned Parenthood in the mind of Jane Smith, we would be leading Jane to assume that their beliefs are just as benign as hers.

If, on the other hand, in promoting our pro-woman strategy, we emphasize our common ground with "pro-choice" advocates and insist that only those who are "pro-abortion" oppose these reforms, we will be helping to clarify the debate and to expose the pro-abor-

tionists for what they truly are—anti-choice and anti-woman. This is
the way to build an alliance with the middle majority, and the first
step in opening their eyes to the fullness of truth.

## SUMMARY

The middle majority are deeply troubled about the moral issue of
aborting the unborn, but this concern is blocked by a greater concern
for the welfare and freedom of women. They see themselves as pragmatists. Because of this, they have hardened their hearts to any moral
appeals on behalf of the unborn. Moral arguments simply won't
change their minds, as is evidenced by over twenty years of pro-life
educational efforts. Yet, at the same time, the middle majority would
welcome a dramatic reduction in abortion rates, if this could be done
without harming the welfare of women.

To successfully address the concerns of the middle majority, our
anti-abortion efforts must become more clearly pro-woman. It is only
by leading the middle majority to the understanding that the welfare
of a mother and her unborn child are permanently intertwined that
we will open their hearts to the unborn.

CHAPTER THREE

# THE POLITICAL OPPORTUNITY

THE abortion debate has typically been framed as a conflict between women's rights and the rights of the unborn. Pro-abortionists have consciously defined the issue in these terms to polarize public opinion and paralyze the middle majority—the "fence sitting" 50 percent or more who feel torn between the woman and the child—so they will remain neutral.

Unfortunately, many pro-lifers are all too willing to accept this characterization of the issue. In practice, they even reinforce it by rushing to announce the conclusion, which the middle majority refuses to embrace, that the right of the unborn child to live must always prevail over the needs and desires of the woman. This conclusion, however morally sound, does not help the middle majority in its search to escape the paralysis of compassion for both the unborn and their mothers.

For pro-abortionists, then, this woman versus "fetus" strategy has been highly successful. This is especially clear in the political arena. By framing the debate in this way, pro-abortionists have attempted to push pro-life candidates into a box labeled "Uncompassionate Anti-Woman Ideologues." Pro-life candidates are quite aware of this trap. Many try to avoid it by down-playing the issue or dancing around it.

Our boldest pro-life politicians, on the other hand, usually try to counter the opposition's focus on women's rights by reframing the debate in terms of the sacredness of innocent human life, to which they may add the importance of better options, such as adoption. While this counter-strategy is often a successful way to display a pro-life candidate's integrity and commitment to ideals, in fact, it only reinforces the original framing which says abortion is an issue about balancing women's rights versus fetal rights. This pro-life strategy shifts the spotlight, but it does not truly reframe the arena which defines the debate's dynamics.

## REFRAMING THE DEBATE

To truly reframe the political debate to our advantage, it is not enough to simply highlight the part of the frame touching on the rights of the unborn. Instead, we must expand the frame to include more parties, so that we can convincingly show that it is we who are defending the authentic rights of **both** women and children. In short, we must insist that the proper frame for the abortion issue is not women's rights versus unborn children's rights, but rather women's *and* children's rights versus the schemes of exploiters *and* the profits of the abortion industry.

By reframing the political issue in this way, we capture the sentiments of the middle majority, which lean toward the rights of women, and thus we reverse the trap. Any politician who opposes our pro-woman/pro-life initiatives can rightly be described as anti-woman. Those who oppose safeguards against coercion are the enemies of freedom. If they oppose our pro-woman/pro-life initiatives, it is they who belong in the box labeled "Uncompassionate Anti-Woman Ideologues."

Reframing the abortion debate in this way is not difficult. But it does require pro-life politicians to become familiar with new facts, arguments, and media "sound bites."

First, the pro-woman/pro-life candidate needs an agenda. The complete details of this agenda are spelled out later in this book. For the purpose of campaigning, however, it is sufficient to declare his or her support for legislation covering one or more of the following needs:

1. Protecting women from being coerced into *unwanted* abortions;

2. Guaranteeing the right of women to make free and *fully informed* decisions about abortion;

3. Protecting the women most likely to be injured by abortion by requiring physicians to properly screen patients for characteristics which would place them at higher risk of physical or psychological complications; and

4. Expanding the rights of injured patients to recover fair compensation for physical or psychological harm resulting from abortion.

All of these pro-woman proposals are impossible for pro-abortion candidates to oppose on pro-woman grounds. The only publicly acceptable way they can oppose these reforms is to deny that these problems exist. But when faced with such denials, the pro-woman/pro-life candidate simply has to point out that (1) the opponent is risking the welfare of women for the sake of preserving the abortion industry's profit margins, and (2) these pro-woman initiatives do not outlaw abortion but simply make abortion providers properly responsible for those problems which are occurring, or at the very least, may occur.

Second, the pro-woman candidate must be prepared to shift every abortion-related question to the issue of the need to protect women from the unscrupulous abortion industry and those who are forcing them into *unwanted* abortions. By shifting all questions to address this need, the candidate can keep the focus on his or her pro-woman/pro-life agenda.

Third, pro-abortion opponents must be challenged to support specific legislation which would protect women from being coerced into *unwanted* abortions. This challenge must be repeatedly and insistently put forth. The goal of pro-life candidates is to force their opponents to either agree to pro-woman/pro-life reforms (and thus alienate their radical pro-abortion supporters) or to oppose these pro-woman proposals (and thus appear to be more interested in protecting the profits of the abortion industry than the freedom of women). This is a win-win position for us, and a lose-lose situation for them.

## COERCED ABORTIONS—A POLITICAL ISSUE

The task of gaining public support for a pro-woman/pro-life platform is not difficult. The issue of coerced abortions, for example, is ripe for the picking.

In my experience, once this issue is raised, everyone, even pro-abortionists, admit that coercion is occurring. It is common knowledge that abortion often suits lovers and parents more than pregnant women themselves. It takes no leap of imagination to understand how these other persons often pressure, badger, and blackmail a woman into accepting an unwanted "safe and legal" abortion because it will be "best for everyone." Even the prominent abortion defender Daniel Callahan, director of the Hastings Center, writes, "That men have long coerced women into unwanted abortion when it suits their purposes is well-known but rarely mentioned. Data reported by the Alan Guttmacher Institute indicate that some 30 percent of women have an abortion because someone else, not the woman, wants it."[1]

This is a powerful political issue. No one can rationally deny that coerced abortions occur, and no politician would dare to defend this practice. Only population control zealots defend forced abortions, but even they are generally reluctant to publicly express this position.

Thus, a pro-life politician who emphasizes this issue will be establishing an area of common ground which will be shared by all people of good will. Pro-lifers will support such defense of women's rights, and the vast majority of those who describe themselves as pro-choice would also agree that an effort to stop coerced abortions is reasonable and necessary.

While a campaign speech may not be the place to define the solution to this problem, the solution is straightforward. Abortionists must be held legally responsible for ensuring that a woman's choice to have an abortion is totally her own and that she is not being pressured into this decision by others. If abortion clinics fail to properly screen their patients, they should be held accountable as "accessories" to the crime of pressuring a woman into an unwanted abortion. If a woman can later show that an abortion counselor added to the pressures which made her feel she "had no choice," or did nothing to protect her from being pressured into an unwanted abortion, she should be entitled to sue the clinic for the wrongful death of her wanted child—which can entail millions of dollars in compensation. The basis for this claim is expanded upon further in Chapter Nine.

## RECLAIMING THE MIDDLE

By a consistent application of the pro-woman/pro-life strategy, we can quickly dispel the notion that anti-abortionists are anti-woman. Instead, we want the word "anti-abortionists" to come to mean "people who think abortion is dangerous." It is this implication which will help create the appropriate doubt about abortion's safety in the minds of the middle majority.

By focusing on the rights of women and the unconscionable abuses of the abortion industry, this political posture appeals to the chief concern of the middle majority—their concern for women. It is also "value neutral" in that it does not attempt to condemn women for abortion. These pro-woman policies, moreover, do not even attempt to "impose" a moral judgment on abortion. Such a moral judgment is deliberately deferred until such time as the general public becomes more fully aware of the dangerous consequences of abortion.

Our goal with this political posture is to make the middle majority see that our goals and their goals can be aligned. Together, we can cooperate in trying to protect women, not judge them. Together, we can begin to make abortion more rare, not by restricting women's rights, but instead by expanding their rights to ensure that their choices are truly free and fully informed. In this respect, those who are truly pro-choice and those who are pro-life share a common concern and a common ground on which to build toward a reasonable solution to the abortion problem.

## SUMMARY

By understanding the priorities of the middle majority, it is possible to align their political support around candidates who support pro-woman/pro-life initiatives. Furthermore, by reframing the abortion debate in a way which puts women and children together on the same side, we shift the balance of the debate to our advantage. When faced with clearly pro-woman initiatives, pro-abortion politicians will be forced to either accede to our reforms, which will doom the abortion industry, or to side with the abortion industry against women's rights, which will doom pro-abortion politicians. Either way, we win.

CHAPTER FOUR

# THE KEY IS IN *ROE*

A political strategy is meaningless if the legislation it achieves is struck down by the courts. While it may eventually be possible to overturn *Roe v. Wade*, our strategy must not depend on this. Instead, we are better served by looking at *Roe* and the subsequent abortion decisions more carefully to see how their nuances can be turned to our own advantage. By working with these precedents, rather than against them, we can pass laws which are within the bounds allowed by *Roe* for protecting women from dangerous abortions.

Furthermore, by carefully defining the issue as one of protecting women's health interests, we can confidently predict the Court's reaction. First, since the Court has already ruled on these issues pertaining to women's rights and the doctor's duties, the judicial principle of *stare decisis* would require it to uphold our pro-woman statutes. In short, the Supreme Court has already painted itself into a corner; we just haven't taken advantage of it yet. Second, any attempt by the Justices to void our pro-woman statutes would clearly place them in the position of protecting abortionists at the expense of women, a position which would outrage the middle majority, whose sympathies are for women, not abortionists. Third, moderates on the Court would welcome a "face-saving" way to get out from under the abortion issue without actually overturning *Roe*. Our pro-woman laws open the door for curtailing abortion on demand without requiring the Court to actually admit its errors.

## PUTTING *ROE* IN CONTEXT

The *Roe* decision was clearly results-oriented. Determined to respond to the concerns of the time, which included exaggerated fears of a "population explosion," environmental degradation, the rise of a welfare state, the emancipation of women, and sexual license, the Court abandoned normal principles of judicial methodology and constitutional interpretation. With an amazing resolve, and no intellectual restraint, the Justices pulled the "right to abortion" out of a vague "right to privacy," which itself lay in the shadowy "penumbra" of the Bill of Rights.

Even supporters of abortion were troubled by the *Roe* majority's merely token attempt to acknowledge constitutional principles and judicial precedent. For example, Arthur Selwyn Miller, Professor Emeritus at the George Washington University National Law Center, stated, "[A]bortion is an idea whose time has come. I applaud the decision ...but do let me shake my head in bewilderment as to how one can make such a decision jibe with orthodox jurisprudence or judicial methodology."[1]

But the lack of constitutional guidance did not mean that Justice Blackmun and his collaborators had totally abandoned the goal of basing their decision on reasoned principles. Indeed, the reasoned principle on which *Roe* was formulated was first suggested by Justices William O. Douglas and Potter Stewart in dissents to the 1970 ruling *United States v. Vuitch*. Both were of the opinion that criminal abortion laws should not apply to physicians acting in their best medical judgment to preserve the health of their pregnant patients.

This argument for the autonomy of physicians had a special appeal to Nixon appointee Harry Blackmun. Before his appointment as a federal judge, Blackmun had been a "doctor's lawyer" for the prestigious Mayo Clinic. Programmed to defend the medical establishment, Blackmun always objected to any "undue" interference with the medical profession.[2] The arguments of Stewart and Douglas appealed to his world view. Whenever a doctor believes an abortion is necessary for a patient, Blackmun believed, the ability of the state to interfere should be severely limited. Indeed, in one of his summary statements in *Roe*, Blackmun writes: "[This] decision vindicates the right of the physician to administer medical treatment according to his professional judgment up to the points where important state interests provide compelling justifications for intervention."[3]

This "doctors know best" approach appeared reasonable and appealing for several reasons. First, there are inherent dangers to abortion. The safety of women is clearly better served by physicians with years of medical training than by radical feminists and bold entrepreneurs who have completed a four-hour workshop on abortion technique. Second, the decision to abort in a time of personal crisis involves a complex interplay of medical, social, psychological and moral issues unique to each woman. The professional opinion of a trained physician who could assist the woman in making a fully free and informed choice is essential to prevent hasty or ill-considered decisions which might result not only in regrets but also in grave physical injuries. Third, the medical profession was highly respected and exercised a great deal of political and social power. In the absence of constitutional principles, a decision based on the dignity and professionalism of physicians would carry with it a sense of reasonableness. In an era when doctors were epitomized by television's competent and compassionate Dr. Welby, placing abortion decisions under the authority of physicians was seen as a practical solution to the abortion question, one which would both prevent abusive profiteering and ensure the safety of women.

## A CONFLICT OF INTERESTS

It is in this context that *Roe* and its progeny are best understood. Though doctors have no special constitutional right to be free of state regulation, it was because of its appeal to the integrity of physicians that the Court's abortion solution had a claim to being reasonable.

This is the cornerstone upon which the "abortion liberty" was built, and its edifice was constructed by a convenient intertwining of the rights of women and the duties of physicians. But this intertwining of rights and duties also resulted in certain conflicts between the woman's and the abortionist's interests. Unlike the co-dependent interests of a woman and her child, the abortion liberty's entwining of a woman's rights with her physician's rights is an unnatural one. While the best interests of the woman and child are always the same, the best interests of a woman and her abortionist are not.

The key, then, to unraveling the "abortion liberty" is to expand the legitimate rights of women so that they are clearly superior to the imputed rights of abortionists. These legitimate rights of women include (1) the right to be protected from contraindicated procedures which would endanger their health, (2) the right to receive the best choice of care options, (3) the right to be fully involved in all aspects of medical decisions affecting their health, and (4) the right to receive full financial compensation for any injuries they incur as a result of an abortionist's failure to respect their rights.

It is noteworthy that abortion was legalized only after pro-abortionists succeeded in promoting their argument that when there is a conflict between the rights of a woman and the rights of her unborn child, the rights of the woman must prevail. Learning from this same strategy, we can apply it here as well. In short, we must promote the argument that whenever there is a conflict between the rights of the woman and those of her abortionist, the rights of the woman must still prevail.

## BASIC RESPONSIBILITY FOR THE DECISION RESTS ON THE PHYSICIAN

Contrary to popular notions, abortion is not a constitutional right which women are free to exercise autonomously. As *Roe* makes clear, "Some *amici* argue that the woman's right is absolute and that she is entitled to terminate her pregnancy at whatever time, in whatever way, and for whatever reason she alone chooses. With this we do not agree."[4]

A woman's request for abortion is always subject to the review and recommendation of a physician, who bears full responsibility for making that recommendation. This is so because the Supreme Court has repeatedly found that abortion has serious health risks, both mental and physical.[5] Therefore, abortion is not an arbitrary right of women but is rather a medical right which derives from her health needs and can therefore only be exercised after appropriate and sufficient consultation with a "responsible physician." It is by thus intertwining the rights of the patient and the duties of the physician that the Court has attempted to simultaneously advance and *protect* the health of women.

Abortion is best described as a medical procedure which women have a protected liberty to *seek* because of their unique health needs.[6] But this liberty is limited by three factors: (1) the physician's duty to protect the woman's health, (2) the state's interest in protecting the woman's health, and (3) the state's interest in protecting "potential human life."[7]

In describing the duties and obligations of the physician, the Court has been very clear. Physicians are free to provide abortion when, in consultation with their patients, it is *medically determined* to be in their patient's health interests. This is not an arbitrary decision; it is a medical decision. This important distinction was made in *Roe* when the Court concluded its decision with the emphatic statement that "the abortion decision in all its aspects is inherently, and primarily, a medical decision, and *basic responsibility* for it must rest with the physician."[8] [Italics added.]

Furthermore, the Court has consistently held that physicians are obligated to make this medical decision in light of a broad range of health issues, including physical, mental, social and family planning concerns.[9] Thus, as a health issue, "*the attending physician*, in consultation with his patient, is free to determine, without regulation by the State, that, *in his medical judgment*, the patient's pregnancy *should* be terminated."[10] [Italics added.]

In order to reach a "medical judgment" that a pregnancy "should" be aborted, the physician is clearly obligated to thoughtfully weigh, on a case-by-case basis, the risks, benefits, and alternative forms of care. This requirement to make an informed medical judgment is intended to protect women from profiteers and to preclude the pros-titution of medical skills, which would occur if an abortion were sim-ply provided on request. The role of the physician as a thoughtful protector of the woman's health was further substantiated when the Court emphasized that its "consistent recognition of the critical role of the physician in the abortion procedure has been based on the model of the competent, conscientious, and ethical physician."[11]

Clearly, a competent and conscientious physician would never allow a patient to self-diagnose her own health problems, much less prescribe her own treatment. In reserving to the physician the final judgment of when an abortion may be performed, the Court requires the physician to protect the patient from the grievous harm which can result from her own ignorance of potential risks and alternatives. And in all cases, the recommendation for an abortion, formed on the basis of her broadly defined health needs, should be "for the benefit, not the disadvantage, of the pregnant woman."[12]

To summarize up to this point, while a woman may initiate a request for an abortion, it is the physician's responsibility, in consul-tation with the patient, to weigh *all* the risks and benefits of every option and make an appropriate medical recommendation. This important, but generally neglected, safeguard in the Court's rulings reflects the fact that the distress of an unplanned pregnancy may lead a woman to make a hasty, rash, ill-informed, or even dangerous deci-sion. It is the physician's role, then, to bring a calm mind to this med-ical problem, to evaluate the patient's problems, needs, and risks, and to offer her the best care possible given all the complex factors involved. Just as a cancer patient is not free to procure chemotherapy without the review and recommendation of a physician, so a crisis pregnancy patient is not free to procure an abortion without the review and recommendation of a physician who will accept respon-sibility for what is "inherently, and primarily, a medical decision."

## THE STANDARD OF CARE FOR ABORTION RECOMMENDATIONS

The above analysis is very important to the issue of medical mal-practice. Abortion practitioners are not free to abandon all responsi-bility for the abortion decision. They may not justify provision of a dangerous abortion on the grounds that "I just gave her what she wanted." They must be able to articulate some basis for arriving at a recommendation for abortion which would reflect due consideration of all the health needs of the woman and the health risks of abortion.

In short, the Supreme Court has set in place specific requirements on the standard of care for abortion providers. It is the burden of the physician to make a medical judgment "in the light of all factors—physical, emotional, psychological, and the woman's age—relevant to well-being."[13] From this it can be argued that the Court clearly intended the physician to become familiar with the patient's health history, problems, and needs. Conversely, the failure to form a medical basis for an abortion recommendation constitutes negligence which endangers a patient's health, and abuse of this medical privilege to provide abortions is a cause for legal action.[14]

In addition, under the Supreme Court rulings, physicians clearly retain the right and duty to refuse an abortion which is contraindicated. This right and duty is also recognized by the Committee on Professional Standards of the American College of Obstetricians and Gynecologists (ACOG), which has reiterated that:

> It is recognized that although an abortion may be *requested* by a patient or recommended by a physician, the final decision as to performing the abortion must be left to the medical judgment of the pregnant woman's attending physician, in consultation with the patient.[15] [Italics added.]

A physician has the right and duty to refuse to perform an abortion which is likely to exacerbate a woman's *physical, psychological, or social problems*. At the very least, a competent physician would insist on delaying an abortion until pre-existing medical or psychological conditions had been treated.[16] The importance of this obligation will be further explored in Chapter Six, where the issue of proper screening will be examined.

## SUMMARY

In the Supreme Court's search to find a rational basis for restricting state regulation of abortion, the Court discovered the "abortion liberty" in the realm of a private relationship between a woman and her doctor. This "liberty" is predicated upon an idealized model of "the competent, conscientious, and ethical physician," who has specific obligations with regard to protecting the woman's well-being.

Though a woman is always free to *seek* an abortion, she does not have an absolute right to procure one. The physician retains the right and duty to refuse to provide an abortion which, in his best judgment, given the patient's unique physical, psychological, and social circumstances, may be injurious to her health. This is precisely the way in which the physician retains his medical discretion and exercises his "basic responsibility" for the abortion decision.[17]

However, the Court has never given the physician this same veto power with regard to childbirth. In other words, while a physician can refuse to perform an abortion for health reasons, he has no right to require or pressure a woman into consenting to an abortion because of the health risks associated with childbirth. In the same vein, he has no right to conceal alternative management options or health risks of abortion in order to "guide" her to choose abortion over childbirth.[18] Indeed, the Supreme Court itself has found that abortion involves such emotional and psychological risks that a decision to forego a previously desired abortion may generally be the safest course of action.[19]

This division of rights can be simply summed up in the following way. The physician is responsible for determining whether or not an abortion is contraindicated and is likely to be injurious to a woman's health. On the other hand, the woman is entitled to be fully informed about risks and alternatives so that she can make the ultimate decision, on the basis of all relevant information, of whether or not to accept the physician's recommendation to abort.[20]

It is notable that the duty of a physician to refuse a contraindicated abortion and the right of women to be fully informed of risks and alternatives so that they can change their minds would both tend to reduce the number of abortions performed. But instead, the number of abortions performed continues to grow. Why? Because abortionists are both violating their duty and denying women their rights. It is this abuse of their medical authority which will eventually destroy the abortion industry.

# CHAPTER FIVE

# DEVIATIONS FROM THE *ROE* IDEAL

ABORTION should not be carelessly dispensed as a panacea. While the Supreme Court has allowed physicians to use abortion as one of their tools in treating crisis pregnancies, it has never suggested that physicians are free to use this tool indiscriminately. Indeed, Chief Justice Burger's statements at the time of *Roe* clearly reflect that it was his personal expectation that physicians would resort to abortion only sparingly.[1] By the time he retired, however, Chief Justice Burger had come to the opinion that, in practice, *Roe* had resulted in the unmitigated disaster of abortion on request. Still, his earlier views do reflect that there was a hope, at least in some quarters of the Court, that responsible physicians would never exploit the despair of women in crisis just to earn a quick buck.

Unfortunately, when a quick buck can quickly turn into an extra hundred thousand, or two, per year, just by working on Fridays and Saturdays, some physicians quickly formed the "medical" opinion that every crisis pregnancy is treatable by abortion. In doing so, they have negligently abandoned their duty and violated the civil rights of women as defined by *Roe*.

## THE TYPICAL ABORTION CLINIC

At this moment, a brief digression is in order for readers who may not be familiar with the workings of the modern abortion industry. Those interested in a more complete description of abortion industry practices, and the personalities and instability of the persons involved, are referred to the chapter entitled "Business Before Medicine" in my previous book, *Aborted Women, Silent No More*.

In contrast to the Supreme Court's Dr. Welby model of a physician who is familiar with his or her patient's history and needs and who compassionately discusses with her the difficulties and options she faces, most abortionists are extremely distanced from their patients and work at a hectic pace. According to Dr. Edward Allred, owner of a chain of clinics performing 60,000 abortions per year:

> Very commonly we hear patients say they feel like they're on an assembly line. We tell them they're right. It is an assembly line....We're trying to be as cost-effective as possible, and speed is important....We try to use the physician for his technical skills and reduce the one-on-one relationship with the patient. We usually see the patient for the first time on the operating table and then not again...[2]

At least 90 percent of abortions are provided in non-hospital facilities. Abortion providers advertise aggressively in the Yellow Pages, offer 800 numbers and discount coupons, and frequently employ a referral network which includes family planning clinics. Often, free pregnancy tests are offered as a way of attracting potential clients who can be counseled toward and scheduled for abortion.

Abortion clinics are essentially self-policing, since the federal courts have rejected most state regulatory efforts, largely on the basis that they infringe on the autonomy of the physician and the privacy of the patient. Thus, there are seldom any substantial requirements for emergency equipment or advanced transfer arrangements to the nearest hospital in the event of a life-threatening complication. Indeed, when complications do occur, many clinics refuse to use ambulance services to transport the patient in order to avoid bad publicity. Instead, the patient is transported in a clinic person's car, often without the aid of a trained medical person during transit.

Under the dictates of *Roe*, any licensed physician may perform abortions. Thus, though many abortionists are obstetricians with extensive training in women's reproductive health, many others are from unrelated fields such as dermatology, psychiatry, or urology.

Unlike other medical practices, abortion clinics universally require payment for the full amount of the abortion prior to rendering any services, unless the costs of the abortion are clearly guaranteed by an insurer. Generally, only cash or certified checks are accepted. There are two reasons for this cash-in-advance rule. First, it shifts the balance of power to the clinic and serves as a deterrent against women who want to change their minds. This is especially powerful in cases where the woman is having an abortion to satisfy the demands of her parents or her boyfriend or husband. She knows that their fury will only be doubled if she goes home not only still pregnant, but also without her money, or with only a partial refund. Second, clinic staff are all too familiar with the outburst of tears, regrets, and anger which sometimes follow an abortion. Some women immediately blame the clinic staff for what they are feeling. If they were not required to pay until after the abortion, such women might refuse to do so.

Typically, there are no licensing requirements for staff persons who are responsible for patient counseling or post-operative care. Qualifications and training are at the sole discretion of clinic owners, though at least theoretically, medically related tasks such as screening, counseling, and informed consent are under the supervision of the responsible physician.

Pre-abortion counseling is usually performed by a clinic-trained staff person. Counseling sessions for groups of three to 20 women are not uncommon, though many clinics do offer individual counseling sessions. Group counseling sessions may last from fifteen minutes to half an hour or more, while individual counseling sessions seldom last more than ten to fifteen minutes.

Most abortion counselors are trained to recognize the fact that the decision to undergo an abortion is difficult, stressful, and often a marginal one. Therefore, to avoid increasing the stress on the patient (and losing a client), counselors are trained to avoid answering questions or providing information which will aggravate the concerns or doubts of a patient. Instead, pre-abortion counselors generally concentrate on reassuring the woman that abortion is her best option. The counselor is trained to take the role of a compassionate friend to help the aborting woman face the unknown and overcome her doubts. The problems which have motivated a woman to seek an abortion may be discussed in a casual manner, so as to provide the woman an opportunity to air her feelings, but they are seldom explored. Alternative methods of problem resolution, such as marital counseling or job relocation service, are rarely discussed at all.

Frequently, a patient's questions and concerns are sidestepped or answered in trivial ways so as to avoid arousing unresolved doubts or fears. When a patient volunteers a statement such as, "I really wish I could have this baby," abortion counselors will generally attempt to refocus her attention on reasons why the abortion is "for the best." As will be discussed later, such ambivalence is a major risk factor for psychological problems post-abortion and may be a contraindication for continuing with the abortion. When a counselor fails to assist patients to fully explore such feelings, that counselor is not only guilty of ignoring a "red flag" for post-abortion sequelae, she is also clearly engaged in the "selling" of abortions to an overtly reluctant patient.

Discussion of abortion-related risks is generally brief, with an emphasis on only a few of the immediate physical risks. Reproductive health risks are minimized, and increased cancer risks are almost certainly never mentioned at all. If psychological aftereffects are discussed at all, women are generally told that they may experience only temporary feelings of mild depression. Emphasis will be placed on the fact that "most" women are not significantly affected and are able to "get on with their lives." The fact that serious psychological sequelae are experienced by at least a significant minority of women (15 to 25 percent) is almost never discussed, even though these complication rates are at least equal to, and probably greater than, the risks associated with most physical complications.

Pre-abortion screening is generally non-existent. Most abortion counselors are not trained to identify all of the pre-existing characteristics which would place a woman at higher risk of negative physical or psychological reactions (see Chapter Six). Proper screening for risk factors, much more follow-up counseling to explain and resolve these risk factors, is a time-consuming task which most abortion clinics shun. Also, extensive pre-abortion screening does not contribute to the number of patients serviced, and would be most likely to result in some patients changing their minds. This lack of screening for known risk factors is symptomatic of a "routine driven" service industry which neglects the individual circumstances of patients.

Another area where many clinics cut corners in order to speed up the process is in the dilatation of the cervix prior to the abortion. The safest technique involves the insertion of laminaria, fibrous seaweed sticks which slowly swell, dilating and softening the cervix. This is the safest and least painful method of dilatation, and it reduces the risks of cervical injury.[3] The alternative is manual dilatation, which mechanically forces the cervix open with a series of progressively larger cone-like dilators. This method involves more pain and tearing of cervical muscles, but it is preferred by many abortion providers because it is faster, involves only one visit, and reduces the amount of time in which the patient can attempt to change her mind.

Since sonograms are rarely used, or even available, the abortion itself is a blind procedure, meaning the physician must work by feel alone. Experienced abortionists with large case loads may work quickly, completing an abortion in ten minutes or less. Local anesthetics are generally preferred to general anesthesia. Afterwards, the patient is held in a recovery room until her post-operative bleeding is under control. Before leaving, the patient will generally be given instructions regarding any warning signs of which she should be aware, such as excessive bleeding, fever, or passing of large clots. Unfortunately, many abortion providers do not keep their patients under observation in post-operative recovery for sufficient time, missing the opportunity to diagnose conditions like uterine atony, which may not be evident until up to an hour after the abortion.[4]

Good follow-up care is considered very important to the prevention of major post-operative complications.[5] But while some clinics offer follow-up examinations one to three weeks post-abortion, many do not.

According to the most widely used textbook on abortion services, "Properly performed in the best setting, abortion offers a second chance....Poorly done, abortion leaves physical and emotional scars for life."[6]

Tragically, all too many abortions are poorly done. This is because the pursuit of high profit margins has displaced concern for the welfare of patients. This is why the aggressive defense of patient's rights is essential to curtailing the shoddy practices which are occurring. For as Justice Blackmun wrote in *Roe*, "If an individual practitioner abuses the privilege of exercising proper medical judgment, the usual remedies, judicial and intra-professional, are available."[7]

## AVOIDING LIABILITY

When critically examined, the typical practices of the abortion industry clearly violate the idealized standards established by *Roe* and the subsequent abortion cases. Instead of "competent, compassionate, and ethical physicians" making informed recommendations for abortion, and fully disclosing to patients all that is relevant to their decisions, we find incompetent, compassionless, unethical technicians dispensing abortions on request without review of risks or consideration of better treatment options.

The abortion industry survives not because it is competent, but because the women it injures are generally so ashamed of what they have done that they don't dare to complain, much less face public humiliation in a lawsuit. This is especially true in the short period of time during which the statute of limitations normally allows malpractice victims to file suit, because it is during this time—immediately after the abortion—that women are most ashamed and most want to put the abortion experience behind them.

The abortion industry is also being protected by laws and judicial standards pertaining to malpractice which tend to favor physicians. For example, in some states, the normal standards for disclosure of risks are interpreted according to the "customary" norms of the medical community. This "community standard" will generally eliminate most opportunities to sue for lack of informed consent. Another example is the requirement placed on the plaintiff to obtain the cooperation of another abortionist to provide expert testimony against the defendant. Since abortionists are loathe to condemn each other, this requirement may pose a major obstacle to recovery.

Furthermore, in all states, malpractice suits are among the most expensive and difficult cases to litigate. Since such cases are usually taken on contingency, attorneys are likely to refuse even a good case if they cannot be confident that they will win a large enough award to cover their expenses. Because of these and other legal hurdles, many women who have suffered injuries for which they would justly be entitled to an award are simply denied the opportunity to have their cases heard.

These hurdles, however, can be removed. Some can be removed by statutes expanding the rights of women injured by abortion, and others can be removed by a more complete adherence to the precedents established in *Roe* and its progeny. These precedents, combined with new pro-women's-rights laws (such as described in Chapter Nine), can be used to define a higher standard of care for abortionists, which will respect the rights of women and protect them from dangerous and unnecessary abortions.

In the next three chapters we will look at three specific areas of negligence, pre-abortion screening, options counseling, and disclosure. We will show how proper conduct in these areas would dramatically reduce the number of abortions performed on women, especially among the majority of women who are most at risk of suffering post-abortion sequelae.

## SUMMARY

The business of abortion has evolved into a streamlined service industry which is far removed from the highly professional model of medical care upon which *Roe* was formulated. To reduce the level of involvement by physicians, clients are allowed to self-diagnose their problems and prescribe their own treatment. To further reduce the cost of counseling, and to avoid time-consuming introspection, risk disclosure is minimized, screening for risk factors is non-existent, and alternatives counseling is presumed to be mostly unnecessary. The result is that women are being exposed to dangerous abortions which are injurious to their best interests.

This substandard level of care has evolved, and thrived, because there are artificial legal obstacles which prevent most women from being able to successfully sue their abortionists. Reform will occur only when abortionists become fully liable for protecting women's health and are held fully responsible for ensuring that a woman's consent to an abortion recommendation is fully free and informed.

CHAPTER SIX

# PROPER SCREENING
# OF PATIENTS

THE demand for adequate screening of abortion patients is one of the most important keys to our pro-woman/pro-life strategy. Proper screening is especially important to women because the vast majority of them fall into one or more high-risk categories.

The duty to properly screen patients prior to abortion is derived both from the physician's obligation to form a treatment plan which safeguards his patient's health and from the woman's right to be given all of the information relevant to her decision to accept or reject his recommendation.

The failure to adequately screen patients for pre-identifying factors constitutes negligence. Additional negligence occurs if a risk factor is identified and not mitigated by proper treatment, referral, or additional counseling. In addition, the failure to tell a woman or, in the case of a minor, the minor's parents of identifiable risk factors is concealment of relevant information and a violation of the patient's right to full disclosure. Thus, the need to hold the abortion industry accountable for proper pre-abortion screening is undisputable.

## IDENTIFYING HIGH-RISK ABORTION PATIENTS

In determining the risks and benefits of management options for a crisis pregnancy, a physician is clearly obligated to make an assessment of risk factors associated with specific physical and psychological adverse reactions.[1] Risk factors for physical complications include uterine abnormalities, multiple gestation, cardiovascular disease, renal disease, asthma, epilepsy, diabetes, venereal infection, intoxication or being in a drugged state, obesity, and other pre-existing conditions.[2]

While the physical risks of abortion are significant, the published literature demonstrates that emotional and psychological complications following an abortion are far more common. While there is wide variation among what researchers define to be "significant" emotional complications, all studies show that at least some women are negatively affected by abortion. Even the most dedicated pro-choice researchers generally admit that "[t]here is now virtually no disagreement among researchers that some women experience negative psychological reactions postabortion."[3] The lowest estimate for adverse outcomes is six percent, with typical reports ranging from 12 to 25 percent, and the highest estimates ranging up to 80 percent.[4]

While there is intense controversy among researchers regarding how frequently women experience post-abortion psychological sequelae, there is general agreement concerning the pre-identifying factors which can be used to predict an increased risk of significant post-abortion psychological distress. Indeed, most of the research on pre-identifying risk factors has been published by abortion proponents, and so these findings are immune from the charge of bias.

The risk factors for post-abortion psychological maladjustments can be divided into two general categories. The first category includes women for whom there exist significant emotional, social, or moral conflicts regarding the contemplated abortion. The second category includes women for whom there are developmental problems, including immaturity, or pre-existing and unresolved psychological problems. A summary list of established risk factors includes: conflicting maternal desires; moral ambivalence; feeling pressured to abort by others; feeling the decision is not her own, or is her "only choice;" feeling rushed to make a decision; immaturity or adolescence; prior emotional or psychological problems, including poor development of coping skills or prior low self-image; a prior history of abuse or unresolved trauma; a history of social isolation as indicated by having few friends or lack of support from one's partner or family; a history of prior abortions; or a history of religious or conservative values which attach feelings of shame or social stigma to abortion. Readers may refer to Appendix A for a more complete list of these pre-identifying risk factors.

These risk factors clearly suggest that the majority of women are predictably at risk of experiencing adverse psychological reactions.[5] The conscientious physician would be legally and ethically bound to consider these risk factors in forming a recommendation, to advise the woman of the existence of these risk factors, and, in at least some cases, to refuse to perform an abortion until these risk factors had been alleviated through appropriate counseling.[6]

Proper pre-abortion counseling should include screening for all of the high-risk factors listed above, notification to the patient of any existing risk factors, and appropriate counseling or referral to care and counseling resources outside the clinic where these risk factors can be addressed or treated.[7] Furthermore, after the intake screening, patients should routinely be instructed about *all* pre-existing risk factors, even those which the patient does not report, because it is well known that abortion patients may conceal a history of prior abortions, coercion, or other relevant information. In anticipation of such concealment, routine disclosure of all risk factors is necessary for the purpose of ensuring that the patient at least has the opportunity to make an informed self-evaluation of her risk profile. Inadequate psychosocial screening endangers patients' health and should be considered sufficient to establish negligence.

## A Look at Motivations Behind This Research

This issue of inadequate pre-abortion screening is one which pro-abortion researchers have virtually handed to us on a silver platter. This was not their intent, of course.

Instead, the real reason pro-abortion researchers have published so much on risk factors is that they have been seeking a way to dismiss the complaints of the troublesome "minority" of women who clearly have post-abortion maladjustments within even a few weeks after the abortion. In order to dismiss these patients, pro-abortion researchers have tried to identify how these women are different from those who appear to be "unaffected" by abortion. Having identified these pre-existing factors, they then argue that it is not abortion which causes these women to have problems; their distress is instead the result of some other pre-existing problem. This "politically correct" view of post-abortion trauma contains a kernel of truth, but it is mostly coated with a lot of "blaming the victim."

It is certainly true that women who are suffering from mental disorders or have previously suffered psychological trauma are more likely to subsequently report more severe negative post-abortion reactions. Indeed, if one thing is clear from post-abortion research over the last forty years, it is that abortion is contraindicated when a woman already has mental health problems. This is true because abortion is always stressful. How well a person copes with this stress depends on the individual's resiliency and the conditions under which the stress occurs. When a woman's psychological state is already fragile, the stress of an abortion can more easily overwhelm her. But the fact that she was more vulnerable to stress than others does not mean that the abortion is not the cause of her psychological injuries.

If a glass plate and a plastic plate are both dropped, the glass plate is likely to shatter, while the same stress may cause the plastic plate to only crack or chip. In either case, the damage cannot be blamed on the material; it must be blamed on the fall. While the *extent* of the damage is related to the nature of the material, the fall itself is the direct *cause* of the damage. In the same way, while the nature of an individual's psyche determines the *extent* of post-abortion injuries, it is the abortion itself which is the *direct cause* of those injuries.

Pro-abortion researchers, on the other hand, insist that post-abortion maladjustments must be blamed on the character flaws of the individual. This "blame the victim" strategy is not new. It is identical to the type of reasoning used during World War I when veterans suffering from "shell shock" were diagnosed by military psychiatrists as "malingerers" or even cowards. In an age when fighting for one's country was romantically idealized as adventurous passage into manhood, this "politically correct" diagnosis was necessary to deflect attention away from the fact that modern warfare was often more traumatic than ennobling. Military officials therefore attempted to suppress reports of psychiatric casualties because accurate reports would have had a demoralizing effect on the public.[8]

In the same way, when pro-abortion researchers are confronted with women who suffer from post-abortion trauma, there is a tendency to blame the women for being "whiners" or "dysfunctional." This judgment is a result of their *a priori* belief that abortion "empowers" women. This bias is so strong that some pro-abortion researchers even argue that women should not be told of any psychological risks associated with abortion because such "demoralizing" information may make them even more prone to an adverse outcome. It is better, they would claim, to be ignorantly optimistic about the future than informed and worried. Essentially, these pro-abortion researchers are arguing that the suffering of a "few" misfits should not be used to raise doubts among the many.

## THE STRATEGIC IMPORTANCE OF SCREENING REQUIREMENTS

The biases of pro-abortion researchers, however, are not nearly as important as their findings. When examined as a body of literature, the information they have handed us actually demonstrates that the vast majority of women fall into one or more statistically significant high-risk categories. The pro-abortionists themselves have clearly established the importance of adequate screening.

These findings have inadvertently placed the abortion industry in a "Catch-22." Failure to screen makes them liable for negligence. Adequate screening, on the other hand, will demand from them far greater attention to evaluation of each case and a much higher standard of counseling to alleviate the risk factors which are identified. In addition, it must be remembered that the physician has a right and duty to refuse to do a contraindicated abortion. If he performs an abortion despite the presence of known risk factors, and the woman subsequently experiences negative emotional consequences, his recommendation to perform a contraindicated abortion would itself be evidence of either incompetence or negligence.

In short, proof that high-risk factors were present at the time of the abortion, whether identified at that time or not, increases the liability of the abortionist. If they were left unidentified, he is guilty of negligence. If they were identified, and the abortionist persisted in recommending abortion, there was again negligence. Whether the abortion caused the subsequent emotional problems or whether it simply triggered the worsening of previously existing emotional problems is mostly a philosophical issue. The relevant fact is that the abortionist knew, or should have known, that the woman's psychological health was at risk.

Another way of looking at the issue of pre-identifying risk factors is to examine how this knowledge *should* affect the standard of care for abortion. A competent physician would properly be expected to (1) provide pre-consent information about the types of psychological reactions which have been linked to a negative abortion experience and the risk factors associated with these adverse reactions; (2) provide adequate pre-abortion screening using the criteria outlined above to identify women who are at risk of negative post-abortion reactions; (3) provide individualized counseling to high-risk patients which would more fully explain why the patient is at risk, along with more detailed information concerning possible post-abortion reactions; and (4) assist women who have pre-identifying high-risk factors in evaluating and choosing lower-risk solutions to their social, economic, and health problems.

## THE DUTY TO LOOK DEEPER

In evaluating a patient's psychological risks, the idealized standard of care established by the medical community does not allow abortion counselors to rely simply on whatever the patient volunteers. Instead, counselors should actively look for "red flags" which would indicate the presence of risk factors. Uta Landy, a former executive director of the National Abortion Federation, encourages counselors to be aware of the fact that:

> Some women's feelings about their pregnancy are not simply ambivalent but deeply confused. This confusion is not necessarily expressed in a straightforward manner, but can hide behind such outward behavior as: (1) being uncommunicative, (2) being extremely self- assured, (3) being impatient (how long is this going to take, I have other important things to do), or (4) being hostile (this is an awful place; you are an awful doctor, counselor, nurse; I hate being here).[9]

Landy also admits that because women seeking abortion are experiencing a time of personal crisis, their decision-making processes can be temporarily impaired. This crisis-related disability may lead them to make a poor decision which will subsequently result in serious feelings of regret. Landy defines four types of defective decision-making observed in abortion clinics. She calls the first defective process the "spontaneous approach," wherein the decision is made too quickly, without taking sufficient time to resolve internal conflicts or explore options. A second defective decision-making process is the "rational-analytical approach," which focuses on the practical reasons to terminate the pregnancy (financial problems, single parenthood, etc.) without consideration of emotional needs (attachment to the pregnancy, maternal desires, etc.). A third defective process is the "denying-procrastinating" approach, which is typical of women who have delayed making a decision precisely because of the many conflicting feelings they have about keeping the baby. When such a "denying-procrastinator" finally agrees to an abortion, it is likely that she has still not resolved her internal conflicts, but is submitting to the abortion only because she has "run out of time." Fourth, there is the "no-decision-making approach" wherein a woman refuses to make her own decision but allows others, such as her male partner, parents, counselors, or physician, to make the decision for her.[10]

The standard of care for pre-abortion screening is further described in *Obstetrical Decision Making*. In the section regarding induced abortion, it clearly states:

> It is essential for the gravida [pregnant woman] to be *fully informed* about alternative resources and options and about the safety and risks of the procedure. Psychosocial assessment and counseling are done at the very first visit [see section on psychosocial assessment]. In addition to the medical history, an *in-depth* social history, including relationships with others, attitudes about abortion, and support systems *must be*

*obtained* at this time....No decision should be made by the gravida *in haste, under duress, or without adequate time and information.* Special attention should be given to feelings of ambivalence, guilt, anger, shame, sadness, and sense of loss....Patients requesting abortion *must also be screened* to uncover any serious medical or psychiatric conditions."[11] [Italics added.]

Under the section on psychosocial assessment, the obstetrician is also told that "he or she needs to be alert to gravid women who are at *greatest risk*, such as those who were victims of child abuse or neglect themselves and those with a history of psychologic impairment, drug dependency, or behavioral problems." [Italics added.]

At least one pro-choice researcher suggests that pre-abortion screening should be used to distinguish those patients who need in-depth counseling from those who need only supportive counseling. Using just five screening criteria—(1) a history of psychosocial instability, (2) a poor or unstable relationship with her partner, (3) few friends, (4) a poor work pattern, and (5) failure to take contraceptive precautions—Belsey determined that 64 percent of the 350 abortion patients she studied should have been referred for more extensive counseling. Of this high risk group, 72 percent actually did develop negative post-abortion reactions within the time frame of the study's follow-up. "From a clinician's point of view," she writes, "this result can be viewed as erring on the right side, for a [pre-abortion screening] system that tends to select more women for counseling than is actually necessary is preferable to the reverse."[12]

Of special concern are cases in which a woman desires to have her child but is submitting to the abortion to satisfy the demands of others.[13] Patients should be carefully questioned, in private, to determine if this risk factor is present, since the abused or coerced patient may attempt to conceal the abuse out of fear. This abuse or coercion can be subtle or overt; for example, her partner or parents may threaten to withhold love or approval unless she "does the best thing." Even lack of emotional support to keep a pregnancy may be experienced as a pressure "forcing" a woman to choose abortion.[14]

In addition, pressure from adverse circumstances, such as financial problems, being unmarried, social problems, or health problems, may also make a woman feel she is being "forced" to accept abortion as her "only choice." If her "only choice" is contrary to her maternal desires, she should be assisted in finding resources and alternatives which may provide her with an option which does not violate her emotional, maternal, and moral needs.

## INSIGHTS FROM PRE-IDENTIFYING RISK FACTORS

If I may be allowed a brief detour, I would like readers to take a closer look at the list of pre-identifying risk factors. These risk factors are very instructive for helping one to understand exactly why abortion patients suffer psychological sequelae.

In the majority of cases, women seeking abortion feel some external pressure to do so. Yet at the same time, 60 to 70 percent of women seeking abortions have moral qualms about abortion itself, and over 60 percent are struggling with a maternal desire to protect their pregnancies.

For these women, abortion is not a glorious right by which they are able to reclaim control of their lives; instead, it is an "evil necessity" which they submit to because they "have no choice." Rather than affirming their own values, these women feel forced to compromise their values. Rather than feeling proud of themselves for standing up for their beliefs, even during in difficult circumstances, they feel ashamed of themselves for being "spineless cowards."

This feeling of self-betrayal is a devastating blow to the woman's self-image and her feelings of self-worth. She is internally divided by an emotional "war" within and against her very self. On one side are her original moral beliefs and maternal desires. On the other side is her abortion experience, which represents a choice to act against those feelings. From this internal warfare, unresolved feelings will unpredictably erupt through out the woman's life and will manifest themselves in a wide variety of psychological illnesses.

## SUMMARY

Few abortionists adequately screen patients for the known risk factors which pre-identify women as being at higher risk of experiencing psychological maladjustments post-abortion. This lack of adequate screening is due to (1) a desire to streamline abortion services and avoid extensive pre-abortion evaluations, and (2) a desire to deny that there are *any* post-abortion problems.

In their efforts to dismiss the "minority" of women, 15 to 25 percent, who are known to have post-abortion sequelae, pro-abortion researchers have thoroughly established that there are pre-identifying factors which can be used to predict negative post-abortion reactions. Proper use of these factors in pre-abortion screening would require much more extensive counseling and care than is normally provided today for 70 percent, or more, of all patients requesting abortion.

In terms of civil action against abortion providers, either the failure to identify known risk factors, the failure to notify the patient of potential risk factors, or the failure to refuse an abortion which was contraindicated may provide grounds for a suit claiming malpractice or reckless endangerment.

# CHAPTER SEVEN

# ALTERNATIVES COUNSELING

I N the previous chapter, we looked more closely at the legal and medical obligations of the abortionist with regard to screening. Now we will look more closely at his obligations with regard to recommending the safest course of action and advising the patient with regard to alternative forms of care.

When a woman comes to a physician requesting an abortion (a form of treatment), her actual complaint (her health problem) is that she is experiencing a crisis pregnancy. But what, precisely, is this problem for which she is seeking help? Is it the "crisis" or is it the "pregnancy?"

When over 80 percent of women seeking abortions report that they would have desired, or at least been willing, to keep their pregnancies if only circumstances were better, it is clear that the notion of a "health problem" should attach to whatever it is that is making a crisis out of the pregnancy, not the pregnancy itself. Clearly, many women would be extremely happy to keep their pregnancy if only they could be relieved of the crisis associated with it. Most actively desire to have children in the future. These women are self-prescribing the "cure" of abortion only because they do not know how to get rid of their present problems without also sacrificing their babies.[1]

When evaluating a patient who is seeking treatment for a crisis pregnancy, it is the physician's duty to identify the underlying "disease"—meaning whatever it is that is causing the "crisis" associated with her pregnancy. Only after doing this can a physician make a knowledgeable and responsible recommendation which will treat, and hopefully resolve, the crisis in the least dangerous and most effective manner. As we will see, just as the cause of the crisis will be unique to each woman, so will the most effective treatment. Furthermore, we will see why it is precisely because they engage in a "one treatment fits all" type of medicine that assembly-line abortion mills are inherently mistreating women.

## AN EXAMPLE OF THE FAILURE TO
## IDENTIFY THE PROPER ALTERNATIVES

Proper alternatives counseling is perhaps best illustrated by example. This is the true story of "Terri," whose abortion of a wanted pregnancy led to drug abuse and prolonged psychological treatment. Adequate assessment of her crisis would have identified alternatives which would have spared her the injuries she and other women have experienced when they felt forced to submit to the "evil necessity" of an unwanted abortion.

Terri had become pregnant by her fiance. Both were happy about it. They had even picked out names and moved up the wedding date. But suddenly, Terri became concerned that her former husband would use the out-of-wedlock pregnancy to take away custody of her two small children. There was no provocation for this fear. Her ex-husband had never even indicated a desire to have custody. Yet this fear that he *might* try to take them reached overpowering proportions and drove her to seek an abortion over the objections of her fiance.

Terri was given an abortion without any screening for the several high-risk factors which are evident even in this short synopsis (a wanted pregnancy, feelings of being pressured to have an unwanted abortion, and objections from her male partner). Nor was her crisis situation accurately identified so that appropriate counseling and care could be provided. In this case, the pregnancy was not her problem; it was fear of the possibility that her ex-husband might seek custody. Proper counseling would have identified the crux of Terri's crisis. She should have been referred for legal counseling and possibly marriage counseling.

What Terri really wanted was a way to keep her pregnancy without losing custody of her other two children. In reviewing her circumstances and options, a competent physician would have helped her to identify this need and find the means to satisfy it. And if no other resolution could be found, the physician, if he decided to recommend abortion at all, would at the very least have discussed the risk factors which exposed her to the greater likelihood of post-abortion problems so that Terri could weigh these risks against the risk of losing custody of her children.

In the end, it was only after Terri was in counseling to recover from her post-abortion psychological disabilities that she discovered that her ex-husband highly valued her as a good mother. He would never have sought to deny her custody of the children. Only in hindsight did she discover that her fears had been groundless.

## CHOOSING THE BEST ALTERNATIVE

Alternatives counseling is not a service which abortion providers are free to dismiss; it is a required part of pre-abortion counseling.[2] In the case of Terri, the abortionist failed to identify that Terri's first need was legal counsel.

Other cases may present different alternatives. For example, when a woman is being pressured into an unwanted abortion by her husband (a high-risk factor), marital counseling would best suit her needs and desires. Similarly, if a teenager is being pressured into an unwanted abortion by her parents, or if she is simply too embarrassed to face her parents alone, interventive family counseling would provide a safer alternative. Is she chiefly concerned about ridicule at her work, or does she fear that she may lose advancement opportunities because of her boss's prejudices? Then she might feel saved from an unwanted abortion simply by being referred to the care of a job relocation service, such as those offered by The Nurturing Network, which would place her into a new and more receptive work environment.

Is she submitting to an abortion only to keep her boyfriend from leaving her? Then she should be helped to understand that the abortion will almost certainly doom their uncommitted relationship anyway (which she will often know already in her heart but be denying in her head), in which case, she will be left with nothing but the regrets. Would any responsible physician subject a patient to the more than 100 physical and psychological risks of abortion simply to satisfy the demands of an irresponsible scoundrel?

Does she want children but simply feel unable to have one now because she has financial problems or concerns about finishing school? Then a referral to the appropriate social services agency might best serve her.

Is she pregnant as the result of sexual assault? Then she should be informed that an abortion is likely to aggravate her feelings of violation and despair, adding trauma on top of trauma.[3] She should be referred to a support group like the Life After Assault League, where she can talk to women who have been in the same situation so that she can learn from their experiences.[4]

All of the patients in the situations described above are actually at high-risk of experiencing severe psychological sequelae from abortion. These women do not want to remain childless. They may even be filled with a longing to have the very baby which is in their womb. But these maternal feelings are being overpowered by pressures from circumstances or people which they feel powerless to resist. They are submitting to *unwanted* abortions because they feel as if they have no other choice. It is the role of the crisis pregnancy counselor to help the woman identify this distinction and to assist her in finding the support and resources she needs to keep her baby.

## THE CRISIS PREGNANCY BUSINESS

While it is true that abortionists see themselves as being in the business of providing abortions, in a legal and professional sense, this is not what their business is really supposed to be. Instead, they are supposed to be health professionals, in the business of helping women manage crisis pregnancies.

As has been previously discussed, the Supreme Court never gave to abortionists the right to indiscriminately dispense abortions on request. It is more accurate to say that the Court insisted that physicians must be allowed to use abortion as simply one of the many treatment options which they may employ. This is an important point because it helps us to clarify precisely what standard for counseling and diagnosis should be applied to crisis pregnancies.

Given the fact that there are more than 100 physical and psychological complications associated with abortion, plus the fact that most women see their unborn child as a living being, the killing of whom involves great moral questions, it is clear that abortion should not be the preferred method of treatment. Instead, it seems obvious under the Hippocratic standard of "first, do no harm," that the physician should, if at all possible, assist the woman in finding a way to keep her child by helping her to find ways to correct the circumstances which make her feel that she has to have an abortion.

At this point, abortionists would object, saying that they are not social workers. They provide abortions, not marital counseling or job placement. But it is precisely because they are artificially limiting the scope of their involvement in their patients' health needs that they are negligent. In *Doe v. Bolton* the Supreme Court declared that the physician's decision to treat a woman's crisis pregnancy by abortion should properly be made "in the light of all factors—physical, emotional, psychological, and the woman's age—relevant to well-being."[5] It is therefore obvious that these same factors must be considered in evaluating and recommending alternatives.

While a physician who treats crisis pregnancies may not be trained to actually provide marital counseling, financial counseling, job placement, or similar services, he or she is presumed to be capable of doing a psychosocial assessment of the patient to identify the root causes of her psychosocial problem. One would also presume that a physician who is specializing in crisis pregnancy care would be capable of making appropriate referrals to outside agencies and resources.

Furthermore, the successful practices of thousands of ob/gyns and general practitioners demonstrate that crisis pregnancies can be safely and effectively managed without abortion. These non-aborting physicians have proven themselves capable of screening and counseling women, with appropriate referrals, so that they can resolve their crises without the risks involved in abortion. The professional care that these non-aborting physicians provide women is clearly relevant to the standard of care which all pregnant women in crisis should receive.

## EXPERT TESTIMONY

It is one of our goals in this pro-woman/pro-life strategy to make this issue of alternatives counseling, and the corresponding duty of recommending the best treatment option, an important issue in abortion malpractice suits. Abortionists should not be allowed to state in their defense that "I simply gave her what she wanted—an abortion." Instead, they must be required to show why they believed abortion was the best choice of management options.

In this regard, however, the abortion industry should not be allowed to establish its own standard of care in isolation from the rest of the medical community. Therefore, it is inappropriate for state courts to disallow as "non-expert" the testimony of physicians who do not perform abortions. This is especially so because abortion is not recognized in the law as a distinct medical specialty. Indeed, the Supreme Court has already determined that abortion is within the expertise of any physician. Requirements for specialization are not, nor can be, required.[6] In essence, then, the Court has already determined that the standard of care for abortion is so routine that *any* licensed physician is qualified to meet this standard. Therefore, one would expect that *any* physician should be accepted as an expert on the standard of care for abortion. If a physician is qualified enough to perform an abortion tomorrow, he or she is certainly qualified enough to testify about the proper standard of care today.

Nor should the testimony of a qualified expert be excluded simply because he or she has never found a sufficiently compelling reason to recommend or perform an abortion. Indeed, the testimony of a physician who rarely, or never, performs abortions in the management of crisis pregnancies may be particularly relevant, especially if he or she has found that other options have always been available which pose less of a threat to the physical, emotional, psychological, or social health of the patient than abortion. Such testimony goes directly to the issue of the appropriateness of the defendant physician's recommendation for an abortion. Indeed, the jury may also consider relevant the fact that, while many women complain that they have been exploited by abortionists, there is no evidence of women complaining against physicians who helped them find alternatives which enabled them to keep their children. This fact alone should suggest the preferred course of treatment.

Furthermore, the standard of care for crisis pregnancy counseling, alternatives counseling, and pre-abortion screening can legitimately be separated from the actual surgical procedure of abortion. This is evident from the fact that all ob/gyns and general practitioners routinely counsel women faced with unplanned pregnancies. This professional crisis pregnancy management includes supportive psychological counseling, options counseling, screening for risk factors associated with each option, and disclosure of risks and options to the patient.[7]

These observations provide compelling reason to expand the pool of expert witnesses available for plaintiffs to call upon in suits against abortion clinics. By eliminating the requirement for testimony from experts from within the abortion industry, we will eliminate a major barrier against women seeking redress. Justice is also better served by clearly placing the burden of proving the appropriateness of an abortion recommendation on the abortionist.

## SUMMARY

In treating a woman faced with a crisis pregnancy, it is the physician's duty to help her find the best solutions to her physical and psychosocial health problems. It is superficial, and negligent, to assume that the pregnancy itself is always the real problem, or that aborting it will always solve a woman's problems without causing additional physical or psychosocial problems. As with any medical condition, there are many alternatives for managing a crisis pregnancy. A proper recommendation must be based on an understanding of the precise factors which make up the underlying cause of this health crisis.

The failure to consider alternative options of care is medical negligence. The failure to provide alternatives counseling is also a denial of the patient's right to full disclosure of risks and alternatives and may invalidate the patient's consent. In the event of a civil suit by an injured patient, abortionists can and should be required to defend their recommendation to abort against the standard of medical care provided by non-aborting physicians. The obligation of proving that a medical treatment is safer or more effective than allowing nature to take its course always rests on those who advocate that form of treatment. The promoters of abortion have failed to meet this obligation.

CHAPTER EIGHT

# THE WOMAN'S RIGHT TO FULL DISCLOSURE

IN *Planned Parenthood v. Casey*, the Supreme Court approved state-mandated informed consent requirements for abortion which are intended to protect the rights of the women as patients.Following this lead, pro-life organizations in several states have successfully lobbied for regulations on informed consent procedures at abortion clinics. This is a positive development, and should be continued.

But not all informed consent statutes are created equal. Indeed, there is the danger, in some cases, that statutory informed consent requirements may be viewed by the courts as establishing a *sufficient* standard for informed consent rather than a *minimum* standard. In such cases, the statute may be construed to protect the abortionist from liability in cases where the patient may have required *more* information than that specified in the statute. Such would be the case when a woman had physical or psychological characteristics which placed her at higher risk of suffering post-abortion complications than a "normal" patient. In such instances, an ill-drafted informed consent law might actually reduce the injured patient's right to recovery.

It is therefore important for pro-lifers to better understand the abortion patient's rights as already defined by the judiciary. This is especially so in states where special informed consent legislation is difficult to pass. In these states, existing statutes and legal precedents can effectively be used to defend and expand patients' rights through civil litigation.

## VARIATIONS IN DISCLOSURE STANDARDS

There are two prevailing standards for disclosure of risks prior to receiving medical care. The first, the so-called "traditional" or "community" standard, is physician-centered and defined by the common and customary practices in the medical community, namely, by what another physician in the same specialty would reveal in a similar situation. The second standard is patient-centered, and is defined by what a "reasonable patient" would find *relevant* to his or her decision to accept or forego a recommended medical treatment.

The traditional, physician-centered standard is best understood in the context of the trust relationship between the physician and patient: "Where the physician-patient relationship is established, the law imposes on the physician a fiduciary duty of good faith and fair dealing; among other things, this duty requires the physician to inform the patient of the nature of his condition and to obtain informed consent as to future treatment."[1]

The "reasonable patient" standard has evolved in recognition of the fact that whenever any bias about any medical procedure exists, it tends to produce a bias in favor of underdisclosure of risks, thereby making a "community medical standard" for disclosure inadequate.[2] Courts have ruled that, "As the patient must bear the expense, pain and suffering of any injury from medical treatment, his right to know all material facts pertaining to the proposed treatment cannot be dependent upon the self-imposed standards of the medical profession."[3] "True consent to what happens to oneself is the exercise of a *choice*, and that entails an opportunity to evaluate knowledgeably the *options available* and the *risks* attendant upon each."[4] [Italics added.] Though the physician may feel strongly about the correct course of action, "it is the prerogative of the patient, not the physician, to determine for himself the direction in which his interests lie," and that requires full disclosure of the nature of the procedure and all the risks and alternatives which a reasonable patient might desire to know in order to make an informed choice.[5] Even complications occurring only one percent of the time must be disclosed.[6]

In all, fifteen states and the District of Columbia have adopted the "reasonable patient" standard for informed consent, nineteen have adopted an informed consent doctrine based on the fiduciary relationship of the physician and patient, and ten have combined elements of both.[7]

Under both standards for obtaining informed consent, it is not sufficient merely to give a patient a laundry list of potential risks. It is the attending physician's responsibility to make sure that the patient adequately *understands* the relevant risks and options and has *sufficient time* to consider them. These requirements, understanding and time, are especially important in dealing with teenagers who have developmental limitations which may prevent them from fully comprehending and weighing the information as quickly as would an adult.[8] In such cases, the patient may need more detailed explanations and more assistance in reviewing the benefits, risks, and options. Failure to ensure that the patient fully understands the risks, or has had adequate time to reach an informed choice, may provide an additional basis of negligence.[9]

Uninformed consent may also occur when a patient is not informed of personal physical or psychological characteristics which would pre-identify her as being at higher risk of suffering one or more post-procedural complications. A patient would reasonably expect to be informed of any high-risk factors pertinent to his or her case and to receive counseling with regard to alleviating these risks. If the patient was not informed of these high-risk factors because the physician failed to identify them during pre-procedure screening, the physician might be guilty of negligence.[10]

If there is inadequate disclosure to a patient, *the consent is invalid* and the physician's actions are a form of battery. In such cases, the offenses of negligence and battery are intertwined.[11]

## THERAPEUTIC PRIVILEGE AND ITS LIMITS

Under both informed consent standards, nondisclosure is justified when the information itself "poses such a threat of detriment to the patient as to become unfeasible or contraindicated from a medical point of view."[12] For example, it may be reasonable to withhold highly stressful information to a cardiac patient when the information itself can cause the onset of a heart attack.

But even when a treatment is lifesaving, the option of withholding potentially upsetting information, commonly referred to as "therapeutic privilege," is very narrow.[13] This option is narrowed even further in the case of an elective procedure, where, by definition, the patient may decline the proposed treatment without dire consequences.[14] When the information does not pose a significant health risk, there is no "therapeutic privilege." Furthermore, no court has ever held a doctor liable for giving too much information.[15] Therefore, it seems reasonable that physicians should err on the side of full disclosure.

When a procedure is elective, then, the only reasons a physician could give for withholding relevant information would be purely self-serving, that is, either (1) to save time, or (2) to avoid losing the sale of one's services.

The application of these principles to the case of abortion is readily apparent. As opposed to therapeutic abortions necessary to save a woman's life, an *elective* abortion is, by definition, never life-threat-

ening. In the latter case the withholding of information is never justified. A decision to forego a previously desired abortion after learning
of possible risks, even remote ones, is always reasonable.[16] Indeed,
the Supreme Court itself has found that abortion involves such emotional and psychological risks that a decision to forego a previously
desired abortion may often be the wisest course of action.[17]

## PRIMACY OF THE REASONABLE PATIENT STANDARD

Abortion is a unique medical procedure.[18] Certainly no medical
procedure has involved more Supreme Court rulings which have
defined its legal nature and the attendant duties and obligations of
the physician. On one hand, the aborting physician is responsible for
ensuring that his recommendation to abort will benefit the patient,
given her unique circumstances and her physical and emotional
makeup. On the other hand, the physician is also responsible for
helping the patient to fully understand the basis for his recommendation, attendant risks, and alternatives so that she can independently reevaluate the situation in the light of his disclosures.

With regard to this latter responsibility, the Court has clearly presumed that the informed consent standard which should be applied
is the reasonable patient standard. "The decision to abort, indeed, is
an important, and often a stressful one, and it is desirable and *imperative* that it be made with *full knowledge* of its nature and consequences."[19] [Italics added.]

This highest standard, which the Court calls "imperative," has
been defined as applying to abortion in order to fully protect both (1)
the freedom of women, and (2) the health of women. These are precisely the two basic rights in which the Court has found a basis for
creating the abortion liberty. Any informed consent standard that is
less comprehensive than the reasonable patient standard would jeop-
ardize the rights of women as envisioned by the Court.

Thus, regardless of the prevailing standard for informed consent in
a particular state, the Supreme Court has determined that a patient-
centered standard must be applied in abortion cases, if not in general, because this standard for full disclosure is integral to the "abortion
liberty."

Provision of this information is necessary to "insure that the pregnant woman retains control over the discretion of her consulting
physician."[20] The content of disclosure is to be measured not by what
the physician deems important but by the right of the woman to

make a fully knowledgeable choice, for "What is at stake is the woman's right to make the ultimate decision, not a right to be insulated from all others in doing so."[21]

To make this "ultimate decision," women must have access to all of the relevant information. It is not the right of the physician to "screen" information for her, but rather, it is his duty, in consultation with her, to help her fully understand his recommendation for abortion so that she can make an informed choice to accept or refuse his recommendation. To apply a standard based on anything other than the primacy of a woman's right to make a fully informed and free abortion decision undermines the constitutional framework in which the Court has labored to define the abortion right.

Law professor Joseph Stuart, J.D., argues that:

> While several states do not accept the "reasonable patient" standard [in general], it seems clear that whatever standard was applied by a state court [in the case of a suit involving abortion] could not fall below the requirements of the abortion right. Furthermore, it would be reasonable to conclude that no standard could ignore the "imperative" of the Court that the abortion decision be made with "full knowledge of its nature and consequences," and that the pregnant woman retain control over the physician's discretion.
>
> To take this line of reasoning a step further: if the factors to be considered should operate for the benefit of the woman and if she should have "full knowledge of the nature and consequences" of an abortion, then it seems that the needs of the patient-pregnant woman would determine the substance of the information disclosed. Therefore, a standard that held a physician only to some common medical practice (whatever that might be) or to some reasonable practice under the circumstances could very well fall short of the consultative model developed through the abortion cases.[22]

If the abortion right is to be construed for the benefit of women, it is difficult to see how a woman's rights are harmed by use of the reasonable patient standard; on the other hand, it is abundantly clear that a woman's rights may be infringed upon by the self-serving "community standard" of the abortion industry. Without the freedom to be fully informed, a woman's right to choose is rendered meaningless. The withholding of information, therefore, is a violation of her civil rights as defined by the Supreme Court.

In their defense, abortion providers may argue that provision of detailed information regarding risks and alternatives is too burdensome. But because the right to choose is held by the woman, not the physician, "the fact that a duty 'makes his work more laborious' is not relevant. The determination that the information given is particularly dissuasive or persuasive is, likewise, not significant, since the duty is to inform and the assumption is that the woman can make the decision for herself."[23]

## THE SCOPE OF DISCLOSURE

As a general rule, the more complex the treatment options and the more dramatic the risks, the more demanding are the disclosure requirements. This is especially true for elective procedures. For example, it may be reasonable to accept a physician's choice of a particular antibiotic without a lengthy explanation of every risk and alternative to that prescription. But in the case of prostate cancer, which can be treated by drugs, surgery, or non-intervention, the patient would properly expect to receive much more precise and detailed disclosure of the risks and alternatives.

Because abortion is a unique medical procedure, involving a very complex decision which encompasses more medical, psychological, familial, social, and moral issues than any other form of surgery, the requirements for disclosure in this case are higher than for any other medical procedure. Indeed, the Court has raised the standard for disclosure to "full knowledge of [abortion's] nature and consequences."[24] This highest standard, which the Court calls "imperative," has been applied to abortion in order to fully protect both the freedom and health of women, which are exactly the two basic rights in which the Court has found a basis for the abortion liberty.

The scope of health risks which should be discussed prior to an abortion should also be consistent with the broad definition of health reasons upon which the abortion right was established, and so should include physical, psychological, familial, and social complications.[25] Indeed, to be fully informed, the Court notes, disclosure should even include the effects of abortion on the fetus. This is evident in the 1992 *Casey* decision, in which the Court stated:

> It cannot be questioned that psychological well-being is a facet of
> health. Nor can it be doubted that most women considering an abor-
> tion would deem the impact on the fetus relevant, if not dispositive, to
> the decision....[This information] furthers the legitimate purpose of
> reducing the risk that a woman may elect an abortion, only to discover
> later, with devastating psychological consequences, that her decision
> was not fully informed.[26]

Furthermore, since abortion is an elective procedure, an abortion practitioner's opinion that one or another risk is not yet firmly established, or has not yet been adequately measured, does not relieve him of the responsibility to disclose to the patient that members of the medical community are concerned about this disputed risk. This is especially true because the abortion practitioner may be biased against believing in the reality of a certain class of risks, no matter how strong the evidence may be, due to his personal and financial interests in advocating for the abortion option. It is the reasonable patient's right to weigh the evidence for or against a contested abortion complication without paternalistic "screening." Indeed, because it is an elective procedure, women are entitled to the full disclosure of even theoretical risks, such as would be given in the case of experimental drugs.

Finally, it should be noted that all disclosures relating to potential risks should include reported complication rates for women undergoing multiple abortions. It is well known that the probability of both physical and psychological sequelae increases with each subsequent abortion. Since over 40 percent of abortions are for women who have previously had an abortion, this information is immediately relevant for a large number of patients. It is also relevant to women having their first abortion since they too may someday be in a position where they will be compelled to consider a subsequent abortion. They must understand that their decision today will affect the risks they may face if they subsequently choose to abort again. Furthermore, it is well known that many women seeking abortions will, out of shame, conceal a previous abortion from their counselors. A standard routine of disclosing risks for multiple abortions is the only way to insure that such "concealers" receive accurate information about the risks they face.

## REVIEW OF MORAL CONSIDERATIONS

Because the Court recognizes the relevance of fetal development information to a woman's future psychological health,[27] we can also infer that abortionists might also be obligated to discuss the relevant moral issues of abortion with a woman. This may be especially true in cases where women have not fully explored their own moral views, and even more true when a woman's decision to abort is clearly contrary to her belief system.

According to bio-ethicist Daniel Callahan, a noted supporter of legalized abortion, reflection on the moral issue of abortion is, in fact, central to the idea of freedom of choice. "How can it make sense to favor the right of choice, but to be morally indifferent about the use of that right?" asks Callahan. While insisting that each woman must be free to make her own decision, he also insists that we must recognize the "moral seriousness of the abortion choice." Indeed, Callahan admits, "Nothing has so baffled me over the years as the faintly patronizing, paternalistic way in which, in the name of choice, it has been thought necessary to protect women from serious moral struggle. Serious ethical reflection...requires thinking carefully about the moral status of the fetus, and about the best way to live a life and to shape a set of moral values and ideals."[28]

Such serious ethical reflection can be considered an important prophylactic against post-abortion psychological sequelae. It is well known that women who have pre-existing moral conflicts with an abortion decision are significantly more likely to experience post-abortion maladjustments. It is entirely reasonable and, I would maintain, necessary to the purpose of reducing post-abortion sequelae to insist that women considering an abortion recommendation confront and work through any moral ambivalence they have prior to the abortion. Unless the woman is able to honestly reconcile an abortion choice with her own moral beliefs, she is certain to experience post-abortion sequelae.

Even the director of the National Abortion Federation, Sylvia Stengle, has admitted in an interview with *The Wall Street Journal* that one in five women having abortions is doing so in violation of her own moral consciences. (This estimate is almost certainly low.) Stengle says these women are a "very worrisome subset of our patients," and admits, "Sometimes, ethically, a provider has to say, 'If you think you are doing something wrong, I don't want to help you do that.'"[29] Stengle does not say how often, if ever, NAF abortionists actually take this ethical stand. Still, it is nice to have a NAF official admit that it is ethically necessary to refuse to do some abortions.

## MORE REASONS FOR FULL DISCLOSURE

Women seeking abortions are often in a state of emotional turmoil, often under conditions of duress from other people, and lacking in knowledge of abortion's risks. Because of the intense urgency of their circumstances, it is all too easy to make a hasty choice just to "get it over with." This tendency toward haste, which too often leads to post-abortion sequelae,[30] can only be corrected by ensuring that women take the time needed to learn every bit of information relevant to their decision.

Full disclosure is especially important for women who are very ambivalent about the abortion choice. Because the decision to abort is often tentative, or even undertaken solely to please others, "upsetting" information may be *exactly* what a woman is looking for as an excuse to keep her child when everyone else is pressing her into an unwanted abortion. In some cases, it may be far easier for a reluctant woman to resist a boyfriend who is pushing for an abortion by claiming that "the doctor says abortion is dangerous." She may rightly feel that this argument, even if exaggerated, will be more effective than, "I want this baby, even if you don't."

The right of women to be fully informed is further accentuated by the fact that abortionists have historically shifted "basic responsibility" for the abortion decision to the patient. Rather than making informed medical recommendations based on case-by-case risk-benefit analyses, abortionists have tended to provide abortions simply on request. Since abortionists cannot be trusted to do a complete risk-benefit analysis, especially if the patient is withholding relevant information, the importance of each patient doing her own risk-benefit analysis is much further amplified. In order to do this evaluation, the patient needs *all* of the relevant information which is available.

## THE DANGER OF BIAS IN THE INFORMED CONSENT PROCESS

Research conducted at abortion clinics has also found that the majority of women seeking abortion have little or no prior knowledge about the abortion procedure, its risks, or fetal development.[31] For most women, the counseling they receive at the clinic is the only information they will receive about abortion and alternatives.

Research also shows that persons involved in crises are especially vulnerable to being influenced, for good or ill, by third parties. This reliance on others, especially an authority figure who appears capable of providing the stressed person an escape from her crisis, is called heightened psychological accessibility.[32]

Because a woman faced with a crisis pregnancy is more vulnerable to the influence of authority figures, she is also more exposed to their prejudices. Thus, the only way to minimize the biases of abortion counselors is to hold them to the highest standards for full disclosure. If counselors instead introduce their own biases, the results can be tragic.

In a retrospective survey of 252 women who experienced post-abortion sequelae, we found that 66 percent of the women said their counselors' advice was very "biased" toward choosing abortion. This is especially important since 40 to 60 percent describe themselves as not having been certain of their decision prior to counseling, and 44 percent stated they were actively hoping to find an option other than abortion during their counseling sessions. Only five percent reported that they were encouraged to ask questions, while 52 to 71 percent felt their questions were inadequately answered, side-stepped, or trivialized. In all, over 90 percent said they were not given enough information to make an informed decision. These omissions are especially relevant since 83 percent said that it was very likely that they would have chosen differently if they had not been so strongly encouraged to abort by others, including their abortion counselor.[33]

Reports of biased counseling are abundant. For example, when asked about clients who express a desire to keep their child, abortion counselor Betty Orr says, "I ask them who is going to take care of the baby while they're in school. Where are they going to get money for clothes?"[34] Other counselors bluntly tell the woman to forget the motherhood fantasy and "get realistic. Medical bills for having a baby will run over three thousand dollars. Do you have that kind of money? Raising a child is even more expensive. It costs over two hundred thousand dollars to raise a child right. Where are you going to get that kind of money?" This kind of "counseling" is little more than a way of reinforcing a young woman's feelings of powerlessness.

Faced with such antagonism, from parents, boyfriends, and their "health-care" advisors, is it any wonder that young women cave in to the unrelenting pressures to abort even when 60 to 80 percent of them would actually prefer to keep their babies?[35] Pressured into "choosing" abortion by Planned Parenthood counselors at the age of 13, Kathy Walker charges, "I felt like my family had no control over anything. My parents felt as deceived as I was; we never really made an informed decision. Planned Parenthood railroaded us.... But nobody ever really asked me what I wanted to do."[36]

In another case, an Indiana Planned Parenthood affiliate ignored the warnings of Kathleen Kitchen's own physician, who believed an abortion could be fatal because she suffered from certain birth defects. Evading two court orders blocking the abortion, counselors procured a dangerous out-of-state abortion for the girl, which resulted in hospitalization for abortion-related complications.[37] These events demonstrate that a pro-abortion bias may overcome even the most basic evaluation of abortion's dangers for high-risk patients.

When physicians or counselors withhold information because they fear the information will lead to an "unreasonable" choice for childbirth, they are inserting their own bias into the decision-making process, a bias that has no medical basis. Such bias is of special concern since the majority of abortion patients are ambivalent about their choice, with up to 84 percent saying they would have kept their pregnancies under better circumstances.[38]

Furthermore, biased pre-abortion counseling can, in itself, be injurious. Substantial evidence suggests that inadequate, inaccurate, or biased counseling increases the occurrence and severity of negative post-abortion psychological reactions.[39]

## UNDERSTANDING THE CAUSE OF COUNSELING BIAS

There are many reasons for bias in abortion counseling. Some abortion counselors have a financial bias. They see themselves as being in the "business" of selling abortions.[40] Some act paternalistically, honestly believing that abortion is the best solution to every problem pregnancy.[41] Still others have a psychological need to see other women choose abortion as they once did, thus seeking affirmation of a choice which still troubles them on some deeper level.[42]

Even more troublesome are those who see abortion as a tool for social engineering. Whether they seek to use it to reduce welfare rolls, to eliminate the "unfit," or to save the world from overpopulation, these social engineers see some "greater good" which is served by abortion, and this greater good may be deemed more important than "a little guilt" or "a few torn uteruses" among the women whom they abort.

Some abortion providers of the social engineering mindset also have misogynist and racist attitudes. Such persons want to promote abortion to prevent "unfit" persons from raising "unfit" children. For example, Dr. Edward Allred, owner of the largest chain of abortion clinics in California, is a staunch advocate of abortion as a method of controlling the population of minority groups:

> Population control is too important to be stopped by some right-wing pro-life types. Take the new influx of Hispanic immigrants. Their lack of respect of democracy and social order is frightening. I hope I can do something to stem that tide; I'd set up a clinic in Mexico for free if I could....When a sullen black woman can decide to have a baby and get welfare and food stamps and become a burden to all of us it's time to stop.[43]

Most of those who are ideologically committed to population control, however, are more circumspect in their rhetoric. But there is no denying the fact that the primary purpose of many "family planning" groups, such as Planned Parenthood Federation of America, is to promote a policy of population control. Any health care services it provides are subservient to that goal.[44]

According to the PPFA's organizational documents, population control "is a most essential step, if not *the* most essential step ... to solve the most critical problems of hunger, deprivation and the hopelessness of poverty, as well as deterioration of our water, land and air."[45] Other PPFA documents declare that population control is also crucial for bringing about world peace.

To such social engineers, population control is a virtual panacea. It is so important that PPFA officials have frequently supported the right of governments to *force* abortion on women who become pregnant without government consent.[46] Even though they once lost U.S. funding because of this stance, PPFA's international affiliates continue to provide assistance to the Chinese government's program, in which unlawfully pregnant women are "handcuffed, tied with ropes, or placed in pig's baskets" while awaiting their forced abortions.[47]

Other examples of abortion proponents who support coercive population control, including forced abortion, are numerous. For example, Lawrence Lader, founder of the National Abortion Rights Coalition, and author of the pro-abortion tract *Abortion* (1966), which was cited as an authority eight times in *Roe v. Wade*, is also a radical proponent of coercive population control. Lader argues that forced population control is "imperative," both at home and abroad, claiming that "We must accept the principle that having a child is no longer a matter of private will, but of public welfare."[48] In a review of the Chinese program of forced population control, which includes compulsory abortions, mandatory sterilization, forced contraceptive implants, infanticide of handicapped newborns, and infanticide of undesirable female offspring, Lader has only the highest praise.[49]

Similarly, former N.O.W. president Molly Yard has defended the Chinese anti-choice policy, saying, "I consider the Chinese government's policy among the most intelligent in the world."[50]

Persons or organizations who advocate coercion, privately or publicly, would certainly not hesitate to conceal or understate the risks of abortion. Indeed, such population control zealots have frequently defended the use of dangerous or insufficiently tested birth control technologies on the grounds that injured women are a "secondary" concern compared to "overpopulation."[51]

Since PPFA's organizational mandate is to reduce birth rates here and abroad, especially among the poor, its "family planning" services are simply a means to that "all-important" end. It is no wonder, then, that patients report that Planned Parenthood's abortion counseling services are even more biased toward abortion than counseling at non-PPFA clinics.[52]

If a few women, or even 80 percent, suffer minor to severe post-abortion trauma, population controllers may deem this a small price to pay for world peace, prosperity, and environmental purity. Abortion is an essential tool for population control, and many are willing to promote it even if it means hiding its risks from their patients.[53]

## SUMMARY

Informed consent standards for abortion must follow the reasonable patient standard. Furthermore, a woman's right to *all* information relevant to an abortion decision cannot be limited by "therapeutic privilege," because abortion is an elective procedure. Indeed, since full disclosure is an integral part of a woman's "abortion liberty" as defined by the Supreme Court, this right must be treated as a basic civil right. Therefore, violation of this right is a violation of a woman's civil liberties and is itself injurious and should be considered grounds for a civil suit.

The importance of maintaining a rigorous standard for full disclosure is demonstrated by reviewing the many biases of abortion providers. Abortion counseling is biased by financial self-interest, paternalism, psychological need, and social concerns which extend beyond the personal needs of the individual patient. When these biases result in directive counseling and the withholding of relevant information, the well-being and autonomy of women is endangered.

# CHAPTER NINE

# THE LEGISLATIVE OPPORTUNITY

THE previous five chapters have outlined the obligations of abortionists and the rights of women as defined by the Supreme Court, professional medical standards, and common law. Some of these arguments can and have been made in medical malpractice suits against abortionists. Even without new state and federal laws, these arguments will be made by malpractice attorneys who hope to develop case law in favor of women who have been injured by abortion. But this process of developing case law is slow and difficult, and it excludes the vast majority of women who are presently suffering post-abortion sequelae. Therefore, to accelerate this trend, federal and state laws should be passed to codify these standards and solidify these judicial precedents which will seal the abortion industry's fate.

Furthermore, the pursuit of this pro-woman legislation will advance our educational objectives. Debate over pro-woman legislation will increase public awareness of post-abortion injuries and provide a vehicle for building common ground with the middle majority. It is also a political opportunity to separate pro-abortion legislators from their pro-choice supporters, who will see them opposing women's rights in order to protect the abortion industry. This debate will also serve as an opportunity to reshape the public's perception of the pro-life movement by showing that we are concerned about the health and well-being of women both before and after abortion.

The long and short of it is simply this: the abortion industry thrives on providing cheap abortions on demand, knowing that very few women will succeed in suing them for physical or emotional injuries. Once abortionists become truly liable for making the abortion recommendation, and truly liable for the physical and emotional injuries which their abortions cause, they will come to the conclusion that abortion is not only bad medicine, it is also bad business.

## STRATEGIC GOALS IN FORMULATING LEGISLATION

Pro-woman/pro-life legislation is first and always centered on advancing women's rights and increasing the accountability of the abortion industry. Even in the drafting of the legislation, we must carefully keep this focus while also seeking ways to eliminate, or at least minimize, opportunities for our opponents to pose as defenders of women.

Our goal is to leave opponents with only one complaint: our pro-woman legislation is simply too burdensome on abortion providers. Without protection from liability for abortion complications, they will complain, the abortion industry will be forced to shut down, and, therefore, women will "suffer" because they are being denied abortions.

To this complaint we will offer a five point response:

1. Isn't the real suffering of a woman who has been hurt by abortion just as important as the *potential* "suffering" of a woman who gives birth to an unplanned child?

2. Our legislation simply gives women a voice in determining if abortion is or isn't safe. We are simply freeing market forces to push the abortion industry into adopting the appropriate standard of care which maximizes safety and minimizes liability.

3. If abortion is as safe as its proponents claim, our legislation will have no effect. It will only cause fewer abortions to the same degree that abortion is dangerous. Only if abortion is very dangerous will it become very rare, in which case women will clearly benefit from fewer dangerous abortions.

4. Even if it does turn out that abortion is too dangerous to be used in most cases, women will still be free to seek it and doctors will still be free to recommend it. The only difference is that our law will encourage doctors to recommend safer options whenever they are available.

5. Our law merely codifies the standards established by the Supreme Court in *Roe* and the subsequent abortion cases. Supporting the right of women to hold physicians liable for abortion-related injuries is the only effective way of making sure legal abortions are safe abortions.

## LEGISLATIVE INITIATIVES

The following sections describe some of the major features of model legislation developed by the author which has been introduced in the state of Illinois. These features should be read in the light of the previous five chapters, which show why these features properly fit with precedent and will dramatically expand the rights of women and the corresponding liability of abortionists. Enforcement of these provisions is almost exclusively through civil redress.

In drafting this legislation, I have been especially aware of the three primary arguments which are used against standard informed consent statutes. These are: (1) the waiting period after disclosure presents an onerous burden to some women; (2) state mandated lists for disclosure force physicians to give women inaccurate or irrelevant information which is simply intended to "scare" them; and (3) most women already have access to all of the information they need and have already made up their minds. Our legislation eliminates, or makes irrelevant, all three of these objections.

## Minimum Insurance Requirements

To protect the rights of patients in the event of an injury, proof that the physician has adequate malpractice insurance, in the three- to five-million-dollar range, would be required before a license to practice medicine could be issued. This prerequisite could be established only for physicians practicing abortion (who are notorious for "going bare") or for all physicians. To be adequate, the insurance policy would need to cover not only negligence, but also other potential causes for a suit regarding abortion, such as a violation of the woman's civil rights.

Justification of this provision for licensing is straight-forward. If a physician does not have adequate malpractice insurance, a woman will be denied the right to recover damages simply because no lawyer can afford to take her case, since there is no guarantee that sufficient assets will be available to pay the award. Furthermore, the lack of malpractice insurance, or "going bare," is simply unprofessional. No hospital allows admitting privileges to physicians who lack adequate malpractice insurance. Similarly, no state should allow uninsured physicians to practice within its borders.

The abortion industry should be held to the highest of professional standards; it should not be allowed to become a collecting pool for misfits who have otherwise been unable to establish a professional practice. Proof of adequate insurance coverage would be required each year when physicians renew their medical licenses and drug prescription licenses.

## Full Disclosure as a Civil Right

Our legislation codifies a woman's right to *all* information relevant to her decision to accept a physician's recommendation. In drafting such legislation, care has been taken to avoid the appearance that state-mandated requirements represent anything more than a minimum standard. Abortion providers are expected to provide any additional information which a reasonable patient might consider relevant, including newly published research findings, photographs or videos of the developing human fetus at various stages of gestation, and especially information which is uniquely pertinent to a particular woman's health needs. While avoiding vagueness, disclosure requirements should be broad enough to allow juries to continue to expand the standard of "relevant" materials as specific cases are brought to trial.

A key feature of our pro-woman legislation provides that if a plaintiff can demonstrate a lack of either full disclosure or voluntary consent, this is a violation of the woman's basic civil rights, for which she shall be awarded damages of not less than $200,000 and not more than $2,000,000. She does not have to show any other injury. Nor is she required to show that the non-disclosed information would have changed her mind. Furthermore, the cause of action in such cases is not one of medical malpractice, which is always difficult to litigate, but is instead a violation of her civil rights which, because her consent was invalidly obtained, culminated in unlawful touch, which is battery.

This base award for violation of a woman's civil rights, of course, can be increased further if physical or psychological injuries are shown to have occurred. But this base award establishes sufficient monetary incentive for attorneys to accept and litigate abortion cases.

## Extended Statute of Limitations

Perhaps the most important step in holding abortionists liable for abortion-related injuries is the need to extend the statute of limitations for filing a suit. The period for filing should not begin until such time as the woman discovers that she has experienced an injury resulting from the abortion and *has recovered from the injury sufficiently enough to properly pursue her case.* This latter provision is very important because there can be a prolonged delay before reproductive damage, cancer, or psychological injuries become apparent.

The precedent for an open-ended statute of limitations for psychological injuries exists in the case law for victims of child molestation.

Under these precedents, psychologically injured persons have been allowed to sue for damages which were incurred several decades previously. These exceptions to the normal statute of limitations exist because the law recognizes that injuries suffered may create a psychological disability which makes it impossible for a victim to seek damages until after that victim has achieved psychological recovery.

In the case of abortion-related trauma, this psychological disability may include very long periods of denial and repression. In an Elliot Institute study of 260 women, 62 percent of women who reported post-abortion problems experienced a period during which they would have denied the existence of negative feelings resulting from the abortion.[1] This period of denial lasted, on average, slightly over five years, with many reporting symptoms of denial lasting more than a decade.

This same study, and others, show that women may also experience disabling levels of shame and anxiety when confronted with anything to do with abortion. Such feelings may result in avoidance behavior. This disability, avoidance behavior, can severely limit a woman's ability to defend her rights. Thus, a woman may be so overcome with shame that she is unable to confide in a lawyer, much less confront her abortionist, even if she has experienced severe physical injuries. Alternatively, even if she does initiate legal action, she may experience an abnormal onslaught of anxiety reactions which may prevent her from continuing with or cooperating in the suit. According to the same Elliot Institute study, women who experienced post-abortion sequelae reported that it takes, on average, 7.5 years before they can even "begin to reconcile" themselves to the abortion experience. Until this time has elapsed, it may not be possible for them to effectively exercise their right to pursue a malpractice claim.

Extending the statute of limitations until after there is sufficient recovery from an abortion-created disability is not only a fair consideration of a patient's rights, it is also good consumer protection policy. Since the risk of psychological sequelae can easily be pre-identified using known risk factors, proper liability for long-term psychological injuries would dramatically improve the quality of pre-abortion screening and informed consent procedures. No physician wants to risk being sued by patients he or she treated ten or fifteen years ago. Therefore, physicians who use abortion in their treatment regimen will be very careful in pre-screening their patients to ensure that they are fully informed of all its attendant risks.

## Liability for the Abortion Recommendation

Our pro-woman statutes clearly reiterate *Roe*'s finding that abortion is "inherently, and primarily, a medical decision." In the event of a subsequent lawsuit, the abortionist can and should be held accountable for having formed a basis for "his medical judgment [that] the patient's pregnancy *should* be terminated." In defending themselves in civil action, abortionists would be required to document the basis for their recommendations to abort, given a woman's particular health needs, circumstances, and psychological risk profile, especially in relation to alternative options for managing the woman's psychosocial crisis. An inability to justify his choice for the recommended treatment would be considered sufficient to establish negligence.

We believe that this issue, that an abortion must be recommended by a physician as the preferred treatment option, will be an important one in many jury decisions. Conversely, the law must also be clear in restating the physician's right and duty to refuse to provide an abortion which, in his best judgment, given the patient's physical, psychological, and social circumstances, would be injurious to her health. This aspect of the law, too, will be relevant to jury deliberations.

## Screening for High-Risk Factors

Prior to making a recommendation for abortion, physicians would be required to properly screen patients for any characteristics which would predict that the patient is at risk of experiencing physical or emotional harm after the abortion. The physician would be legally and ethically bound to consider these risk factors in forming a recommendation, to advise the woman of the existence of these risk factors, and, in at least some cases, to refuse to perform an abortion until these risk factors had been alleviated through appropriate counseling. An inadequate evaluation of a woman's medical needs and psychosocial condition would be considered sufficient to establish a finding of negligence.

In essence, our pro-woman bill establishes a two-tier process of disclosure. There is standard disclosure, according to the reasonable patient standard. But if screening discloses any high-risk factors, the abortionist is expected to provide additional counseling above and beyond the normal standard, or to refer the patient to a third party, in order to (1) alleviate these predisposing risks, (2) discover a safer course of care, or (3) document and certify why the abortion is recommended over other options for crisis management.

This touches on another *political* benefit of this bill compared to traditional informed consent bills. Our bill recognizes that each woman is unique in her needs and relative risks. It simply requires clinics to treat each woman accordingly, which they claim to be doing already. Indeed, one of the pro-abortionists' standard arguments against reading off a state-mandated laundry list of risks and alternatives is that such lists do not respect the unique circumstances of each patient. This bill accepts their argument, and insists that they live up to their own idealized standard for individualized counseling and accept legal liability when they do not.

### Burden of Proving Adequate Disclosure

In the event of a lawsuit brought on the basis of lack of informed consent, the burden of establishing the sufficiency of the disclosure should fall on the physician. Video-taped recordings of the pre-abortion counseling would be advised, a copy of which should be given to the client. Furthermore, the failure to disclose potential complications which did in fact occur should be considered presumptive evidence that either (1) the physician negligently evaluated the patient, (2) the physician was incompetently ignorant of risks which should have influenced his recommendation, or (3) the physician deliberately withheld relevant information in order to guide the patient toward his own pre-determined choice.

In addition, if a pattern of inadequate disclosure to patients can be established, this may be construed as evidence that the physician was involved in deceptive trade practices, in which case the plaintiff may be entitled to triple damages.

Here it is worth noting that if the courts were to decide that there must be a better defined standard for determining what risks must be disclosed, a two-study rule, patterned after an FDA standard, could be mandated. According to this FDA standard, if any two studies link a substance to cancer, the substance must be listed as a potential carcinogen. These studies can be drawn from international literature and can include studies on animals. In the case of abortion, this same standard could be adopted, requiring disclosure of any complication reported in two or more studies as potentially associated with abortion. The adequacy of the studies would not be at issue. The relevant point is simply that a patient might have a reasonable basis, drawn from at least two studies, for believing that the reported complication may be related to abortion.

## Sufficient Reflection Time

A major objection to standard informed consent laws is that 24- or 48-hour waiting periods represent a substantial burden to women, who are then required to make two trips to the abortion clinic. They argue that most women have already had adequate time to consider their decision and already know all that they need to know when they arrive. Rather than argue with them, we once again not only give them what they want, but *more* than they want.

Our model legislation requires that the abortionist must simply certify that the woman has had "sufficient reflection time." Our definition states that "sufficient reflection time" normally requires no less than 24 hours, but that even this period for reflection can be waived if the abortionist certifies that the patient has demonstrated adequate maturity, possessed prior knowledge of all the information which she would have been given, and has already given the information due consideration.

The catch is this: if the abortionist provides an abortion with less than 24 hours of reflection time, then, in the event of a suit for lack of informed consent, the abortionist is liable for triple damages. He would also face the additional burden of proving the appropriateness of his decision with evidence establishing that the patient was mature and had adequately considered all the relevant information, and therefore did not require additional reflection time.

Politically, this solution defuses all of the objections to a mandatory waiting period. Here, nothing is mandatory except good medical judgment. The right to "sufficient reflection time" is already part of the common law interpretation of informed consent procedures. This law simply states that for a complex decision such as abortion, this period of reflection normally takes at least 24 hours. However, because the state "respects" their medical opinions, abortionists are free to waive even this nominal period for reflection if they are willing to accept greater liability for allowing a rushed decision. Obviously, because their chief concern is money, they will not accept this increased liability. Instead, they will voluntarily choose to require a 24-hour period for reflection.

Another advantage of this approach is that the standard for "sufficient reflection time" is related to the maturity and intellect of the particular patient. In the event of a subsequent suit, this leaves the door open for another charge of negligence. Specifically, a plaintiff's attorney may be able to show that for a particular woman, whose cognitive abilities were impaired by low intelligence, immaturity, or emotional stress, the requirement for "sufficient reflection time" might require two weeks rather than only 24 hours. Again, since the burden of evaluating the patient's understanding of the disclosed information rests on the physician, the abortionist becomes liable for defending the basis for his opinion that the woman had "sufficient reflection time."

## Abortionists' Responsibility for Brochures

Informed consent laws in most states have sought to guarantee disclosure by mandating that women receive a brochure prepared by the state describing fetal development, risks of abortion, and alternatives. Typically, these brochures have been prepared by the state's department of public health.

This approach has been fraught with difficulties. First, the writing of these brochures has been highly politicized. In some cases, pro-abortion bureaucrats have actually attempted to use the law to benefit the abortion industry by exaggerating the dangers of childbirth while understating the risks of abortion. Still another problem with these brochures is that their very existence tends to shift responsibility for disclosure from the physician to the state. Defense attorneys for the abortionist can argue that provision of the "official" state-prepared brochure satisfies all of the abortionist's responsibilities for disclosure.

Our legislation avoids these pitfalls. First, we emphasize that a brochure is required as an aid to disclosure, but that it is not a substitute for full disclosure, which may vary from case to case, and that in every instance, the adequacy of the disclosure must be certified by the attending physician.

Second, each clinic is free to prepare its own disclosure brochure, or it may purchase copies from a third party, which might be either a pro-abortion source or an anti-abortion source. In any event, the abortionist is individually liable for ensuring the adequacy of the contents and for supplementing or updating the contents with additional printed materials.

In the brochure itself, only general topics are mandated: "Your Legal Rights," "Resources to Help You," "Development of the Human Fetus," "Risks Which May Be Related to Abortion," and "Characteristics Which May Place You at Higher Risk." Abortionists are free to fill in these sections in whatever way they feel is accurate and sufficient, knowing that they are also completely liable for the accuracy and sufficiency of their statements. The only exception is the section on legal rights, where the law mandates very specific statements regarding the physician's obligations and the woman's rights, including her right to sue for any lack of full disclosure or other violation of her rights. In the event of a suit against the abortionist on the basis of inadequate disclosure, a jury would use the reasonable patient standard to judge the adequacy of the abortionist's disclosure document.

Politically, this approach robs pro-abortionists of the arguments that (1) the state is incompetent to give medical advice, and (2) doctors should not be "forced" to recite a list of risks developed by state bureaucrats which may be inaccurate or outdated. Both charges are true. Therefore, our approach gives abortionists complete freedom regarding specific content, but also makes them totally responsible for full disclosure. In essence, we ensure quality not by dictating the exact contents of disclosure but by increasing the liability risks for inadequate disclosure.

In practice, the safest way for abortionists to minimize liability will be for them to give more information than necessary, which is as it should be. Indeed, because they will actually be held liable for the contents of their brochures, they will be far more motivated to provide full disclosure than would be public health officials who are subject to political pressures.

## The Abortion Information Depository

To assist both abortionists and plaintiffs' attorneys, our model legislation requires the state department of public health to maintain an Abortion Information Depository. Anyone, in particular, those who believe abortion has risks or who offer safer alternatives, can deposit date-stamped information and data which should be available for consideration by patients seeking abortion. The legal presumption will be that abortionists are familiar with the materials in the Depository.

In the event of a lawsuit, the clinic-prepared brochure can be compared to the contents of the Depository. The jury would then decide if there is anything in the Depository which a reasonable patient would have found relevant to her decision but that was not disclosed. If so, the plaintiff has made her case.

## Certification of Voluntary Consent

Abortion providers would be held legally responsible for certifying that a woman's choice to have an abortion is totally her own and that she is not being pressured into this decision by others. If abortion clinics fail to properly screen their patients for signs of coercion, they have been negligent. Furthermore, if a woman can later show that an abortion counselor added to the pressures which made her feel she "had no choice," or did nothing to protect her from being pressured into an unwanted abortion, the clinic would be held accountable as an "accomplice" in the crime of pressuring her into an unwanted abortion.

### Liability for Wrongful Death

If a plaintiff's testimony establishes that her pregnancy was in any way wanted, or, conversely that the abortion was in some way *unwanted*, such testimony shall entitle the woman to seek damages for wrongful death—a claim which can entail multi-million-dollar awards. There are several reasons for this.

First, if the pregnancy was wanted, the abortionist failed to intervene to protect the woman from the individuals or circumstances which were making her feel forced to undergo an unwanted abortion. This, in turn, demonstrates that there was failure in the process of screening, counseling, and consideration of alternatives better suited to the woman's desire to keep her pregnancy.

Second, if one accepts the pro-choice position that "personhood" attaches to the unborn child only when the woman mentally decides that she wants or loves the child, then a child who is killed during an *unwanted* abortion is a person of value. While it is possible that a mother could feel forced to consent to the killing of her wanted child, it is impossible that she could *freely* consent to such an act. Therefore, no matter how dire the circumstances, if the woman believes that she is aborting "her baby" as opposed to "fetal tissue" she is losing a loved one and should have been protected from this loss.

Third, contrary to popular notions, the Supreme Court never ruled that human life does not begin at conception. Instead, the Court has decided that the "difficult question of when human life begins" cannot be resolved by the mandate of the state; therefore, the state may not "override" the rights of a woman by "adopting one theory of life."[2] In other words, the Court has insisted that the subjective views of the individual woman take precedence over the views of the state, at least up until the point of viability in the third trimester.[3]

Clearly, if state legislatures may not impose one legal theory regarding the beginnings of life on women, then neither can state courts. It is improper, then, for a civil court to deny a mother the right to seek damages for wrongful death of her unborn child. Such a ruling would improperly restrict the rights of a plaintiff by imposing "one theory of life" upon her. Instead, if the subjective standards of *Roe* are to be consistently applied, a woman should always be entitled to recovery for the wrongful death of her unborn child if she can provide testimony that the abortion occurred after such time as she subjectively believes human life begins. Her charge of wrongful death would be further substantiated by testimony regarding factors which made her feel forced into an unwanted abortion or by evidence showing that she was denied information which would have changed her mind. In short, if we are to be ruled by a subjective view of when human life begins, then this subjective view must operate both ways—both to allow for abortion and to allow for charges of wrongful death.

Finally, women who have had abortions who subjectively believe that the aborted child was a being of value are confronted with a high risk of developing psychological sequelae. This one risk alone should be sufficient to deter a responsible physician from performing an abortion.[4] In such cases, then, compensation for wrongful death is fair because the emotional pain and suffering of a mother who loses a wanted child to abortion may be just as great as the suffering of a mother who loses her child to a careless driver.

If capricious and tyrannical courts refuse to allow awards for wrongful death, legislation should be sought which would set generous minimum levels of compensation for the emotional pain and suffering which results from an unwanted abortion.

### Withdrawn Consent

It is not uncommon for patients immediately before or during the abortion procedure to get "cold feet" and withdraw consent. In interviews with 300 Australian women, psychologist Lawrence Fulton found that three of every four tried to stop the abortion at the last minute. Fulton attributed this finding to pre-surgical anxiety-reducing drugs which allowed deeper feelings of ambivalence to surface.

In many of these cases, patients have been inaccurately told that "it's too late," and the abortionist has insisted on continuing with the procedure. In other cases, the physician will momentarily pause but pressure the woman to make up her mind in haste: "Get on the table now, or get out!"

Because even a temporary withdrawal of consent is clearly an indication that the patient is experiencing deep and unresolved conflicts about her decision, continuing an abortion in such cases is inappropriate and irresponsible.[5] In these circumstances, our model law would require the abortionist to immediately cease the operation and transfer the patient to a hospital for evaluation and treatment by another physician to determine if the pregnancy can be saved. Even if the woman changed her mind, again, and requested that the abortion should be completed, the operation could not be resumed or even rescheduled until the woman received more extensive screening and counseling. This provision would guarantee that a vacillating patient would take the time necessary to resolve her conflicted feelings.

## Payment Procedures

It is common practice in the abortion industry to obtain payment for the abortion in advance. This requirement for up-front payment is unheard of in any other medical practice and is clearly unprofessional. It is also potentially coercive in that it may deter women from changing their minds for fear of not getting their money back.

According to our model legislation, a woman's consent to abortion is voluntary only if she is not required to pay any amount for the abortion procedure, or pre-abortion counseling, until after the procedure has been completed. Abortion providers may, however, request proof of an ability to pay before providing any services. If, after screening and counseling, the woman decides against the recommendation for an abortion, she would be liable for no more than $50 in counseling and surgical preparation fees.

## Reporting of Cases Involving Potential Child Molestation

Whenever a person seeking abortion is a minor, the abortionist would be required to determine if the pregnancy did result, or may have resulted, from an act of incest, forcible rape, or *statutory rape*. If there is reason to believe that the pregnancy is a result of one of these criminal acts, the abortionist would be required to report the case to the appropriate law enforcement officials and child protection authorities.

This provision is especially important in order to protect minors from exploitation by older males. According to one study of teenage births in Kansas in 1992, of 29 babies born to 10- to 14- year olds in Kansas, 20 (69 percent) of the fathers were over the age of 18. Similarly, of 937 babies born to girls 15-17 years of age, 781 (83 percent) were fathered by adults over the age of 18. Clearly, the state has a public policy interest in prosecuting adult males who prey on minors.

In addition, child protection authorities may need to investigate home environments when fourteen-year-old girls seeking abortion have been made pregnant by a 23-year-old man. As Linda Martinez, who brought these statistics to my attention, comments, "If parents accepted money for allowing a man to have sexual intercourse with their young child, they would be charged with several crimes. But when they allow it at no charge, is it okay? No, it's not okay. It's neglect! Parents may not be able to prevent it ahead of time, but if they refuse to cooperate with law enforcement after the fact, they should face neglect charges themselves."

Linda also suggests that laws governing prosecution of statutory rape and indecent liberties with children should be modified in a manner similar to laws against spousal abuse. These modified laws allow prosecution without the cooperation of the victim. Prosecution should not be stymied simply because the girl refuses to cooperate, whether out of fear of the abuser, or because she loves her seducer. This is especially true in the event that the minor becomes pregnant. Whether the child is born or aborted, blood tests can be used to establish paternity, which should be entirely sufficient for obtaining a conviction.

This law not only would provide an effective means for intervening on behalf of a young girl who is being sexually exploited, it may also provide her with the opportunity to escape from an unwanted abortion. This is especially important because minors are more likely to be coerced into unwanted abortions, especially in cases of incest. Furthermore, a vigorous prosecution of statutory rape charges, combined with financial liability for the child and the young mother, will deter the victimization of minors and may ultimately do more to reduce births among minors than other state programs which simply promote contraception and abortion.

## Expert Testimony

Our legislation also expands the right of plaintiffs' attorneys to call upon expert witnesses outside of the abortion industry. Specifically, the statute distinguishes between the technical-medical aspect of induced abortion and the separate issues of screening, counseling, disclosure, and making a medical recommendation. With regard to the latter, physicians or qualified persons who provide care for women in crisis pregnancies would be allowed to testify as expert witnesses. With regard to the technical-medical process used for the induced abortion, any physician skilled in D&C, D&E, evacuation techniques, instillation, prescription of labor-inducing drugs, or other medical techniques which are substantially similar to the method employed for the induced abortion at issue would be allowed to testify as an expert. The testimony of a board-certified obstetrician-gynecologist would normally be allowed as expert testimony.

### Liability for Referrals

Any physician, health care worker, or family planning agency which makes referrals for abortion would be held as jointly liable for all of the obligations of this law. Any party who makes referrals to an abortionist outside of the state would be solely liable for all provisions of our statute, including the requirements to guarantee full disclosure, voluntary consent, and adequate reflection time. Finally, any abortion provider advertising in the state would be considered as doing business in the state and would be held liable for satisfying the requirements of the statute.

### Guaranteed Jury Instructions

To avoid the risk that jury instructions will fail to adequately define the woman's rights and the physician's duties, the counsel for either party would be able to demand that the jury be given a copy of our pro-woman legislation to aid them in their deliberations. This feature ensures that juries have an opportunity to more fully appreciate the intent of the legislation and the broad rights which it grants to women.

## FEDERAL LEGISLATION

While pro-woman legislation can be pursued in the individual states, many of these principles can also be enacted through federal legislation. Following the Republican congressional victory of 1994, this author proposed to pro-life congressmen the enactment of the Full Disclosure Act, which would define the abortion patient's right to full disclosure as a civil right under federal law. The central aspects of this act are described in the appropriate sections above.

In summary, the Full Disclosure Act would codify the reasonable patient standard for all cases of abortion in all fifty states. It would specifically require notification of all pre-identifying risk factors and disclosure of all optional ways of correcting the physical, emotional, familial, social, or economic problems associated with the pregnancy. Women who are denied their civil right to full disclosure would be entitled to a compensatory award of not less than $200,000 and not more than $2,000,000 without having to prove any other injury, though this award could be increased if additional injuries were proven.

On a smaller scale, this same standard could be specifically applied only to agencies receiving federal health and family planning grants. Planned Parenthood and the like have insisted that the "Gag Rule" forbidding federal funds from being spent on counseling for abortion prevents them from providing women with the option of abortion, which they are "ethically" bound to provide. Since we want to respect their ethical standards (especially since they are so rarely seen), the "Full Disclosure Rule" would simply insist that once they bring up the topic of abortion, they become legally and financially responsible for providing *full disclosure*. This Full Disclosure Rule would include all of the provisions described above with two additional stipulations. First, the grant recipient would be solely responsible for all amounts awarded to a plaintiff for violation of the full disclosure requirements. Second, violation of the full disclosure requirements would automatically make the offending agency, and any parent agency, ineligible for federal funds under all funding Titles, for any programs, for a period of ten years.

It should be noted that this same strategy can be used to stop *any* pro-abortion legislation. Pro-woman/pro-life candidates merely need to amend the legislation to expand women's rights against the abortion industry. For example, when President Clinton came into office, the pro-abortionists were pushing hard for the Freedom of Choice Act. The centerpiece of this act was the provision that states "may not restrict the right of a woman to choose to terminate a pregnancy." Pro-abortionists hoped to use this bill to protect abortion in the event that *Roe* was reversed. *Roe* wasn't reversed and so the push for FOCA died. If it is ever revived, pro-abortion enthusiasm for the bill would immediately dissipate if a simple amendment were added, namely, "No State may restrict the right of a woman, or her survivors, to recover damages in civil action, at any time, from an abortion provider for any physical, psychological, emotional or social injuries associated with the abortion." This amendment to FOCA would strike down all statutes of limitations on civil actions against abortionists and would eliminate all malpractice caps on awards for abortion-related injuries—all while expanding women's rights, which is ostensibly the goal of the bill. Any debate of such an amendment would place supporters of FOCA in the very awkward position of claiming that the right of women to sue for abortion-related injuries must be remain limited in order to protect the viability of the abortion industry. Clearly, they would not want to openly debate this amendment, but neither could they afford to let it pass into law. Thus, this amendment would be a "poison pill" which would force them to withdraw their bill.

## TAKING BACK CHOICE

Readers by now have noticed that I like to take the battle onto our opponents' ground. If we are right, and they are wrong, then even the smallest kernel of truth which lies in their arguments can be built upon to destroy their false god. They claim to be concerned about the welfare and autonomy of women. We claim to be more concerned, for the very good reason that abortion is injuring women, not helping them.

In the same spirit of stripping away their rhetoric and winning back the ground that they have claimed for themselves, I believe we should also take back the terms "freedom of choice" and "reproductive freedom." The pro-abortionists don't have a copyright on these terms. We can and should use these terms properly, as opposed to the skewed way in which they have been used by pro-abortionists. We must do battle over these terms to emphasize the fact that we are the ones who are really defending the right of women to make an *informed* choice; we are the ones who are defending the freedom of women to reproduce without fear of being coerced into *unwanted* abortions. For this reason, and others described below, I believe our pro-woman/pro-life legislation should be called the Freedom of Choice Act. We should openly battle for the privilege of defending the freedom of choice.

Some pro-life strategists dislike the idea of a pro-life bill called the Freedom of Choice Act because they fear it would only "confuse" grassroots supporters. But this confusion can easily be cleared up through the network of pro-life publications. Furthermore, legislators can easily screen calls of those who object to the "Freedom of Choice Act" to determine if the caller's intent is to support the right of women to sue abortionists or to support the right of abortionists to be safeguarded from lawsuits.

More importantly, by calling our pro-woman bill the Freedom of Choice Act. we will actually be forcing the process through a momentary confusion which leads to greater clarity. This name focuses attention on the fact that our bill in no way limits the rights of women who seek abortion. Instead, it increases the rights of women by simply ensuring that their decisions to accept a recommendation for abortion are fully voluntary and fully informed.

We can even hope that in the aftermath of the outrage over our "stealing" of their slogans, feminists will begin to think more deeply about how to respond to our efforts. In the process of formulating a response, they may actually begin to realize that this bill really does expand the rights of women. This will lead them to an even deeper confusion: "If this bill expands women's rights yet infringes on the liberties of abortionists, maybe women's rights and abortionists' rights do not march in lockstep. Maybe there are abuses which need to be corrected!"

Furthermore, the symbol of "choice" has a lot of appeal to the middle majority, thanks to the millions of dollars spent on public relations by pro-abortionists. There is no reason why we should not be bold in capturing this banner for our own cause, especially given the form and intent of our bill, which truly does enhance choice. As discussed in the second chapter, the middle majority would be quite content with legislation which guarantees voluntary and informed choice for women while at the same time making abortion more rare. Calling our pro-woman/pro-life bill the Freedom of Choice Act just adds to its appeal.

Finally, win or lose, by engaging in a public "wrestling match" over which side is representing freedom of choice for women, the middle majority will undergo a healthy disorientation. The clear-cut stereotypes which they have been fed by the media will be disrupted. The line of issues separating pro-abortionists from anti-abortionists will be confused. The banner of "choice" will become torn in two, with each side claiming ownership, and it will no longer be possible to lead the middle majority simply by advocating "choice."

When this conflict is engaged, the idea of "choice" will be less mesmerizing because its meaning will be less clear. To sort out the sides and the issues, the middle majority will be forced to reinvent its stereotypes. It will be forced to examine what each side means by "choice," what the choice means, and how the choice is made. This type of confusion is healthy because it leads to greater clarity of thought, which is exactly what we are trying to achieve.

In short, win or lose, by adamantly pushing our own Freedom of Choice legislation and boldly proclaiming its name, we will be breaking the grip of pro-abortionists on "choice." Their years of public relations efforts to build up the hypnotic power of the word "choice" will be scuttled. Indeed, much of the public's love of "choice" will be turned to our advantage because the middle majority are naturally inclined to support the right of women to informed choice and the establishment of safeguards against coerced abortions. We should not be hesitant to use the words with which they are comfortable to attract their support for legislation on which we share common ground.

## SUMMARY

This chapter discussed model legislation for the Freedom of Choice Act, which would expand the right of women to full disclosure of all information relevant to abortion, expand their right to redress if full disclosure is denied to them, and establish safeguards to prevent women from being coerced into unwanted abortions. Since various studies have placed the incidence of women being "forced" into abortions by others at between 30 and 60 percent, this anti-coercion feature is very important to protecting the freedom of choice of women.

In our public defense of this legislation, pro-woman/pro-life advocates must be extremely clear about the purpose of this legislation. This statute is not designed to discourage women who are seeking abortions; it is designed to protect women from unwanted or dangerous abortions. If a woman really wants an abortion, and her physician has determined that it will be safe and beneficial for her to have one, this law will not impede her in any way. But for those women who are feeling forced into unwanted abortions, this law will ensure that they get all the information they need to make the choice that best serves their needs.

If abortion is safe, this law will make it safer. If abortion is dangerous, this law will give women the right to police dangerous abortion providers simply by expanding their rights to sue their exploiters.

It is our personal belief, as proponents of this legislation, that as the dangers of abortion become better known, fewer women will choose it and fewer doctors will recommend it. This is our pro-life goal. If we are wrong, and abortion is safe, and women are happy with abortion services as they exist, then this legislation will have no concrete effect. The bottom line, then, is that this bill only serves to increase the standard of care given to women seeking abortion. Who can oppose that? No one, except the abortion profiteers and social engineers do not want to be bothered with the real needs of women.

# CHAPTER TEN

# A HEALING STRATEGY

Laws protecting women's rights will not be effective unless women will actually exercise these rights. As we have previously suggested, however, the majority of women who suffer psychological scars from abortion are too injured to bring lawsuits against their exploiters. They feel so much shame that their first impulse is to bury their pain by hiding it and denying it. Their second impulse is to believe that they deserve to suffer for what they have done.

This is one of the ways in which abortion is like rape. Both rapists and abortionists injure women in a way which creates so much shame that their victims actually help to conceal the crime. Furthermore, the victims of rape and abortion are both inclined to blame themselves for the "stupidity" of having put themselves into the hands of their abuser. Focused on self-blame, they often ignore the fact that the abuser had an obligation to respect their rights. This is especially true in the case of abortion, where the abortionist, who at least in theory is supposed to be acting in a professional manner, has an obligation to protect his patients from making a hasty, ill-informed, or dangerous decision.

Before women will aggressively pursue their rights against abortionists, then, we must create an environment which is conducive to post-abortion healing. The living victims of abortion must be helped to find psychological, emotional, and spiritual healing. It is only from this position of recovered strength that post-aborted women can properly exercise their right to redress, not just to compensate themselves, but to protect the rights of others.

While this need to promote post-abortion healing is essential to the legal leg of our pro-woman strategy, it is even more essential as an aspect of promoting the Christian renewal of our society. Compassion and aid to post-aborted women must be given not because it empowers women to sue abortionists, but because it is the right thing to do. The former is a byproduct of the latter, which must be done purely for its own sake.

## Removing the Plank from Our Own Eye

Before we can develop a healing environment for others, it is essential that we first heal ourselves. We, the pro-life movement and the Church, must learn to replace any traces of judgmentalism with compassion, prejudice with understanding. We must learn to see those who have undergone abortions not as different from ourselves, but as identical to ourselves. We must find the humility to see that without the overflowing grace of God, under the right conditions and the right pressures, we too would be capable of abortion, if not worse.

We also need to remember that our concern for unborn children should always be one with our concern for the unborn child's mother. As previously discussed, this is necessary because by God's natural ordering of things, an unborn child can only be nurtured and protected by the mother. All that the rest of us can do is to nurture and protect the mother. To make this point in another way, the best way we can live out our concern for the unborn child is through actions taken on behalf of the unborn's mother. It is only in serving her needs that we can serve her child.

From another perspective, while we can and should mourn the deaths of the children killed by abortion, we should really be more concerned about the ravages of abortion on the souls of the women and men who have been touched by this sin. This argument will be elaborated upon further in Chapter Twelve. For now it is enough to share the insight of a crisis pregnancy counselor who once told me, "When I began this work, I was mostly concerned about the unborn. But after working with so many young girls who have had abortions, what saddens me most is how abortion destroys the joy of their youth, and strips away every last shred of their innocence. Nothing can make a young girl feel more worthless and despicable than having killed her own child."

I sincerely believe that this attitude is the only one which has any hope of creating a pro-life society. By applying generous doses of sympathy, understanding, and charity toward those who have been involved in abortion, we will create a ripple effect which will truly transform the world.

## Reducing Judgmentalism

Women who have had abortions are either filled with humility or shame. The forgiven feel humility; the unforgiven feel shame. The former have found humility in a repentance which requires the acknowledgment of one's guilt, one's weakness, one's flaws. But for the many, shame is a manifestation of denial. To protect their denial, many become resentful, defiant, and even hateful of everyone who aggravates the feelings of guilt which they are trying to deny. They feel that no one can understand them, and they fear that everyone is prepared to condemn them.

This is our task then: to reduce feelings of shame by increasing our own level of understanding and compassion. Through compassion, we seek to eliminate the hurdles women and men face along the way to repentance. This is the path they must travel in the search for post-abortion healing. It is therefore extremely important for the pro-woman/pro-life movement to concentrate its public relations efforts on counteracting the image that pro-lifers are judgmental and replace it with a message of understanding and compassion. This message must be prominent in all of our campaigns, but it must especially be proclaimed in our churches.

Clergy should be encouraged to give entire sermons on the need for understanding and compassion for those who have had abortions. This can be done without in any way condoning abortion. Using as examples the testimonies of women who have chosen abortion, congregations can be reminded of how, in times of great stress, people do even those things which they most abhor. With examples of women who have been literally dragged to unwanted abortions, and those who simply gave in under the weight of many pressures, people should be helped to see that women are not always fully culpable. This does not lessen the seriousness of abortion, but it does lessen the tendency to judge and blame.

Church communities need to be reminded that we need not judge *why* people have had abortions—they will do that for themselves, perhaps more harshly than we would. Nor do we need to dwell on the humanity of the child or the sinfulness of abortion, because these truths are implicitly known by all who have been involved in abortion. Whether they acknowledge their sinfulness or defend their abortions as "necessary," everyone, on some level, knows the truth of what happened. A life was destroyed.

For many, this is a truth which they dare not look upon. Attempts to force them to confront it only aggravate anxiety, fear, resentment, and anger. In short, walls go up. On the other hand, showing them that we have learned the truth of what abortion does to women, and men, makes walls come down because *this* is what they know, *this* is what they feel and have experienced. The knowledge that one's church community understands what one has experienced is itself healing.

## BUILDING BRIDGES WITH EMPATHY

Through this approach of taking down walls of defensiveness, post-aborted women and men can be led to the truth they most desperately need, the truth about forgiveness. They need to hear that, in repentance and reform, there is freedom and new life, even after suffering the greatest of shames. They need to discover hope in the message of our non-condemning acceptance of them as our brothers and sisters. After all, since Christ Himself is offering them forgiveness, who are we to cast the first stone? In short, the message of forgiveness must always precede the message of life's sanctity, for it is only after they feel forgiven, or at least taste its hope, that post-aborted women and men can bear to look directly at the truth about their unborn children.

To succeed in creating a healing environment, we must begin by teaching others how to understand their pangs of doubt, their ambivalence, their grief. In the process, we will also be helping the post-aborted members of our churches to understand their own confused and buried feelings. Even if some post-aborted members cannot admit having had these feelings themselves, they will immediately recognize that what we are saying must be true at least for "others." This is very important, for by even this small step of admitting that the pain of "others" is real, they are opening a door through which they may eventually recognize their own need to heal buried feelings of remorse.

Most of all, we, their church community, must be ready to cry with those who are aware of their loss. We must graciously acknowledge their need and desire for healing and share with them the certainty of God's freely offered forgiveness. We must assure them that our faith does not condemn any of us to a life of shame. All of us are sinners, but through God's mercy, all of us can find peace again.

## A HEALING ENVIRONMENT BUILDS STRENGTH

By promising compassion, we break the paralyzing bonds of shame. By minimizing shame, we welcome repentance. By creating a more healing environment, we will be enabling more people to seek post-abortion healing. In helping post-aborted women and men to move beyond denial, resentment, and shame, we will also be helping them to become active witnesses for the sanctity of life. This is a good end in and of itself. But it is also good for the Church and the pro-life movement.

The psychological and spiritual healing which can follow an abortion is never automatic. As with all healings of the spirit, it is always the result of the Lord's initiative and the sinner's response in faith, including sincere regret, a change of heart, and acceptance of God's forgiveness.

Those who experience post-abortion healing strengthen the Church. In finding forgiveness, they find humility and a restoration of their faith. Many become deeply spiritual. Having experienced the depths of despair, they become marvelous witnesses to hope.

They also strengthen the pro-life cause. They are the voice of experience, the unimpeachable witnesses of abortion's dangers. As readers of their stories know, there is no more powerful testimony on behalf of the unborn, in condemnation of abortion's exploitation of women, and in the appeal for social and political reform than the testimony of post-aborted women.[1]

## TOWARD CRITICAL MASS

In physics, critical mass is the point at which a fusion reaction takes place and becomes self-perpetuating. I pray for the day when the post-abortion healing movement will reach "critical mass." At that point, there will be an explosion of interest in, and demand for, post-abortion healing services. On that day, public empathy for post-aborted women and men will have overcome the pro-abortion bias against "traitors" who speak out against abortion. On that day, movie stars, athletes, politicians, and other public figures will be able to publicly confess their guilt over past abortions and proclaim their healing to others without fear of destroying their careers.

Everywhere, the witness of post-aborted men and women will be leading others to seek and accept post-abortion healing.

As mentioned earlier, post-abortion healing will also propel post-abortion litigation. As more and more women and men find healing in post-abortion forgiveness, more and more will be sufficiently freed from the slavery of shame to bring legal action against the abortionists who have injured them. Increased litigation will, in turn, draw more attention from the media to the issue of abortion's dangers, and all of this together will destroy pro-abortionists' most potent myth: the claim that abortion is safe.

Still another aspect of post-abortion healing which should not be missed is its impact on family members. Many people remain silent about abortion in general because they do not want to hurt loved ones who they know have had abortions. But when these loved ones begin to witness to the grief abortion has caused in their lives, this same loyalty among family members which previously fostered silence will now encourage these other family members to speak up and support reform. This effect should not be underestimated. For every woman who has had an abortion, there are numerous people who remain neutral on abortion, or hide their pro-life sympathies, out of deference to her feelings. Every post-aborted woman who is healed brings with her new allies in our battle. This is our key to a broad segment of the middle majority who are presently avoiding involvement in the abortion debate.

## SUMMARY

Millions of men and women silently carry the grief of a secret abortion in their hearts. They are silenced by shame. They are silenced by the belief that they are alone and no one can understand their pain. Indeed, they fear that "it's just something wrong with me. No one else feels this way after an abortion."

These walking wounded need to learn that we do understand. They need to know that it is normal and necessary not only to grieve after an abortion, but to seek emotional and spiritual healing. It is our obligation, as Christians, to help them escape their feelings of shame and to find peace in God's forgiveness. Most of all, we must help them to forgive themselves.

It is critical, therefore, that the pro-life movement and the Church break through the media-imposed image that we are judgmental and condemning of those who have had abortions. Our rhetoric must hold fast to defense of the twin truths of the sacredness of human life and God's love for all sinners, among whom we number ourselves. Perhaps we should invest in bumper stickers which read, "Abortion always Kills. God will always Forgive."

We need to overcome the fear that, by stressing God's forgiveness, we will be encouraging women to abort now and seek forgiveness later. I believe this is an unwarranted fear which stifles the display of understanding and compassion which is truly needed to create an environment conducive to post-abortion healing. It is only through such a healing environment that we will finally build a pro-life society. Only then, when the grief and suffering abortion causes to women, men, families, and society is known by all, will abortion be not only illegal, but unthinkable.

# Chapter Eleven

# Conquering Despair

THE idea that "abortion is an act of despair" is one of the key points I have always tried to stress in my writing and speaking engagements.[1] Despair is not only the driving force behind most abortion choices, it is also the greatest obstacle to post-abortion recovery. Until pro-lifers understand this, they will never be effective at helping women in crisis.

In describing the despair which leads women to abort, Frederica Mathewes-Green of Feminists for Life of America gives us this compelling word-picture: "No woman wants an abortion as she wants an ice cream cone or a Porsche. She wants an abortion as an animal caught in a trap wants to gnaw off its own leg."[2]

This quote is so powerfully accurate that it has even been reprinted by Planned Parenthood. Why? Because pro-abortionists have long wanted to diffuse the notion that women abort for selfish or casual reasons. They want the public to sympathize with the desperation of women seeking abortions because they want to convert sympathy for women into support for abortion.

Actually, the fact that most women agonize over the decision to abort is one of the few areas for finding "common ground" in the abortion debate. Most, if not all, counselors and researchers, on both sides of the political issue, would agree that most abortion decisions involve elements of fear and despair.

But simply because a woman agonizes over an abortion decision does not make the decision morally acceptable, not even to the women themselves. In fact, post-abortion research suggests that the more a woman agonizes over making an abortion decision, the more she is likely to agonize over the abortion afterwards. Maternal desires, moral doubts, and feelings of being exploited do not disappear after an abortion. They continue. They grow. They become sources of constant reflection or stifling avoidance. They can even become the source of a crippling self-condemnation.

## ESCAPE THROUGH SELF-DESTRUCTION

Returning to Mathewes-Green's analogy of an animal gnawing its leg off to escape a trap, we see that abortion is actually an act of self-destruction. When pro-abortionists view a woman in this desperate situation, their solution is to offer the woman a clean, legal way of cutting off the offending leg—after all, they believe there are too many unfit "legs" in the world already.

But what abortion counselors fail to tell women who are choosing abortion is that the loss of their "leg" will leave them crippled. Just like many amputees, they will experience the feeling of a "phantom leg." This missing part will leave them less whole and less capable. And at times this missing piece will cause an indescribable ache and a flood of uncontrollable tears. In escaping the trap, they will have lost a part of themselves.

Contrast this approach to that of crisis pregnancy centers where pro-lifers are committed to finding a way to open the jaws of the trap to save both the woman and her "leg." Pro-lifers insist that there is always room for hope. There is always a way to avoid a destructive amputation—a way which, in the long run, will be appreciated by both her and her "leg."

What we see in these two perspectives is the difference between despair and hope. Despair inevitably leads us to accept abortion. Hope always leads us to embrace life.

Hope is a virtue. It is centered on God, the source of all hope. Despair is a sin against hope. It is one of Satan's greatest weapons.

## THE WEAPON OF DESPAIR

Despair involves a loss of faith and trust in God. In the case of abortion, the desperate woman has lost faith in the promise that God has a plan for her life and a plan for her child's life.

Desperate people try to take control. They try to save whatever they can by doing whatever needs to be done—which may include betraying their own values. For example, when the Nazis undertook the extermination of millions of Jews, the sheer magnitude of their task required them to develop ways of soliciting the cooperation of the victims. There were too few soldiers to contain millions of rebellious Jews. So it was necessary to manipulate their victims so that they would choose to cooperate for at least one day at a time. The Nazis did this by exposing the Jews to *limited* threats; the victims were always left with the bit of hope that by submitting to the present indignity, there was something else which could be saved. According to sociologist Zygmunt Bauman:

> At all stages of the Holocaust, the victims were *confronted with a choice* (as least subjectively—even when objectively the choice did not exist any more, having been pre-empted by the secret decision of physical destruction). They could not choose between good and bad situations, but they could at least choose between greater and lesser evil....In other words, they *had something to save*. To make their victims' behavior predictable and hence manipulable and controllable, the Nazis had to induce them to act in the 'rational mode.' To achieve that effect, they had to make the victims believe that there was indeed something to save, and that there were clear rules as to how one should go about saving it.[3]

These choices were presented in a way that discouraged reflecting on the decisions from a moral perspective. Instead, the victims were pressured to make *rational* decisions based on the rational need to "save whatever we can."

Using this demonic strategy, the Nazis encouraged the empowerment of Jewish ghetto leaders who would see to the needs of the people, coordinate distribution of medicine and materials, maintain morale, etc. These same leaders were then manipulated into cooperating with the Nazi extermination program. They were confronted with the agonizing choice of cooperating with the Nazis or witnessing the slaughter of their people. At first, the cooperation was in "small" things, maintaining a ghetto police force, providing lists of names, selection of ghetto residents to be sent to "resettlement" projects, providing transportation to pick-up points, and the like. In some cases, when the Nazis wanted to punish the entire community for some infraction, Jewish leaders were even forced to select and arrest the desired number of victims who were to be publicly executed by the Nazis. And always, no matter what the request, the leaders were told that by cooperating they were saving the lives of the majority who remained. Leaders who didn't cooperate were eliminated. Leaders who did cooperate saved their own lives and those of their families, at least for a time, and were left to agonize over their complicity.

The similarity between Nazi manipulations of the Jews and the abortionists' manipulation of women faced with crisis pregnancies is striking. Just as the Jews were forced to choose between losing everything or just a little, so abortion counselors encourage the victim-woman to view "this pregnancy" as a threat to everything she has—her relationships, her family, her career, her entire future. She is assured that by sacrificing this one thing (a tiny unborn child), she can save the rest. During this process, the victim-woman is urged to view the abortion decision not as a moral choice, but as a rational choice of "saving what you can."

But in fact, just as those who reluctantly cooperated with the Nazis discovered, the bargain is a false one. The demands on ghetto leaders to sacrifice more and more victims never stopped. And so it is with the post-aborted woman. After her child is destroyed, she faces self-condemnation, lower self-esteem, difficulty with relationships, substance abuse, career problems, a cycle of repeat abortions, and more. Often she experiences an intense desire for replacement pregnancies to atone for her lost child, and she becomes a single parent—the very problem she sought to avoid in the first place—but now she also has to deal with the emotional scars of an abortion.

## THE DEVIL VERSUS CHRIST

It is significant how differently Christ and the devil appear before and after any sin, in this case, abortion. Before the abortion, Christ stands, with his arms outstretched to block the way, saying, "Do not do this thing. The sacrifices you must make now will be rewarded a hundred fold. I offer you life, so that you may live life abundantly. Place your hope in Me and I will not abandon you."

The devil, on the other hand, insists, "You must get rid of it. Look at all you will lose.... You have no choice. You have already gotten yourself into this problem. Now you must get yourself out. Do this one thing and then you will be back in the driver's seat of life. Things will be the way they used to be."

Christ asks us to trust in a plan for our future which we do not yet fully understand; Satan urges us to act *now*, to take control, to save what we already have. Christ asks us to make a moral decision rooted in hope; Satan asks us to make a "rational" decision based on present needs, desires, and fears.

But after the abortion, how do they appear? Afterwards, Christ continues to offer hope: "Come to me. I want to share your tears. I want to comfort you. Know that all is forgiven. See, your child is in My arms waiting for you to join us when your day is completed."

Satan, on the other hand, continues to fan the flames of despair. He who pretended to be on her side now stands as her fiercest accuser. "Look at what you have done! You have murdered your own child! Can there be anything worse than that? There's no hope for you now.

You are nothing. You're beyond redemption! You may as well seek what little comfort you can in the bottom of a booze bottle, in the silence of suicide, or in the embrace of an affair. And if you get pregnant again, you've already had an abortion once, so you might as well do it again—it may even help you to get tougher and more immune to this pain. It makes no difference now. You've proven you can murder. Nothing can be worse. And, oh, how you must hate those people who led you to this. Your boyfriend, your parents, your doctor. There is no one you can trust. There is no one who can love YOU—*a murderer*. You are alone. Your best hope is to bury your past. Hide it from others. Hide it from yourself. But remember it will always be yours *alone* to bear."

Before the abortion, Christ condemns it and Satan makes excuses for it. After the abortion, Satan is the one condemning it while Christ wants to forgive it.[4]

This is the devil's bargain. He encourages women to submit to abortion in order to avoid losing what they already have. But once they have chosen it, he tries to keep them trapped in despair so as to strip away everything else. Indeed, Satan pumps as much despair into their lives as he can generate. And not only into their lives, but into the lives of the child's father, and grandparents, and siblings, and everyone else he can touch with the poison of abortion. His purpose is threefold: to generate misery, to encourage more sin, and to create doubt in the unfathomable mercy of God.

## DESPAIR AND FORGIVENESS

For many post-aborted women, the forgiveness of God is a precept which they can mouth, but which is difficult for them to digest. How can *they* be forgiven? The horror of their sin is so great. Many know that they must believe in God's forgiveness, and they do so in an act of faith. But how can they *feel* forgiven, when every instinct in their nature says they cannot be forgiven, even *should not* be forgiven?

I certainly do not have a complete answer to this complex question, but I do believe we can offer more than simply the truth that "God can forgive any sin, even abortion." While this is a revealed truth, it is also a conclusion for which we can develop a greater appreciation if we look at some of the reasons behind this truth. As we look, I believe we will discover not only truths which must be shared with post-aborted men and women, but also truths which explain why our focus must be on ministering to them, not accusing them.

Assume that I am on a joy ride, speeding along for thrills. I see a flash of light. A bump. And I know I've killed someone. I run to the victim. He's dead. An innocent man has been killed because of my negligence. My guilt is very real and well deserved. But a moment later my victim jumps to his feet alive and uninjured. Now the guilt is gone! I am spared, not by my virtue, but by *his* immortality.

In just the same way we have all been forgiven of murder. Because of our sins, of whatever type, each of us is guilty of crucifying Christ. Because of our sins, He was killed on the cross. His blood is on our hands. Yet on Easter Sunday, He rose from the dead. He is not dead at all! The guilt has been lifted.

## WORDS TO A GRIEVING MOTHER

"But my child did not rise from the dead," a post-aborted woman complains. "She is truly dead, and I am guilty of her death." But to such a woman I would respond that this is another example of her guilt being twisted into despair.

Death is an experience, not a state of being. For "God is not the God of the dead but of the living. All are alive for Him (Luke 20:38)." When your child was killed by abortion, he or she *experienced* death. But your child is not *dead* in the sense of destroyed. Your child, like us all, is immortal. Death cannot keep her down.

C.S. Lewis explains it well when he writes, "There are no ordinary people. You have never talked to a mere mortal. Nations, cultures, arts, civilization—these are mortal, and their life is to ours as the life of a gnat. But it is immortals whom we joke with, work with, marry, snub and exploit—immortal horrors or everlasting splendors." Damned or glorified, all people live on (Matt. 25:46).

Therefore, like Christ, your child lives. Your guilt can be removed precisely because God has already preserved your child from destruction. He lives! She lives! They all live in Him!

Remember, your abortion was a result of your failure to trust God. In giving you that pregnancy, God was giving you the opportunity to love. But you rejected this gift because you did not trust God's plan for you. This lack of trust and obedience is at the root of all sin, yours and mine. So it is only right that the reparation for abortion is found not by clinging to guilt and despair, but by trusting in God's love. You failed once in rejecting His gift of a new life. But now He has a new plan for you, a second gift which He passionately desires for you—the gift of His forgiveness, the rebirth and renewal of your spirit.

To refuse God's mercy is to refuse His love. Don't insult Him by refusing His forgiveness. Accept God's forgiveness, not because you deserve it, but so that God can use you as an instrument for showing the abundant glory of His mercy. Accepting the gift of God's forgiveness is actually a humble thing to do. It is your first step toward an obedience which is rooted in both faith and hope, and it is your only escape from the tar pit of despair.

## THE WORST EVIL

In a sense (and I write this asking the reader's forbearance for my inability to express this more precisely), since immortal persons cannot be destroyed, the greatest tragedy in killing is what this sin does to killers. This does not deny that the killed have been unjustly deprived of life, but we know that God will be merciful toward these innocent victims. We should be more concerned about the eternal fate of killers.

Even Socrates, a pagan philosopher, recognized that, in terms of preserving the nobility of our character, inner virtue, and our very souls, it is better to suffer evil from others than to do evil ourselves. Specifically, Socrates argued that those who do unjust acts are becoming unjust; those who reject their obligations to others are becoming irresponsible.

Because he believed that moral character was more important than physical well-being, Socrates believed that harm which is done to one's body is less important than harm done to one's "inner self" as the result of immoral choices. In the case of abortion, he would argue, the harm done to the mother's soul is a greater moral evil than the physical wrong suffered by the unborn child, who remains innocent.

There is nothing in this argument which is contrary to Christian thought. Indeed, Scripture teaches not only that it is preferable to suffer evil than to commit evil but that those who suffer from wrongdoing can even rejoice in being called upon to share in the suffering of Christ (1 Peter 4:13-16). As we have suggested above, and will discuss further in the next chapter, the unborn child who suffers physical harm from abortion is an immortal being whose innocence will be recognized and rewarded by God. But the spiritual damage done to those who are involved in abortion, directly or indirectly, individually or socially, is immeasurable.

Let us look at the spiritual meaning of abortion from another perspective. We begin by recognizing the Judeo-Christian teaching that children are always a gift from God. Because God is the author of all life, no child is conceived by accident. Each has a part to play in God's design. This providential purpose includes not only the child's destiny, but the destiny of those whom the child's life touches. For parents, the conception of a child may be intended to lead them to greater generosity, responsibility, and understanding of the meaning of unconditional and sacrificial love. (Even in the case of experimentation on *in vitro* human embryos, God allows these human lives to be conceived so that scientists and the eugenicists who fund them can prove their depravity and thereby justify their final judgment.) No life is created without a purpose. It is our role to simply find and cooperate with that purpose.

Thus, whenever we reject the gift of new life, we are rejecting a gift from *God*! Obviously, this is an insult to the Giver. But it is an insult which will be mercifully forgiven. And, as members of the body of Christ, we are called upon to be mirrors of God's mercy and ambassadors of His forgiveness. While we can do nothing for the unborn children in heaven, there is much we can do for the women and men who have been so morally wounded by abortion.

In brief, without in any way diminishing the horror of abortion, I am confident that children killed by abortion are in the enviable position of living in the glorious presence of Christ. Furthermore, if the salvation of souls is the greatest of goods, then the damnation of souls is the greatest of evils. Thus, the greatest evil of abortion lies in the spiritual damage it inflicts on the women, men, and families (and politicians) who are ensnared by it. It is these bleeding, bruised, despairing, and even rebellious souls who are most at risk. It is they to whom Christians need to reach out with the good news of forgiveness and hope.

## SUMMARY

The greatest tragedy of abortion is that it separates men and women from God. The despair which drives women to abortion is also used to make them doubt God's mercy, which, in turn leads to an embracing of atheism. For some sinners, the fear of hell makes them hope for a death of annihilation: "When it's over, it's over." For those trapped by despair, this is their only hope, the annihilation of self. This is why so many post-aborted women directly seek death through suicide. Others court death's semblance in abusive relationships or the mind-deadening effects of drug or alcohol abuse. Still others just run from life, burying themselves in everything from pointless work to joyless parties—anything that distracts them from reflection.

Abortion is, of course, not the only sin which separates us from God. But to those who have had one, it almost always creates the biggest rift. To return across this chasm, they need our help, offered graciously and abundantly. In giving them hope, we will be giving them back to God.

# CHAPTER TWELVE

# TRUSTING GOD'S MERCY FOR UNBORN CHILDREN

THERE is still one more hook of despair which Satan can use to deny peace of mind to the mothers and fathers of aborted children. This is the fear that even if God can forgive them, their unborn children will be deprived of heaven because they were denied baptism.

This fear that unbaptized infants will be denied heaven is also used by Satan to build a wall of separation and prejudice between pro-lifers and the post-aborted men and women. Not a few Christians have coldly turned their backs on those who have had abortions, believing that they have deprived God of the souls of their unborn children. They may not wish the post-aborted ill, but they cannot bring themselves to offer them comfort, either.

These are two reasons why the issue of the final repose of the unborn is a very important one, not only for those who seek post-abortion healing, but also for the pro-life movement as a whole. First, if we truly believe that the unborn are in heaven, then anger and resentment will be dissipated. Second, concern for the living, those who suffer the guilt of abortion, will not only be easier, it will be more compelling.

## THE ISSUE: THE NECESSITY OF BAPTISM

The question of salvation for the unborn arises from an interpretation of Christ's solemn pronouncement to Nicodemus that "no one can enter into God's kingdom without being begotten of water and the Spirit" (John 3:5). The necessity of baptism is further supported by Christ's statement, "The man who believes in it [the good news] and accepts baptism will be saved; the man who refuses to believe will be condemned" (Mark 16:16). Note, however, that condemnation is pronounced for those who *refuse* to believe. Nothing is said regarding those who have not had the opportunity to believe. Indeed, we are also told that no one will be judged guilty simply because of their ignorance (John 9:41).

What are we to make of this, then? Baptism by water is clearly the way God has given the Church for bringing new members into His Body. When it can be done, it ought to be done. However, God's mercy is not limited by human failings, nor are His means limited by the physical reality which defines human interaction. Indeed, it is clear in Scripture that God has at least one other way of bringing sanctifying grace to those who have died without having the opportunity to receive baptism by water.

The most obvious example of unbaptized persons who were saved is that of the Old Testament saints, including the patriarchs, the prophets, and untold others. For the sake of these departed, Christ went in death to preach to them "in prison" (1 Peter 3:19) so that they "might live in the spirit in the eyes of God" (1 Peter 4:6). Yet another example is shown in the good thief, who followed Jesus into Paradise (Luke 23:42-44) without the benefit of baptism by water.

In fact, the Church has always recognized that martyrs who die for the faith before they have the opportunity to be baptized are reborn in a baptism by blood rather than water.[1] Baptism by either water or blood has been recognized as having the same efficacy and the same source. This view was defended by the prominent Christian apologist Tertullian around 203 A.D., who wrote:

> We have one and only one Baptism in accord with the Gospel (Eph. 4:4-6) …[But there is] a second font, one with the former [water]: namely, that of blood, of which the Lord says: "I am to be baptized with a baptism" (Luke 12:50, Mark 10:38-39), when he had already been baptized [by water]. For He had come through water and blood, as John wrote (1 John 5:6), so that he might be baptized with water and glorified with blood. He sent out these two Baptisms from the wound in His pierced side (John 19:34), that we might in like manner be called by water and chosen by blood, and so that they who believed in His blood might be washed by the water. If they might be washed in the water, they must necessarily be so by blood. This is the Baptism which replaces that of the fountain, *when it has not been received*, and restores it when it has been lost.[2] [Italics added.]

Tertullian's argument that baptism by blood can be a substitute for baptism by water is further supported by the fact that Christ offered the sons of Zebedee the baptism of suffering as one with the cup of salvation (Mark 10:38-39). Furthermore, Scripture tells us that before Christ's death, John's baptism by water was only a baptism of repentance (Acts 19:4, Luke 3:3). It was only after Christ's baptism in blood that the baptism of water was raised up to become a baptism with the Holy Spirit (Acts 1:5, John 16:7).

Clearly, then, the understanding that God has a means to save

.those who through no fault of their own have been denied the opportunity of baptism by water is not novel. Indeed, it is revealed by Scripture. Therefore, if we are to properly interpret Christ's insistence on baptism by water, we must admit that it is a binding command on the living, while recognizing that this precept does not preclude God from offering some other spiritual means of rebirth for those who die without this opportunity.*

## GOD'S SPECIAL LOVE FOR CHILDREN

We know as part of our revealed faith that God desires the salvation of all (1 Tim. 2:4, Rom. 8:32) and that his mercy endures forever (Psalm 136). Though all are stained by original sin, all whom Christ claims for Himself will live in Him (1 Cor. 15:22-23). That Christ should not claim the unborn as His own is unimaginable, contrary to both reason and revelation. Furthermore, Paul teaches that God's mercy and providence extends even to the unborn, who have done neither good nor evil (Rom. 9:11), and Christ himself repeatedly expressed His special love of infants and children.

> And they brought unto him also infants, that he would touch them: but when his disciples saw it, they rebuked them. But Jesus called them, and said, "Suffer the little children to come unto me, and forbid them not: for of such is the kingdom of God" (Luke 18:15-16).

See how Jesus describes heaven; it is filled with infants such as these! And are not His words a warning against those who would forbid these children entry into His heavenly kingdom? And look at yet another occasion:

> [The disciples asked Jesus:] "Who is of greatest importance in the kingdom of God?" He called a little child over and stood him in their midst and said: "I assure you, unless you change and become like little children, you will not enter the kingdom of God....See that you never despise one of these little ones. I assure you, their angels in heaven constantly behold my heavenly Father's face....Just so, it is no part of your heavenly Father's plan that a single one of these little ones shall ever come to grief." (Matt. 18:1-2, 10, 14)

---

*What this way is has not been fully revealed. On the other hand, since it is a spiritual baptism which is outside the responsibilities of believers on earth, it is not something about which we need to know the details. It is enough for us to know that it is possible. Once this truth is recognized, we can then confidently trust God's mercy and justice.

Other renderings of this last line are that none of these little ones should ever "perish" or be "lost." These passages suggest a promise of universal salvation for the innocents, for (1) they are numbered among the greatest of importance in God's kingdom, (2) their angels pray for them before the Father, and (3) the Father wills that none of them should be lost. Notice also that the small child standing before Christ was unbaptized.

Reason, too, demands our acknowledgment of God's saving grace for the unborn. Christ's love is so great, He died to bring salvation to sinners who deserve nothing (Romans 5:6-9). Yet, if He would save sinners like us, would He not do at least as much, if not more, for the unborn who have not sinned?[3] Of course He would. Those who doubt it must defend the absurd notion that God's judgments are less merciful than human judgments.

## THEORIES OF SALVATION

While the method of salvation for the unborn is not revealed, there are some theories which are useful to consider, remembering always that they are only theories. Some Christian theologians speculate that at the moment of death, God enlightens the minds of the "incompetent" so that they can freely choose for or against Him. This possibility would be analogous to the free choice for or against God which the angels made at the time of their creation.

Others believe that children who die without formal baptism, or other incompetents who are incapable of understanding or freely choosing baptism, acquire salvation through a "vicarious baptism of desire"—that is, through the desire of their parents, the Church, or someone else. Along these lines, it is a common practice within the post-abortion healing movement to encourage mothers and fathers of aborted children to offer a solemn prayer in which they entrust their children to the care of Jesus. This is an important part of the healing experience for many women and men. There have also been reports of mystical experiences in which the dedication of the aborted child was prompted by an interior voice of the Holy Spirit,[4] and others who have prayerfully dedicated an aborted child to God have reported remarkable healing for the post-aborted mother and father or relatives who were not even aware that the prayer was made.[5]

Another theory, which was once widely taught in Catholic parochial schools, is that of Limbo. Contrary to popular belief, this theory has never been a dogma of the Catholic Church. It has always been nothing more than a theological speculation which offers one possible solution to the puzzle of God's judgment of unbaptized innocents.

According to the Limbo theory, God's justice precludes punishment of the innocent, but the requirement of baptism precludes the unbaptized from enjoying the actual presence of God, heaven. Given these two constraints, one can conclude that God must at least supply these souls with a place where they enjoy a state of natural happiness, free of all suffering, where they would lack only the beatific vision of God. This place would be analogous to the place where Abraham and Lazarus were at rest prior to the opening of heaven by Christ (Luke 16:22).

While Catholics are free to believe in Limbo, the official Catechism encourages believers to hope for more, trusting that God has another means for admitting unbaptized innocents into heaven.[6] Indeed, the teaching documents of the Catholic Church exclude any theory which would hold that salvation of unbaptized innocents is not possible.[7] Most recently, in fact, Pope John Paul II has written in a major encyclical on abortion that *"nothing is definitively lost* and you [the women and men who have procured abortions] will also be able to ask forgiveness from your child, *who is now living in the Lord."*[8] [Italics added.] In short, while the Catholic Church does not teach the salvation of aborted children as a dogmatic certainty, it strongly encourages us to hope for their salvation through trust in God's mercy.

## THE HOLY INNOCENTS

Nancyjo Mann, the founder of Women Exploited by Abortion, once suggested that the slaughter of infants has always preceded the coming of a savior. Infant boys were slaughtered by Pharaoh before the coming of Moses. The infants of Bethlehem were slaughtered by Herod, who sought to prevent the Messiah from gaining his throne. Perhaps, she speculated, the slaughter of millions of babies by abortion throughout the world is a precursor to Christ's return.

No one knows when the Second Coming will be (Mark 13:32). Indeed, the moment we begin to feel certain that we do know is the moment we almost certainly prove that we are wrong (Mark 13:33). Throughout the ages, Christians have looked at the world's sinfulness and said, "Certainly He will come to judge us now." Our age is no different. Few Christians would doubt that the horrors of our generation demand judgment. But while we should all pray for Christ's return tomorrow, we must never neglect our task of building up His kingdom today.

It is true. This sinful age, with its own slaughter of innocents, will not be allowed to go on forever. God will not be mocked. So there are only three possibilities: (1) Christ will return; or (2) God, who is the Lord of History, will crush our modern civilization, adding its dust to the ruins of all the other proud empires which have gone before us; or (3) to glorify God's own Mercy, the Holy Spirit will conquer our love affair with death by bringing about a time of awakening, healing, and spiritual renewal. I do not know which of these God has ordained, His return, our culture's destruction, or our culture's spiritual healing. I do know that we, His followers, can only contribute to the latter. This is our task now, as it was from the beginning, to spread the good news of God's mercy and forgiveness.

But I have strayed a bit. My real reason for bringing up the Holy Innocents who were slaughtered by Herod is that they have been traditionally considered as assured of heavenly repose by virtue of the fact that they died in an attack on Christ. This was a form of martyrdom. They did not die in defense of their faith, for they did not know it, but rather as victims of mass murder directed against the Messiah.

If we believe the Holy Innocents are in Heaven, then this belief, too, should encourage us to believe in the salvation of the unborn who die by abortion. For whether Christ's return is imminent or not, abortion in our culture is clearly the result of a diabolical attack on Christian values. In the larger scheme of things, it is an attempt by Satan to usurp the Lord of Life and install a cult of death. It is an attack against the Body of Christ, His Church, which includes the vast majority of aborting women and men, who belong to the Church by virtue of their own baptisms. In this attack on Christ's body, unborn children are the innocent casualties. It is therefore reasonable to assume that, like the Holy Innocents, they too are baptized in their own blood, and in this way, will be brought into a share of Christ's own bloody baptism.

## SUMMARY

We must be confident of God's mercy, not only toward us, but also toward the unborn. If God has mercy on anyone, certainly He will be merciful with them.

Those who seek post-abortion healing must recognize that fears about the salvation of their unborn children are a temptation toward despair—a temptation which must be resisted. If they desire to be reunited with their aborted children, they must not worry about the salvation of their children, but rather about their own salvation, to which end they must build up lives of faith, *hope*, and charity. Of these, the virtue of hope precludes doubts about whether God will have mercy on the unborn.

For those who seek an end to abortion, confidence in God's mercy toward the children killed by abortion should undergird efforts to minister to those who have lost their children to abortion. By helping them to find spiritual healing, we will be helping them to become instruments of God's will. As His instruments, it is they, speaking with the wisdom of their own experiences, who will bring an end to abortion. We must remember that this is their battle even more than ours. By helping them, we help the cause of respect for all human life.

CHAPTER THIRTEEN

# HEALING, PUBLIC RELATIONS, AND RESEARCH

THE third leg of our pro-woman/pro-life strategy requires us to increase our efforts in the area of research and education relevant to the negative effects of abortion on women, men, siblings, family structures, and society at large. This leg of our strategy is closely tied to the first two (legal issues related to redress, and post-abortion healing) in that (1) it will define key issues of the political debate, which in turn will bring about the right to redress legislation we seek; (2) it will present new findings of fact regarding post-abortion injuries, which will affect judicial interpretations of the law; and (3) it will increase public awareness of the need for post-abortion healing.

Another important aspect of this public relations effort is to redefine public perception of the pro-life movement and the Church, showing that we are *both* pro-life and pro-woman. This means demonstrating to the public that our opposition to abortion is motivated not only by a desire to protect the unborn, but also by our desire to safeguard the rights, dignity, and health of women.

## OBSTACLES TO BE OVERCOME

At present, there are perhaps a dozen organizations which offer training in post-abortion counseling. One of the largest is the National Office of Post-Abortion Reconciliation and Healing (NOPARH) in Milwaukee, which provides counselor training for Project Rachel, a post-abortion healing program offered in most Catholic dioceses. Vicki Thorn, the director of NOPARH, estimates that they have trained over 3,000 mental health counselors and clergy in post-abortion counseling during the last six years. Thousands more have been trained through PACE, Last Harvest Ministries, Victims of Choice, Post-Abortion Ministries, and Open Arms. Because of these efforts, most crisis pregnancy centers now offer post-abortion counseling.

Not all of the people who have received training as post-abortion counselors, of course, are active in post-abortion ministry. Many clergy, for example, may work with only a few women per year. But these figures show that we are at the stage at which we have the counseling resources to minister to far more women than are presently being served.

How many women are receiving post-abortion counseling each year? We simply don't know. This illustrates how even the most rudimentary research in this field has not been done because of a lack of funding and coordination. Still, all post-abortion counselors agree that we are only reaching a small fraction of the women who need help, mostly because post-aborted women simply do not know that help is available.

In the area of research, most of what has been published about post-abortion reactions has been published by pro-choice or pro-abortion researchers who have limited the scope of their investigations to areas where they can control the political impact of their findings. Because a similar body of research done by abortion critics is lacking, the defenders of abortion currently dominate the scientific literature on abortion. This places us at a great disadvantage in the legislative hearings, the courts, and the press room, because pro-abortionists can argue that "most experts" (theirs) disagree with the concern that abortion is injurious to women.

Because there is no coordination or funding of anti-abortion research, even many of the most simple research tasks have not been undertaken. For example, there have been no systematic polls of post-abortion counselors to provide even rudimentary estimates of how many women and men are seeking counseling each year. Similarly, no one has yet done a study on what risks women would want to be informed of when contemplating abortion. What do women themselves consider to be relevant? This data would be invaluable to efforts to pass informed consent legislation and in malpractice suits against abortionists. Still another simple poll should be done to quantify public receptivity to the issue of coercive abortion. Such data would help to define our public relations campaigns. Research projects dealing with more specific topics are listed in Appendix D.

Researchers who are critical of abortion, including Dr. Vincent Rue, Dr. Philip Ney, myself, and others, have been mostly unable to attract the funding necessary to do the kind of in-depth studies which abortion defenders have been deliberately avoiding. There are many reasons for this inability of abortion critics to find funding for post-abortion research.

First, there is a widespread prejudice within government and academia against any research which might tarnish the image of abortion's safety. Such research is feared because it would "merely provide ammunition to anti-abortion activists."[1] This same "pro-choice" bias is found among the major private foundations which normally fund mental health research. At pro-abortion foundations, grant applications for research into abortion's aftereffects are automatically suspect; they do not serve the foundation's social agenda. The few grants which are given are restricted to carefully selected pro-abortion researchers whose work is billed as being necessary to refute the findings of anti-abortion researchers.

When grant proposals to fund post-abortion research have been sent to religious foundations, even strongly pro-life ones, our experience has been that these proposals are refused because the mandate for most Christian foundations is to fund service projects or evangelization, not research. The value of "academic" research is not immediately apparent to foundation directors who have not seen, by personal experience, how such research can dramatically affect the cultural and political climate of America. On the other hand, the liberals who dominate academia and most secular foundations do recognize the tremendous influence of research and the need to develop the credentials of "experts" who support their views. This is exactly why social research which advances the liberal agenda is so readily funded.

Finally, even large pro-life organizations have not funded post-abortion research because, as a general rule, they have higher or more immediate priorities. There is always some pro-abortion or pro-euthanasia initiative which demands the focus of their efforts. Thus, while they encourage the efforts of pro-life researchers, they have seldom provided any financial support.

As a result of all these obstacles, what little pro-life research has been done has mostly been funded out-of-pocket by the researchers themselves. This situation severely limits the scope of their studies and the time-frame for completion. Furthermore, in the last several years, there have been a half dozen graduate students who have done post-abortion research for their dissertations. But while their work has been excellent, little of their research has been submitted for publication in professional journals. Worst of all, there is no funding available to encourage or help these young scholars to pursue post-abortion research after they leave the university.

Overall, instead of a coordinated effort for exploring post-abortion trauma, we have a haphazard one. What is amazing, to me at least, is how far we have gotten with so few resources. Over the last six years, I have frequently claimed to colleagues that with five million dollars and five years of effort, we could generate such an immense body of literature documenting abortion sequelae that the issue would no longer be disputable. This may *not* have been true ten years ago. But now we have the advantage of over a decade of experience in post-abortion counseling. We know exactly what we are looking for in the whole range of aftereffects. We only need to apply this knowledge to studies of the general population. But until such research is done, pro-abortion groups like the American Psychiatric Association can continue to justify their claims that "abortion is safe for the majority of women" by hiding behind the distorted conclusions of the pro-abortion researchers who currently dominate this field.

The same problem of underfunding and lack of coordinated effort is also plaguing outreach efforts to those who need post-abortion healing. Again, considering that there is not even one well-funded organization promoting post-abortion education and outreach (most of these dozen or so groups work out of a volunteer's home with budgets of well under $20,000 per year), it is absolutely amazing how much has been accomplished. Even with these underfunded, under-staffed, and uncoordinated efforts, we now know that the public is very responsive to our message. Just imagine what could be done with full-time staffs and a multi-million-dollar budget.

## THE POST-ABORTION HEALING AND RESEARCH FOUNDATION

In order to coordinate, fund, and focus our efforts, I believe the pro-life movement must cooperatively support the formation of a national center to support post-abortion research, education, and outreach. This center would not replace any existing or future organizations involved in post-abortion work, but would instead be a servant to these organizations so that they can do their work more effectively and with better funding. For the purposes of discussion, I shall call this organization the Post-Abortion Healing and Research Foundation.

For reasons to be described later, the Foundation would be direct-ly involved in research and education efforts, but it would not become involved in counseling for post-abortion healing. Instead, it would cooperate with, provide support services for, and offer refer-rals to those agencies which do provide post-abortion counseling ser-vices. Along with other activities, the Foundation would:

- Coordinate post-abortion research activities, identify qualified professionals to undertake unmet research needs, provide grants and technical support to complete these projects, and assist in placing these research findings in appropriate academic journals;

- Maintain a library of all relevant publications and journal articles pertaining to post-abortion issues;
- Develop, publish, and disseminate post-abortion educational materials, including brochures, newsletters, and a peer-reviewed academic journal addressing post-abortion issues;
- Provide a clearinghouse for post-abortion information for pro-life groups, lobbyists, legislators, and abortion malpractice attorneys;
- Issue press releases, set up interviews, place public service announcements, develop a list of press contacts sympathetic to post-abortion issues, and otherwise serve as a public relations representative for post-abortion efforts;
- Identify and educate foundations which are sympathetic to these needs and provide a grant writer and fund raising consultant to assist post-abortion healing ministries in their fund-raising efforts;
- Develop a mailing list of individual donors and subscribers who support the Foundation's post-abortion research, education, and outreach activities and provide these individuals with educational materials;
- Provide the Foundation's mailing list of supporters to post-abortion healing ministries and assist them in developing their own lists of financial supporters;
- Support the development of a unified group of post-aborted women who have achieved healing and can bring their public witness to bear in the secular press and in the political arena;
- Develop materials specifically designed to assist clergy in addressing the abortion issue in a way which reduces the defensiveness of those who have been involved in abortion and which helps to strengthen their desire for reconciliation and healing;
- Provide one or more lobbyists to educate state and federal legislators about post-abortion issues and the need to advance legislation which would safeguard women and men who would otherwise be injured by abortion;
- Publicize post-abortion healing opportunities to attract and encourage those in need to seek healing and reconciliation;
- Provide a 24-hour intervention and referral service for post-abortion persons in crisis.

## LIMITS OF THE FOUNDATION

As mentioned above, it would not be the purpose of the Foundation to replace or compete with any existing or future organizations. Instead, its purpose would be to assist these other organizations in their efforts, especially in their efforts to raise operating funds and expand their outreach programs.

There are two major reasons for this limit on the Foundation's charter. First, I honestly believe there are tremendous advantages to having a hundred small organizations headed by a hundred different leaders. This distributed effort encourages innovation and the development of important leadership skills. The Foundation should never compete with any of these efforts, but should aid them. It can best provide this aid by being a collection point and clearinghouse of information, a meeting place for communication, and a vehicle for undertaking cooperative efforts.

Second, unlike research and public education, post-abortion counseling cannot be directed from a single national office. The counseling of women and men is a local process. A hot-line to provide emergency help to a post-aborted woman who is suicidal, for example, is important, but it is not a substitute for the kind of counseling that women and men really need, which requires a human face and a human touch.

In addition, the form and content of post-abortion counseling varies, depending on the beliefs and personalities of both the counselor and the post-aborted woman or man. This is another important reason why the Foundation should stay out of the counseling business and should instead encourage and support *all* post-abortion ministries.

All post-abortion counselors recognize the spiritual needs of post-aborted men and women. Some are licensed counseling professionals. Some are clergy. Some are post-aborted women, and some are simply compassionate people who have learned all they can about helping women to find post-abortion healing. Within this mix, some embrace modern psychological insights and techniques, while others are critical of psychological models and confine their programs to Bible studies exploring issues of grief and forgiveness. Some rely solely on peer discussion circles where women and men can share their personal experiences, and still others use all of these techniques.

Despite philosophical and theological differences regarding the best way to assist women in finding post-abortion healing, all of the present post-abortion ministries share a common vision of the importance of the post-abortion issue to making our country truly pro-life and pro-woman. I believe that all of these organizations would support the need for a more united effort of education and lobbying for reform, especially if this united effort does not attempt to force their healing efforts into some common mold.

For all of the reasons listed above, I envision this Foundation as a support vehicle for healing ministries, not a competitor or endorser of one model over another. When making referrals, the Foundation should advise callers about all the organizations available to help them, encouraging callers to consider each of these organizations in their search for a counselor in whom they can have confidence.

In summary, it is unnecessary, and potentially divisive, for the Foundation to become involved in counseling or promotion of one counseling method over another. But by providing fund-raising and other support services to post-abortion ministries, and by concentrating its in-house activities on research, education, and advocacy issues, the Foundation will fill a tremendous gap in our efforts to promote post-abortion healing and awareness.

## ESTABLISHING THE FOUNDATION

The long-term funding for the Foundation should be through grants from corporate and private foundations and donations from private individuals. But to launch this effort quickly and effectively, the most ideal scenario would be to have it receive start-up support from all the major pro-life organizations and pro-life religious denominations. Each group would be asked to contribute support according to its ability to do so. Perhaps each group would pledge to do one fund-raising appeal to its members to support establishment of the Foundation.

Besides the obvious value of coordinating post-abortion efforts, there would be other, more immediate advantages to a coalition-based effort. First, as briefly discussed in Chapter One, the post-abortion effort is one which is ideologically supported by both "pragmatists" and "purists." The establishment of the Foundation, broadly supported by all sections of the pro-life community, would provide a real opportunity to foster unity, something which we all crave.

Second, the formation of a coalition-based Foundation would also provide us with a media event which could demonstrate (1) pro-life unity and (2) rising concerns about the safety of abortion. Indeed, if pro-life leaders came together in a press conference to announce their combined support for an important "new" pro-life strategy, even the pro-abortion media would give this announcement broad coverage. Though the hostile press would certainly underreport our evidence and give more space to pro-abortionists reiterating that abortion is "safe," it would nonetheless be anxious to report this "major strategy shift" if only to warn the public about our new "anti-choice tactics." But even if pro-abortionists got five paragraphs explaining that abortion is safe and we got only one line saying it's dangerous, the seed of doubt is planted. Why would pro-lifers be putting all this money into this new effort unless they really thought they could win it?

Thus, even before the Foundation actually did anything, the debate would begin. Critical attention would be called to the question, "Is abortion safe or isn't it?" Working with the press, the Foundation would fan the flames of this debate with new research findings, publications, and press releases, all of which would demand responses from the opposition. Sooner or later, as the evidence for our side was rapidly gathered, the pro-abortionists would no longer be able to run from the debate with blanket denials. The debate would then be joined in earnest. At that point, their loss would be assured.

The other side already knows that the safety of abortion cannot stand critical examination. This is exactly why they must rely on blanket pro-abortion pronouncements. Although even the existing facts are not on their side, they are the ones who are dominating the interpretation of these facts, especially through the AMA and APA. Our job is to expose their cover-up and to show that their claims of concern for women are pure hypocrisy. But we won't succeed unless we have an organized and well-funded effort.

Just as Planned Parenthood has the Alan Guttmacher Institute as a research arm, which publishes studies supportive of their population control agenda, so the pro-life and pro-family movement needs its own research arm (or arms) to publish studies which respond to this skewed vision and support our agenda. The Alan Guttmacher Institute has developed tremendous credibility with academia and the press on all questions related to family planning. There is no reason why our own post-abortion research institute could not establish itself as an equally authoritative voice on issues relating to abortion's aftereffects. But credibility will not be achieved simply by publishing review articles criticizing the research of pro-abortionists. We must fund our own projects, gather our own data, and develop our own panel of experts in a wide variety of disciplines.

In short, I believe that the Post-Abortion Healing and Research Foundation (or whatever it might be called) should be a coalition-

based effort, with trustees chosen to represent the many supporting pro-life organizations. In order for this Foundation to be viable,
it would need to be non-political and restricted in scope. This limitation will prevent it from posing a competitive threat to the "ter-
ritory" of existing pro-life groups. Instead, the Foundation would
directly assist pro-life groups equally by providing new and crucial
data which individual groups could not collect on their own. In
this way, the Foundation would offer us a mechanism for establishing both a real and a symbolic point of unity among pro-life
groups.

There is no shortage of talented and qualified researchers who are
willing and ready to critically examine post-abortion sequelae. There
has simply never been any financial support for them to do so.
Given five years of solid financial support, we could have over fifty
studies which, together, would destroy once and for all the myth
that "abortion is safe." On every front, this research could help us
achieve our goal, and, in my opinion, it is worth the investment,
even if it means diverting pro-life funds from other political and
educational activities.

Obviously, if this national center for post-abortion research and
education cannot be established as a coalition effort, it should be
established as an individual effort. I and others have tried to do this,
but we have not had any significant success. Our failure has been due
to (1) inadequate contacts with people or foundations capable of raising the necessary funds, and (2) an inability to fully articulate our
vision in a two-page cover letter. This is one of the reasons for writing this book. It is my hope that it will help to attract the attention of
the "movers and shakers" who can turn vision into reality. If you are
that type of person, or if you know someone who is, I ask you to join
us in this effort to establish a major center for post-abortion research,
education, and outreach.

But if, as is likely, you are person of only modest means and influence, then (if you will excuse my inserting a brief advertisement) I ask
that you give some small support for our minor center for post-abortion research and education, the Elliot Institute. The Elliot Institute
doesn't have the staff or funds necessary to shake our nation from its
slumber, but through our small research and education projects, like
those reported upon in The Post-Abortion Review, we are making
some little headway. It is our prayer that through our modest efforts,
eventually the importance of establishing a major research and education institute will be recognized. Any support you can give to this
work would be greatly appreciated.

## Summary

Post-abortion efforts, in all areas, are severely underfunded and unorganized. There are no organized public relations programs and no sympathetic funding sources to support research. Post-abortion healing groups are plentiful, but their outreach efforts are severely limited by lack of funding, staff, and coordination.

There is a desperate need for a central clearinghouse to coordinate professional public relations efforts, research projects, and fund-raising campaigns to assist present and future post-abortion ministries. The formation of a central Post-Abortion Research and Healing Foundation would provide an opportunity to increase pro-life unity. It would also be an important mechanism for advancing every aspect of our pro-woman/pro-life strategy.

# CHAPTER FOURTEEN

# A MORE DYNAMIC STRATEGY

A major theme of this book has been that the pro-life movement has failed to recognize the true importance of post-abortion issues. I believe this oversight has mostly been caused by inertia. It is human nature to continue doing what has been successful in the past.

Recall that the pro-life movement developed as a natural response to the pro-abortionists' efforts to decriminalize abortion. After *Roe*, the goal of the movement was to once again make abortion illegal by judicial appeal, legislative victories, or constitutional amendment. This effort was motivated by the desire to safeguard the sanctity of human life. The central argument was, and continues to be, that the unborn child's right to life must supersede any lesser rights or desires of the child's mother. This goal and argument are deeply ingrained in all that the pro-life movement has done. This way of thinking has become second nature to pro-lifers.

The strategy for pursuing this goal has also been straightforward. In a much oversimplified sense, this strategy is illustrated in Figure A.

Money is raised from like-minded people. It is spent in educational and lobbying efforts to increase public sympathies for the moral imperative of protecting human life. This public relations campaign is designed to: (1) directly deter abortion by making women more aware of their unborn child's humanity; (2) encourage election of pro-life candidates who will support pro-life legislation; and (3) encourage like-minded people to support more of the same.

The focus of this strategy has always been on the humanity of the unborn. The theory behind this effort is that the hearts of people will be opened by the truth.

Though this traditional strategy has fallen far short of its ultimate goal, it has met with considerable successes. It has been very successful at blocking major pro-abortion initiatives such as public funding of abortion. It has also kept alive moral awareness of abortion's evil. The vast majority of people understand that abortion involves the killing of a human life, and most are at least troubled by this fact. The fundraising efforts of the pro-life movement have also been reasonably successful. Millions of supporters respond regularly to appeals for support in defending the unborn.

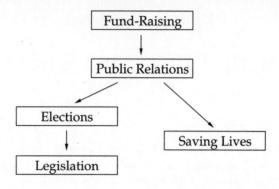

*Figure A*
*Traditional Pro-Life Strategy: Focuses on stimulating concern for the unborn.*

Within this traditional strategy, post-abortion issues are generally an appendage, not a vital organ. The idea that women are victims of abortion is now widely accepted, but they are most often viewed as secondary victims. Even in informed consent statutes, the emphasis by pro-life sponsors has often been placed on disclosing the humanity of the child to the woman in order to appeal to her conscience.

This traditional pro-life strategy has been successful at motivating like-minded people to volunteer, to vote pro-life, and to donate to the cause. But it has failed in its attempt to swing the middle majority of Americans—those who are simultaneously both anti-abortion and pro-choice. The hearts of the middle majority are hardened toward the unborn because they are focused on the needs and autonomy of women. To gain their support, we must talk about the people whom they are chiefly concerned about: women.

## REDIRECTIONAL, NOT COUNTERCULTURAL

Persons skilled in the martial arts learn to use the momentum of their opponent to their own advantage. Similarly, we must learn the art of cultural judo. Rather than fighting human nature, and the trends of our culture, the pro-woman/pro-life strategy uses these trends to our own advantage.

First, we must tap into our society's hypersensitivity to women's rights. By establishing that there are at least some women being victimized by abortion, we can drive a wedge between feminists and population controllers. Politically, the victims of abortion are unas-

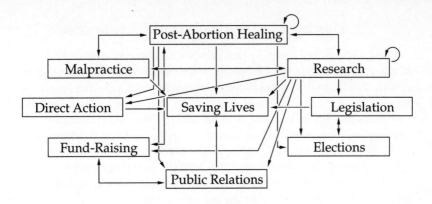

**Figure B**

*ProWoman/Pro-Life Strategy: Focuses on women suffering from unwanted abortions.*

sailable. The pro-abortionists would be pilloried for any direct attack against the integrity of women who are simply bearing witness to their own personal experiences. (Secularists are always sensitive to new classes of victims because they are bound by their faith in subjective realities to respect the claims of every self-professed victim.) The pro-abortionists' only defense is to claim that women only rarely suffer from abortion. Our task is to demonstrate the opposite, or at least to insist that something must be done to protect the "minority" of women who are being hurt and exploited.

Second, we must also tap into the trend toward increased individual autonomy, especially in the field of patients' rights. What right do abortionists have to paternalistically withhold information which might affect a woman's abortion decision? None.

Third, we live in a highly litigious society. People are already conditioned to believe that if they have been injured by someone, especially a doctor, they may have a legal claim. Whether this trend is motivated by a desire for justice or by greed, it is a trend which can be used against the corrupt abortion industry.

Fourth, we live in a society where "saving face" is more important than proclaiming the truth. Pro-abortion politicians and judges feel bound by their past positions on behalf of "a woman's right to abortion." The only face-saving way in which they can support laws regulating and restricting abortion is on the basis of "newly discovered information" about the health risks of abortion.

When these dynamics are harnessed to the cycle of post-abortion healing, which leads to the spread of more post-abortion healing, we will have an unbeatable dynamo for destroying the sacred idol of abortion.

## A DYNAMIC, SELF-PROPELLING STRATEGY

As is shown in Figure B, the pro-woman/pro-life strategy has a much greater interplay of reactions than the traditional pro-life strategy. In this interplay, there is the dynamic force of positive feedback. Success in one area increases success in other areas, which leads to still more success in the first, and on and on. Whereas the traditional strategy of increasing public concern for the unborn has been like pushing a boulder uphill, I believe the pro-woman/pro-life strategy is like pushing a boulder downhill. Once the initial resistance is overcome, existing trends in our society, as outlined above, will provide all the energy necessary to propel us to our goal.

Those who have read the previous chapters will immediately grasp most of the interconnections which are indicated. I will only briefly summarize them here with mention of a few additional points which have not yet been covered.

### Dynamics of Healing

As previously described in Chapter Ten, by creating a more welcoming and forgiving environment, we will be encouraging more people to seek post-abortion healing. Those who seek and receive reconciliation with God and themselves will strengthen both the pro-life movement and the Church. They and their family members will be freed from self-imposed silence and will become actively anti-abortion. Some will file lawsuits, individually or in class action suits. Many will support the pro-life movement with both their money and their time. Speaking with the voice of experience, their voices will be heard far better than our own. Most importantly, these individuals will be an example of hope to others who suffer from post-abortion denial or guilt. Their healing will encourage still more healing. Finally, their witness of how women are victimized by abortion will have profound effects on the political process and, ultimately, on the kind of legislation which is passed.

### Dynamics of Direct Action

Pro-life rescuers, and even sidewalk counselors, have been denied the right to defend their actions in court with any reference to abortion. This has largely been done on the premise that rescuers are motivated solely by a desire to protect the unborn. Since, under *Roe*, the unborn have no rights, any testimony regarding motives associated with the unborn is excluded by the courts as immaterial.

But direct action to inform women of abortion-related risks involves a party, the woman, whom the court is bound to recognize as having rights. Furthermore, as our pro-woman public relations campaign is actively pursued, judges and jurors will be more likely to be receptive to this motivation for direct action. The necessity of disclosing to women the risks of abortion may also prove useful in combatting FACE.

Perhaps even more important to the direct action movement is the healing of post-aborted women and men. For example, in Washington, D.C., on January 23, 1989, a sit-in rescue was led by pro-life women, all of whom had themselves had abortions. The media censored the fact that these rescuers were all "dissatisfied customers." But if, in their burgeoning numbers, the women and men who have recovered from post-abortion trauma should seek to emulate this type of protest to protect other women from the same fate, the courts and the press could not ignore this effort for long.

## Dynamics of Public Relations

Public relations campaigns which focus on the exploitation and suffering of women will appeal to the concerns of the middle majority (see Chapter Four). By focusing first on our efforts to make legal abortions safer, the middle majority will eventually realize that abortion can never be safe. By drawing their attention to women who are being forced into unwanted abortions, the middle majority will eventually realize that almost all abortions are unwanted; women want real choices which empower them to have their children, not to destroy them in an act of despair.

This public relations campaign is important to reshaping our image as both pro-woman and pro-life. The middle majority can identify with this. What they cannot identify with is judgmental condemnation of women. This perception of pro-lifers as condemning of women must be overcome by a sincere and all-out effort to show our understanding of the pressures women face who are considering abortion. We must also highlight our empathy and support for women who have had abortions. By successfully moving to a pro-woman/pro-life stance, we will attract more and more financial and political support from the middle majority.

## Dynamics of Research

It is no secret that post-abortion research, from a critical pro-life perspective, has benefited immensely from the success of the post-abortion healing movement. The willingness of women to share and explore their own abortion experiences laid the groundwork for our understanding of post-abortion trauma. These research findings, in turn, will continue to help post-abortion counselors to better understand their clients' needs and to thereby serve them better.

The opportunities for post-abortion research are almost unlimited. So is the impact. As the dangers of abortion are better documented and publicized, post-abortion research will (1) increase the political pressure for laws regulating pre-abortion disclosure, screening, and the protection of high-risk abortion patients; (2) increase the number of women qualified and willing to sue for abortion-related injuries; (3) increase the total liability, and win-ability, of malpractice suits against abortionists; and (4) increase the insurance premiums for abortionists.

New research is also an effective tool for expanding our public relations efforts with the least use of advertising dollars. New research is news. This news will be reported in both the religious and secular press. This news, in turn, will increase public awareness of the need for post-abortion healing. Not only does this increase the number of women seeking help, it also increases the level of understanding of the general public. By increasing understanding, we increase empathy for the victims of abortion, which in turn creates a more healing environment, which again makes it easier for even more women to seek healing.

Furthermore, better documentation of abortion-related injuries not only increases the liability of abortionists, it also decreases their resolve. More than one abortion provider has reported quitting the abortion industry because of concern that more women were being hurt than they helped. Anti-abortion propaganda to the contrary, not everyone in the abortion industry is motivated solely by greed. Many abortionists and support personnel can be touched by the truth of how abortion destroys the lives of women and their families. They live with the stress of assisting in abortions because they cling to the hope that they are helping women. Take away this illusion, and they will see that they are only participating in the perpetuation of a pure evil.

## SUMMARY

The traditional pro-life strategy is a countercultural movement. It is engaged in an uphill battle because pro-lifers are perceived to be fighting against women's rights.

The pro-woman/pro-life strategy reverses this field of battle. By fighting under the banner of women's rights advocates, we gain the political high ground—which, when combined with the moral high ground of the pro-life position, is an impregnable position. In addition, by aligning the interests of the middle majority with our own, and by promoting post-abortion healing, we will also enjoy the advantage of a much larger supply of reinforcements to strengthen our efforts.

No part of the analysis above is intended to denigrate the value and effectiveness of the traditional pro-life strategy. It has worked, and it continues to serve an important function. The traditional approach is especially good at moving latent pro-lifers into action—to volunteer, to vote, to donate.

But we need to move beyond preaching to the choir. We need to preach to the middle majority in a voice they will hear: concern for women. By appealing to this concern, we can draw them into becoming supporters of our pro-woman/pro-life initiatives. At that point, they will begin to become latent pro-lifers, and, finally, we may hope, they will become active pro-lifers.

It is a step-by-step process. But once the initial steps are taken, it is also a downhill process, with the dynamics of human nature and cultural trends working to our advantage.

Finally, I would reemphasize that we can pursue this pro-woman/pro-life agenda without compromise. We need not, and cannot, acknowledge any fundamental "right" to abortion. But we can insist that just because abortion is legal, women should not be denied their right to be protected from dangerous and unwanted abortions. The abortion "right" must not be allowed to supersede women's rights.

We will know that the end is near on the day when the focus of the abortion debate shifts from the issue of women's rights versus the rights of unborn children to the issue of abortion's risks. At that point, the safety of abortion will be permanently suspect in the public mind. Any future claims of safety will be viewed with as much skepticism as the tobacco industry's claims that cigarettes are safe.

When we succeed in establishing this question mark, we will simultaneously have succeeded in establishing the need for reevaluating the whole abortion question. In this reevaluation, the middle majority will be faced with the determining question: If women aren't being helped by abortion—if women are being hurt—then why are we allowing their children to be killed?

The destruction of the unborn has only been tolerated because it is believed that abortion benefits women's lives. But if there is more pain than benefit, the sacrifice of children to abortion is purely an abomination. Thus, in any reevaluation in which the deaths of the unborn are joined together with the real pain and suffering abortion causes women, men, and their families, the abortion "liberty" will certainly lose.

CHAPTER FIFTEEN

# THE POLITICAL DYNAMICS

E ACH element of the pro-woman/pro-life strategy eventually plays into the political process. This includes the processes of passing legislation, enforcing the laws, and judging the laws. As previously described in Chapter Three, the pro-woman/pro-life strategy is the most effective tool for defeating pro-abortion candidates and electing pro-woman/pro-life politicians. By focusing on women's rights legislation, we turn the table on pro-abortion politicians and force them to take a stand. Do they stand on the side of women injured by abortionists? Or are they defending abortion industry profits at the expense of women? This is the crux of our political campaign. In this chapter, we will expand our discussion of the political dynamics of the pro-woman/pro-life strategy in light of the previous chapters.

## WORKING WITH *PRO-CHOICE* POLITICIANS

Almost nothing is more certain to raise the ire of pro-lifers than a politician who declares, "I'm personally opposed to abortion, but I support every woman's right to choose for herself." Pro-lifers condemn such statements as two-faced pandering. If a person honestly believes abortion is wrong for themselves, they insist, he or she should also believe it is wrong for everyone. For those of us who are convinced of our duty to live according to clear moral principles, such statements are clearly irrational. But to the middle majority, who are themselves ambivalent about abortion, they actually mirror their own mixed sentiments.

As discussed in Chapter Two, there is a significant difference between those who are pro-abortion and those who are pro-choice. It is also clear that many politicians are truly pro-abortion. They seek to use abortion as a tool for social engineering: a means of reducing welfare costs, urban crime, and population growth among the "unwanted" portions of our society. For these pro-abortion politicians, the "personally opposed, but" line is simply that, a line, which appeases the sensibilities of the middle majority. These pro-abortion politicians will not be swayed by appeals to justice for women. Our only leverage with them is their fear of losing votes if they are exposed for protecting abortion industry profits at the expense of injured women.

But many other politicians are truly creatures of the middle majority, falling into one or more of the groups which we have described previously. They are honestly troubled by abortion, but they refuse to judge women or restrict them. These politicians are actually our potential allies, if we can show them that our pro-woman/pro-life proposals will serve *both* women and the unborn.

## CHAMPIONS OF CHOICE

Frankly, we anti-abortionists must not only reclaim our right to represent the interests of women, we must also claim our role as champions of choice. The word "choice" is not the copyrighted property of our opponents. Indeed, it is the pro-abortionists who support coercive population control who are the true enemies of reproductive choice.

In addition, it is only pro-abortionists who oppose the full disclosure of abortion's risks to women. Most people understand that a woman's "right to choose" means nothing without a corresponding "right to know." How can a "pro-choice" legislator say that she is protecting the right of women to choose and at the same time insist that women should be paternalisticly "protected" from knowledge about risks which may affect their choice?

We must, at least for strategic purposes, affirm that there is a middle ground occupied by those who are sincerely trying to be both pro-choice and pro-life. Indeed, it is in our strategic interests to support the building up of the so-called "common ground" organizations which support our pro-woman/pro-life agenda but fall short of a blanket condemnation of abortion. Why? Because the middle majority sees two radically opposed groups on either side of the abortion issue, with no articulate voice in between to negotiate a compromise.

Instead of attacking those who try to hold the nuanced position of being pro-choice and pro-life, we want to encourage them and respect them, acknowledging that they are at least people we can work with. Indeed, we want to see leaders who represent the middle majority grow in influence so that they can help us to show that it is the pro-abortionists who are the true radicals. We want the public to see that pro-life and pro-choice people can work together on pro-woman reforms which reduce dangerous and unwanted abortions. Then the public will begin to see that it is only the pro-abortionists who are resisting all reasonable reforms.

I am *not* saying that all pro-life groups should suddenly turn around and take a "pro-choice/pro-life" stance. Nor should they give up the goal of a straight-out ban on abortion. That would be an abandonment of a moral duty to affirm in the nation's law the inalienable right to life. Even if our pro-woman/pro-life laws resulted in every abortion clinic closing its doors, there would still be a very valid purpose served in codifying the rights of the unborn. In addition, it would be a strategic mistake for the pro-life movement to drop all calls for a total ban because the continued tension between the two extremes gives politicians in the middle greater reason to support a middle way, namely our pro-woman/pro-choice/pro-life legislation.

## DIVIDE AND CONQUER

From a political perspective, what we ideally want is to help lend credence to the notion that common ground organizations represent an important segment of the middle majority. We may disagree with their inability, or unwillingness, to address the fundamental moral issue of abortion, but we should express our respect for their honest desire to protect women's health and prevent unwanted and contraindicated abortions. They are reasonable people with whom we can work.

Preferably, common ground organizations representing the middle majority would be the principal sponsors of pro-woman statutes such as the Freedom of Choice Act described in Chapter Nine. These reforms should also receive the enthusiastic support of groups such as Feminists for Life, Women Exploited by Abortion, and other pro-life women's organizations. Major pro-life groups, on the other hand, would be quite justified in taking a positive but more restrained stance. Pro-life "extremists" should reservedly support these pro-woman initiatives because they "at least save women from unwanted abortions," but they should continue to loudly proclaim that they will continue to work for laws to eventually ban all abortions: "We oppose any implications that this law recognizes that women have a right to abortion. There is no such right. But until abortion can be made illegal, we support efforts which will make it safer and which will protect women from feeling pressured into unwanted abortions."

What we want is to encourage the view that the pro-woman laws described in Chapter Nine and Appendix C are middle-of-the-road, common ground initiatives. By offering the middle majority a "common ground" alternative which respects their mixed pro-choice and pro-life views, we will split them away from the pro-abortionists who oppose even the most sensible regulations.

In addition, by encouraging the development of common ground, pro-woman groups, we offer politicians the support of pro-choice organizations which will stand behind their votes for our pro-woman/pro-life initiatives. In these bills, we are not asking them to abandon their history of voting for "women's rights." We're asking them to continue that history and vote for the authentic rights of women to be protected from dangerous and unwanted abortions. We do not want these politicians to feel that a vote against the abortion industry will leave them unprotected from accusations of "flip-flopping." Common ground, pro-choice/pro-life organizations give these pro-choice politicians a safe-haven. While they may be attacked by Planned Parenthood and the ACLU for overburdening abortionists with "too much" liability, we want them to be able to explain to voters, "This was a pro-choice bill brought to us by groups like Safe, Legal and Rare, Women Exploited by Abortionists, and even by some feminist groups (namely, Feminists for Life). This was a good, common sense bill, which protects the right of women to make an informed and free choice. The only ones who are upset are those few abortion providers who have been taking shortcuts at the expense of women."

Instead of condemning the efforts of those who try to establish a middle ground, we want to encourage their efforts. In some cases, there are pro-life leaders who can and should help provide leadership for this coalition effort. After all, there are no inconsistencies in these two claims: (1) abortion can only be "safe, legal, and rare," when women are protected from dangerous abortions and are given the medical advice they need to freely choose safer alternatives; and (2) the unborn child has an absolute right to life which the state is obligated to protect. The first claim is both pro-choice (mostly) and pro-life (secondarily); the second is strictly a pro-life claim. Those of us who support both claims can and should work with those who only support the first. Indeed, as I have argued previously, the attainment of this first goal will inevitably lead to the second.

## RESTORING PRO-LIFE FEMINISM

If we are ever to divide and conquer the opposition, pro-lifers, as well as political and religious conservatives, must resist their knee-jerk aversion to the word "feminism." Admittedly, this word, as it is currently used, carries with it a lot of negative connotations. It is most commonly associated with the agenda of the radical left, including abortion, lesbianism, and the denigration of both men and the nuclear family. But none of these are inherent to the definition of feminism. Instead, they are a modern aberration.

According to Webster's, feminism simply means "organized activity on behalf of women's rights and interests." This is what we are about. If you and I support efforts to protect the dignity and rights of women, then we have a right to call ourselves feminists just as much as anyone else. Indeed, based on the historical record, we have more of a right, because the original 19th-century feminists were both strongly pro-life and pro-chastity.

Many of the early feminists were orthodox Christians. Indeed, a conservative morality was often the motivating force behind these early feminists' demands for reform of un-Christian attitudes and laws which allowed the suppression of the weak. The rights they demanded for women and minorities included the abolition of slavery, the right to own property, the right to participate in government, opportunities for advanced education, equal employment opportunities and equitable wages, and, above all, the right to be treated as persons possessing the common human dignity endowed upon all people by our Creator and God. These are all beliefs which, I assume, every pro-lifer would affirm.

Furthermore, feminism's founding mothers condemned abortion for the same two reasons we condemn it. First, they insisted it was immoral to kill an unborn child. Susan B. Anthony, Victoria Woodhill, and virtually every other noted feminist leader of the last century described abortion as "infanticide" and "child-murder." Second, they asserted that abortion was just another tool by which women were exploited. While they did not exonerate women from the crime, leaders such as Matilda Gage charged that "most of the responsibility for this crime lies at the door of the male sex" who beg, cajole, and even force women to have abortions. Her contemporary, Elizabeth Cady Stanton, similarly charged that abortion was a "degradation of women," more often than not foisted upon them by men anxious to avoid the responsibility for the children they had fathered. Similarly, Alice Paul, the author of the original Equal Rights Amendment (1923), stated that "abortion is the ultimate exploitation of women," the escape route men use to avoid responsibility for their own sexual acts. None of these feminists would have been shocked by research from the 1980's which shows that nearly 60 percent of women feel "forced" into abortions by others. They would, however, be shocked by how feminism has been perverted into a pro-abortion vehicle.

It was not until the mid-60's that feminism's egalitarian principles were abandoned to make room for abortion. At that time, population control zealot Lawrence Lader convinced a reticent Betty Friedan, the founder of the National Organization for Women (NOW), to adopt abortion as a central element of "neofeminism." (Lader, not so incidentally, was the founder of the National Abortion Rights Action League (NARAL), and he has repeatedly supported the state's right to force women to undergo unwanted abortions for population control and eugenic reasons.)

According to Lader, "It was the surge and fervor of neofeminism that paved the way for the abortion movement. Each was essential to the other." He gives Friedan singular credit for "pushing an abortion plank" into NOW's agenda at its 1967 convention, even though "a lot of delegates resigned" because of it.[1]

Friedan's decision to embrace abortion as part of the modern feminist agenda was a strategic choice. In return for accepting a leadership role in the stalled abortion movement, "neofeminism" gained the support of population controllers and leaders of the sexual revolution who, in turn, provided financial and political muscle to aid the budding feminist movement. The right of women to "control their own bodies" also provided an essential focus for the movement's ideology. Since that time, young feminists have been taught to see abortion rights as the overarching *symbol* of their pursuit of bodily and social independence. Without this freedom, they are told, they are enslaved by their biology.

But not all feminists were willing to abandon feminism's traditional pro-life stand. One such feminist was Pat Goltz, who was called before a tribunal of her local NOW chapter and "excommunicated" because of her vocal pro-life views. In 1972, Pat Goltz and Cathy Callahan founded Feminists for Life of America (FFLA).

Since its founding, the FFLA newsletter, *SisterLife* (now *The American Feminists*), has published many of the most articulate and logically consistent articles available in defense of the rights of both women and their children. These pro-life feminists are the true heirs of 19th-century feminism, continuing in the tradition of their predecessors to embrace the Judeo-Christian ethic of respect for all persons. They have looked through "pro-choice" ideology to the reality of abortion. They have seen what it does to the child, to the woman, and to society, and they say unequivocally that it is wrong.

At the same time, pro-life feminists are bold in their call for justice and equality in the world. They have remained a voice for the authentic rights and dignity of women, without degenerating into the "neofeminism" which has become equated with the advocacy of abortion, lesbianism, pornography, witchcraft, and goddess worship. Instead, they maintain a truly feminine vision of their rights and duties as sisters, mothers, and workers, which is proudly described in their slogan, "We are homemakers, and the world is our home."

While the members of Feminists for Life range across the entire political spectrum, I believe most orthodox Christians would be comfortable with their limited purpose and political positions. Because Feminists for Life of America provides a very articulate voice in defense of authentic pro-life feminism, I believe pro-lifers should do all they can to help build up the membership and influence of FFLA.[2] No organization is in a better position to challenge the National Organization for Women's claim to represent authentic feminism.

It has always puzzled me why pro-life groups haven't published monthly bulletins urging their supporters to join Feminists for Life. If we want to dilute the influence of pro-abortion feminists, we should help to build up the influence of pro-life feminists. If we help FFLA grow to the size of NOW, which only has a membership of 150,000 or so, we will be helping to show America that the pro-abortion feminism represented by NOW is a dying philosophy. By helping to expand recognition of FFLA, we will be offering safe refuge to the many young women who feel compelled to hide their pro-life sentiments in the closet. A larger voice for FFLA will challenge the ambivalent feminists, of which there are many, to reconsider what abortion is actually doing to women.

Most importantly, the work of FFLA is essential to split feminists, or at least a large portion of them, away from the population controllers who form the true base for the pro-abortion movement. We have every reason, and right, to claim that we are the ones who are advancing women's interests and women's rights.

In our rejection of abortion, we are more truly feminist than the modern "neofeminists" (as Lader called them) who have usurped the name of feminism for themselves. We desperately need to get this authentic view of pro-life feminism before the many young women in our high schools and colleges. These young women have a natural desire to articulate their demand for respect. For many, this is most easily done by attaching themselves to the notion of feminism, which, they are falsely told, is grounded in "reproductive freedom" and the "right" to abortion. By expanding public awareness of pro-life feminism, we can save these young women from this self-destructive view of women's rights. Instead, we want them to be drawn to the ideals of pro-life feminism, which says that they can and should demand the respect of men, but that this cannot be done by demanding the right to kill their unborn children.

The only true feminist is a pro-life feminist. Women who are pro-abortion simply misunderstand or are misusing the word "feminism"—which, if it means anything at all, is an expression of egalitarianism. But how can there be equality for all at the expense of the unborn? Clearly, authentic feminism is a pro-life movement. Let the women who support abortion find another name for their narcissistic and nihilistic philosophy. I'm sure Rush Limbaugh will be glad to lend them a few.

## Women Exploited by Abortionists

A final strategic point regarding political coalitions is drawn from Lawrence Lader, the founder of the National Abortion Rights Action League. In advocating for legalized abortion, Lader believed it was necessary to personalize the "enemy." For Lader, this was done by focusing attacks against the Catholic hierarchy—not the laity, but just those "celibate old men" who opposed abortion simply because it gave them a way to "control" women.

While we may laugh at Lader's characterization, we should not ignore his strategic advice for personalizing the enemy. In our case, we want to emphasize that pro-woman/pro-life laws are necessary to protect women from the abortion profiteers who shamelessly exploit women in crisis situations. While Women Exploited by Abortion should remain a healing ministry, we need another organization called Women Exploited by Abortionists, which would be purely a political and lobbying organization.

As I envision it, Women Exploited by Abortionist's agenda would be (1) to help increase the public perception of abortionists as "sleazy" money-hungry opportunists; (2) to reinforce the social stigma which prevents more doctors from becoming abortionists; (3) to advocate for pro-woman laws which would protect women from dangerous and unwanted abortions; (4) to help expose and defeat pro-abortion politicians who oppose pro-woman reforms; and (5) to provide public education about the inherent dangers of abortion and the need to support and advocate safer alternatives.

As a key common ground organization which would be introducing pro-woman/pro-life legislation, Women Exploited by Abortionists' official position would be a nuanced pro-choice/pro-life position. They would affirm that women suffer post-abortion problems precisely because they lose their babies in an abortion, but they would not support laws which would make physician induced abortions illegal for the reason that doctors can be held accountable for its abuse. Their position would simply be that if women's rights are adequately protected, and women are fully informed, no woman would choose to have an abortion.

This common ground position would also maximize its ability to represent *all* women who have been injured by abortion. This is important because many women who have been injured by abortion are nonetheless reluctant to condemn abortion in general. Who are they to condemn abortion for others? Thus, to avoid feeling like hypocrites, they are willing to warn women about the suffering which follows abortion, but they are unwilling to support laws which would criminalize it. While they may have differing views about the legal status of abortion, these women deserve a voice in the debate regarding how to make abortion safer and more rare. Thus, Women Exploited by Abortionists' official position would be similar to that of the National Rifle Association: "It's not vacuum aspirators which are dangerous; it's the people who wield them."

## SUMMARY

By understanding the priorities of the middle majority, it is possible to align their political support around candidates who support pro-woman/pro-life initiatives. Furthermore, by reframing the abortion debate in a way which puts women and children together on the same side, we shift the balance of the debate is shifted to our advantage. When faced with clearly pro-woman initiatives, pro-abortion politicians will be forced to either accede to our reforms, which will doom the abortion industry, or to side with the abortion industry against women's rights, which will doom pro-abortion politicians. Either way, we win.

To expand the opportunities for effective coalitions against the pro-abortionists, mainstream pro-lifers must support the development of common ground organizations which include both pro-life leaders and leaders from the middle majority who are legitimately pro-choice (as opposed to pro-abortion). Support should also be given to pro-life organizations, such as Feminists for Life, which have a special strategic role to play in dividing the opposition.

To help build this coalition effort, established pro-life groups will need to make sacrifices and room at the top. The leaders of new organizations must be entrusted with true leadership roles and the power to make decisions regarding legislative goals. They should neither be dismissed as "Johnny-come-lately's" nor exploited as puppets for the old guard. In short, pro-life leaders must be willing to set aside egos, detach themselves from the "turf" they have labored so hard to build up for their own organizations, and be willing to share their valuable mailing lists.

For the sake of both women and the unborn, everyone within the pro-life movement, both high and low, must be willing to become servants to the women and men who, because of their own personal experience, are best able to speak against abortion. This is done not by telling them what needs to be done. Instead, no matter how uncomfortable it feels, we must get on our hands and knees so that they can use our backs to climb to a higher position where their voices will be heard by all.

# CHAPTER SIXTEEN

# WHAT WE CAN HOPE TO ACHIEVE

THE ultimate political goal of the pro-life movement has been to pass a constitutional amendment which would recognize the right to life of all human beings from the moment of conception to the moment of natural death. It has been our hope that such an amendment would reverse the ravages of *Roe*. But would it?

Prior to *Roe* there were between 100,000 and 200,000 illegal abortions each year, of which 90 percent were done by physicians.[1] Indeed, the term "back alley abortion" refers not to abortion done *in* back alleys, but to entering a physician's office, after hours, *through* the back alley so as to conceal the fact that the office was open for abortions. Even if we could reverse the clock to pre-*Roe* conditions, a hundred-thousand-plus illegal abortions per year would still be a large number. But since the clock cannot be reversed, the number of illegal abortions following a Paramount Human Life Amendment would be much higher than the pre-*Roe* figures. Pro-abortionists are much more organized today. Not only would they establish a massive referral network for illegal abortion, they would also begin promotion of self-abortion techniques.

In addition, there is every reason to believe that the courts and legislatures would seek other ways to ignore or skirt the intent of a Human Life Amendment. In many European countries, for example, the essence of the Human Life Amendment is already in their constitutions. The unborn child is officially recognized as a human being, with constitutional rights, whose life the state is obligated to protect. At the same time, however, European courts and legislatures, while discouraging abortion or even defining it as an inherently illegal act, have allowed that it need not be punished. In Germany, for example, the state is not obligated to prosecute "illegal" abortions that were sought for extraordinary "health" reasons, including cases where the abortion was thought necessary to avoid grave injury to the "general social situation of the pregnant woman and her family."*

In other words, even if the unborn is recognized as a person under the law, there are still rationales which can be exploited to excuse abortion as the "necessary" sacrifice of one person's life for the sake of another's. There is every reason to believe that the pro-abortionists would pursue this alternative course. Thus, passage of a Human Life Amendment will not end the battle; it would simply shift the terms of the debate. We would have the advantage, but not the victory.

What is the solution then? We must instill in our society a universal awareness that abortion is always dangerous to women, no matter how desperate their circumstances. This knowledge must be translated into tough liability laws. We need laws, like those described previously, which will hold those who perform abortions, whether legally or illegally, as well as those who promote self-abortion techniques, accountable for all the pain and suffering, physical and emotional, which are bound to result.

## THE PROBLEM BEFORE *ROE*

As mentioned above, there were between 100,000 and 200,000 illegal abortions per year prior to *Roe*. Many of these were performed on "hard core" aborters, women who were determined to have an abortion at any cost. But many more, perhaps most, were performed on

---

*Mary Ann Glendon, *Abortion and Divorce in Western Law* (Cambridge, MA: Harvard University Press, 1987), 28, citing the decision of the Federal Constitutional Court of the Federal Republic of Germany.

Glendon's review of European law is very important for demonstrating the naivete of those who imagine that a Human Life Amendment will bring an end to legal abortion in America. Different countries have used different rationales, but the case of West Germany is especially important because Articles 1(1) and 2(2) of the Basic Law of Germany encompass all of the principles that are incorporated in the proposed Human Life Amendment in America, plus more (including not only a fundamental right to life, but also the inviolability of human dignity, and the right to develop one's personality). Indeed, the West German Constitutional Court has upheld the legal status of the unborn child under these articles of the German constitution and has affirmed that the government must affirmatively seek to protect the unborn child, even to the point of using criminal sanctions. However, while at all times obligated to discourage abortion, the state is free to allow exemptions from criminal prosecution in cases where the woman is faced with an extraordinary burden. However, in allowing such exceptions, the state must uphold the general ideal that the termination of the pregnancy is a "wrong."

As Glendon summarizes the German Court's position, "What is important is that the *totality* of abortion regulations—that is, all criminal, public health, and social welfare laws relating to abortion—be in proportion to the importance of the legal value of

women who felt they had "no choice" because of the pressures they were facing from circumstances or other people. The rate of negative physical and psychological reactions was nearly as high then as it is now.[2] But then, even more than now, women had no recourse against the abortionists who had injured them.

Then, as now, the doctors and midwives who performed illegal abortions did so without any attempt to screen women for risk factors. They did nothing in the way of alternatives counseling or education in fetal development. Their chief concern was only to do the abortion without causing major physical injury to the woman, if only to avoid any investigation into their activities.

Then, even more so than now, a woman who suffered post-abortion complications had no recourse for suing her abortionist. She had been a party to an illegal act. How could she expect financial compensation when it was she, or her family, who had solicited an illegal abortion? While abortionists faced the risk of jail (but only if the woman was willing to confess to having had an abortion), they did not face the risk of civil suit. The result is that abortionists, then as well as now, could injure patients, physically and psychologically, and seldom be called to account. Not only were their patients too ashamed to confront them, they also had no standing in court.

Remember, too, that then as now, abortionists were in the business of abortion not for humanitarian reasons, but for the money. If money is what most motivates abortionists, it is reasonable to assume that the best way to deter them is to instill in them the fear of losing every-

---

life, and that, as a whole, they work for the continuation of the pregnancy" (28). The State may make broad exceptions for allowing abortion to preserve the psychosocial health of the mother when no other "reasonable" alternative can be demanded of her as long as the state clearly registers its disapproval of abortion in principle.

In essence, the German constitution has been interpreted as making all abortions illegal in principle, but also as allowing the legislature to provide for broad exemptions from prosecution (33). According to Glendon, this compromise would seem to hold that abortion is never justifiable, but is often excusable. "It is one thing to recognize, as did Aristotle, that when we do what we ought not to do under pressure that overstrains ordinary human nature, pardon is appropriate. It is another matter to say that extenuating circumstances can make an otherwise wrongful act rightful" (33).

In short, German law, at least in theory, is very protective of the unborn child's rights. But, in practice, it allows broad exceptions for abortion, especially in the first trimester if the pregnancy poses a "serious hardship that cannot be averted any other way." Even in the second and third trimesters, abortion is excused from prosecution when the pregnancy poses a serious threat to the woman's physical or mental health which cannot be averted in "any other way which she can reasonably be required to bear" (31). If the same type of interpretation were applied to an American Human Life Amendment, as it very well could be, the result would be less than that for which its pro-life advocates are hoping.

thing they own. With these thoughts in mind, I would now like to suggest what I believe is a more comprehensive political goal for reducing abortions far below even the pre-*Roe* level.

## A FORMULA FOR A PRO-LIFE SOCIETY

To achieve a total pro-life victory, it is not enough to make abortion illegal, we must make it *unthinkable*. Unthinkable for pregnant women. Unthinkable for the loved ones to whom they will turn when faced with a crisis pregnancy. And unthinkable for the profiteers who would otherwise exploit women's despair by offering illegal abortions.

There are many parts to this process. One part of it involves developing greater moral awareness of the injustice of aborting innocent human lives. Another part is increasing public awareness of the physical and psychological dangers of abortion. Another part is offering more loving support for men and women faced with the difficulties which surround unplanned pregnancies, sexual assault pregnancies, or pregnancies where the child is suffering from a congenital or developmental disability. All of these steps are rather obvious, but the political implementation of them is not.

### A Human Life Amendment

An important step in the political process is the passage of a Human Life Amendment. While we cannot expect such an amendment alone to stop all abortions, legal or illegal, the law does teach. Individual views of right and wrong *are* guided and reinforced by social norms which are defined in the law.

In addition, our bloody history of abortion demands a solemn renunciation of this evil in just the same way that slavery was renounced by the Thirteenth Amendment. A Human Life Amendment is our way of passing on the wisdom gained in today's struggle to future generations. It is a bookmark in history, our way of saying, "Remember the blood and injustice of our day. Let it never happen again."

### Liability

In practice, however, a Human Life Amendment is likely to be the last step in our pursuit of a pro-life society. The first step, which can be accomplished right now, is simply increasing accountability for abortion-related injuries, which has been discussed at length in previous chapters.

Proper liability for abortion-related injuries will cause most profiteers to close their doors. A quick abortion is an unsafe one, and profiteers will not be willing to take the time with women it requires to do adequate pre-abortion screening and counseling. Among the abortion providers who remain, litigation risks will force them to employ better screening and alternatives counseling. This will be truly beneficial to women, since most high-risk patients will be channeled to resources which can help them advance their own interests while preserving their ability to bear and care for their children. In other words, through pro-woman legislation alone, the worst "hacks" will be forced out of business. The remaining abortionists will be appropriately circumspect about selecting the lowest-risk patients, namely, those who are least likely to be injured and least likely to ever sue them, even under a virtually open-ended statute of limitations.

Indeed, if physicians are held fully liable, and women's broad health needs are truly served, there may actually be fewer abortions if it remains legal than if it were to once again be made illegal. Remember, 90% percent of illegal abortions were done by physicians. Thus, the one advantage of legality is that it provides a mechanism for accountability. Through applying a strict code of accountability, abortion can be both legal and rare—very rare.

### Liability for Self-Induced Abortions

One way in which the pro-abortionists will try to skirt accountability is by teaching women to do self-abortions, which are inherently dangerous. Pro-abortionists, such as Pat Maginnis, were doing this in the '60s, and they are fully prepared to do it again.[3] Then, when women die from these self-abortions, the pro-abortionists will seek to exploit their deaths (for which they are responsible) by arguing that these women wouldn't have died if low-cost "safe" abortions were readily available from physicians. But in order to keep abortions cheap and "safe" (or at least safer than self-abortion), physicians need to be protected from liability for post-abortion injuries.

To stop the "self-abortion" movement, we must pass laws which recognize that self-abortion is inherently dangerous. Those who teach it or supply equipment for it are exploiting women in crisis. Criminal sanctions for endangerment and wrongful death should be established wherever possible. But more importantly, quick and easy civil redress must be available. Whether she suffers only a mild guilt or the loss of her uterus, a woman who attempts or completes a self-abortion should be entitled to huge awards against teachers, publishers, manufacturers, or distributors of self-abortion materials and literature upon whom she relied. A plaintiff should only be obligated to prove that a defendant taught self-abortion techniques, encouraged self-abortion, or knowingly manufactured or sold goods intended for use in self-abortion.

### Legal Standing of Women Seeking Abortion

In the event that a Human Life Amendment is passed or a future Supreme Court decision restores to states the right to regulate abortion, should women be subject to criminal prosecution for seeking or undergoing an illegal abortion?

Prior to *Roe*, no woman was ever prosecuted for having an illegal abortion. One reason was that the woman's testimony was needed to prosecute the abortionist, who was always the prosecutor's primary target. Another reason, at least during some periods of our history, was that there was a presumption in the law that no rational woman would freely choose to kill her own child. Therefore, the fact that she was seeking an abortion suggested that she was not acting freely. She was either being compelled into the act by a third party, or she was acting out of psychological duress. Because she was not acting freely, she could not be held fully culpable for her actions—unlike the abortionist.

I believe this viewpoint is the best one from which to view future cases of illegal abortion. Excepting bizarre circumstances, such as a Satan worshipper deliberately becoming pregnant to engage in a "sacramental" abortion, women should not be prosecuted for seeking or having obtained illegal abortions. Criminal sanctions should generally be reserved for abortionists, those pressing for an abortion, those who attempt to procure abortion for a woman, and those who exploit women by advocating self-abortion techniques.

Indeed, under the most ideal circumstances, we *want* a woman contemplating abortion to be able to talk to a doctor about why she "needs" an abortion in just the same way that we want a woman contemplating suicide to talk to a doctor about why she "needs" to die. We should not throw people in jail just because they're filled with despair. We want them to receive counseling, love, and care. In at least some cases, women who engage in grisly self-abortion attempts have been suffering mental disorders which include other symptoms of self-mutilation and self-destructive behavior. Such women should not be imprisoned. Instead, they should receive counseling until they are no longer a threat to themselves or their children.

## Liability for Illegally Induced Abortions

Whenever an abortion is illegally performed by a third party, whether it is a physician, a midwife, or some other person, there should be stiff criminal sanctions against the abortionist. In addition, however, the criminal abortionist should be held civilly liable for the wrongful death of the unborn child, for endangerment of the mother, and for any additional physical or psychological injuries which the mother experienced. In short, not only should women who undergo an illegal abortion be excluded from criminal prosecution, they should be allowed and encouraged to seek financial retribution from the abortionist without any time limits on filing their suit.

## Legal Standing of Physicians

When and if abortion is ever subject to state regulation, non-physicians should automatically be subject to criminal prosecution as described above. The situation with physicians, however, will remain more complicated.

Assume that the Human Life Amendment is passed and the right of the unborn child to live is recognized as equal to the life of the woman. What should the law require in the case of uterine cancer, where a delay in removing the diseased uterus (which would result in the death of the unborn child) is likely to cause the mother's death? To complicate matters further, what if doctors believe that by delaying surgery by another 30 days, the child can be saved but the disease will by then be so advanced that the mother will almost certainly die? Or, what if there is a case where neither is likely to die, but delaying childbirth threatens to expose the mother to a permanent disability, whereas inducing premature labor threatens to expose the child to permanent disabilities? Would the law allow the woman and her physicians to choose to maximize the care of one party when it would impose a risk to the other?

My point is not to resolve these conflict situations. I am simply pointing out that such conflict situations will always arise, very rarely perhaps, but they will arise. And when they do, a Human Life Amendment will not automatically provide all the answers. Nor is it guaranteed that district attorneys or juries would enforce a total ban on abortion when the circumstances surrounding the decision are threaten the mother's life.

When such conflict situations arise, some women would readily die, or at least risk a close encounter with death, rather than consent to a therapeutic abortion. They would freely give their lives for their child. Most of us would applaud such a woman's self-sacrificing bravery. Unfortunately, there are a few who would accuse such noble women of foolishness because they "owe" their lives to the care of the children already at home.

Matters are further complicated when neither the woman nor the child can voice her opinion. What should be done if the husband/father insists that if a choice must be made, his wife's life must be spared? And what of the physician, who is faced with both moral and legal liabilities? To protect himself, might he not consider even a moderate threat to the woman's life as reason enough to mention therapeutic abortion?

But once we concede that any therapeutic abortions are allowed under the standard of a Human Life Amendment, where can we possibly draw a line? Exactly what level of threat to the mother's life justifies killing an innocent child? If the law condemns a man who throws another man out of a one-person lifeboat to save himself, how can it countenance sacrificing either a mother or her child for the sake of the other?[4] Indeed, the allowance in state laws for therapeutic abortions is exactly the loophole which pro-abortionists expanded to justify providing abortions to "save" women from suicide and other psychosocial health risks.

Prior to *Roe*, one method used to avoid abuse of therapeutic abortions was the establishment of hospital committees which would review the appropriateness of a physician's recommendation for a therapeutic abortion. One problem with this approach was that many committees became nothing more than a "rubber stamp" process for approving every request for a "therapeutic" abortion. Another, and equally serious, problem is that the very existence of committees tends to dilute moral responsibility for decisions. Committees provide individuals with a way to avoid personal responsibility by appealing to the "authority" of the committee. Right and wrong is reduced to a majority vote. Furthermore, with each decision to allow an abortion (or euthanasia), the physicians and bio-ethicists who make up the committee become more psychologically committed to justifying past decisions. This inevitably leads to a creeping extension of exceptions to the rule.[5] "We allowed it in that other case, and this case is only slightly different, so there is no reason not to allow it here too."

Some may wonder why we should even bother worrying about these rare exceptions. After all, if we stop 99.9 percent of all abortions through a Human Life Amendment, haven't we essentially won the battle? No. Because allowance for any therapeutic abortion creates ambiguities which will result in ongoing judicial and political battles.

I believe that what we are seeking are clear moral lines which uphold human dignity but still allow for human fallibility. We must also recognize that political laws, which gain their credibility from public consensus, cannot always demand adherence to the highest standards of moral behavior—otherwise, we would all be in jail. Furthermore, within reasonable limits, the law can accommodate difficult moral decisions without embracing moral relativism. If a pregnant mother of five has a 20 percent chance of surviving if she waits for surgery until after 24 weeks of pregnancy (which is still very risky for her premature child), but a 70 percent chance of surviving if the cancerous uterus is removed now, what is she obligated to do? Reasonable moral arguments can be mounted for either choice. But ultimately, who, other than God, can stand in judgment? In such cases, or even less complicated ones, the law must be flexible.

Yet, flexibility in the law is exactly the starting point for abuses, which brings us back to the original problem. How does one regulate "therapeutic" abortion?

Part of the answer, I believe, is to forbid any compensation for therapeutic abortions. While the reference escapes me, I recall seeing that this idea was first advanced in the late 1950's by a physician who favored expanded access to legal abortion. This physician's view was that abortion was sometimes necessary, even for psychosocial reasons. But abortion clearly results in the destruction of a human life, he argued; therefore, it was unethical for anyone to ever profit from it. His position, as I recall interpreting it, was that physicians should be free to do an abortion when they felt it was necessary, but there should never be any question of mixed motives. Abortions should only be performed when they were done as acts of charity. Anything else would be scandalous profiteering.

While I disagree with this nameless physician's assessment of how often abortion may be "necessary," I do respect his integrity. In deference to the life which is lost in even a life-saving abortion, there should be no exchange of money.

I believe this principle provides us with one way of preventing the abuse of therapeutic abortions. In short, the law should have criminal sanctions against any form of compensation for therapeutic abortion. This provision, which eliminates the profit motive, is even further strengthened by the financial liability which physicians would still face for screening, full disclosure, and alternatives counseling.

I believe the second mechanism for preventing abuse of therapeutic abortions is the grand jury. Statutes protecting the unborn should, wherever possible, be very specific about the circumstances where therapeutic abortions are allowed, such as in the case of an ectopic pregnancy. But the statutes should also provide physicians with latitude when confronted with unique or unforeseeable situations, such as might arise as the result of multiple injuries in an automobile accident. In such cases, wherever a medical decision results in the destruction of an unborn child, the physician would be obligated to bring the case to the attention of the district attorney for automatic review by a grand jury.

For the reasons discussed above, I oppose the use of standing committees of "experts." A grand jury of average citizens, however, is an excellent means for keeping marginal abortion decisions within the realm of moral reason. Physicians and bio-ethicists could present arguments for or against a particular decision, but it would be the members of the grand jury who would decide whether there was unreasonable "discrimination" against the unborn child or the mother. Because the members of a grand jury would always be different, this system avoids the problem of creeping exceptions, which occurs when review committees are made up of professionals who have a psychological investment in past decisions.

If a grand jury found that the reasons for recommending and performing the "therapeutic" abortion were inadequate, the physician would be arraigned to face criminal charges. But if there was no history of abusing "therapeutic privileges," there was no compensation received for the abortion, the abortion was promptly reported to the district attorney, and there was at least some reasonable claim of "necessity" for the abortion, the physician would be charged with nothing more than a misdemeanor. In this way, the grand jury's purpose would not be to intimidate physicians, but rather to remind them that they are accountable; they must be prepared to explain their decisions to destroy a life, both to their community and to their God.

Under such a system, physician-induced abortions would remain legal for therapeutic purposes. In theory, the physician might even be free to recommend abortion for broadly defined health reasons. But abuse of this privilege would be prevented by (1) making compensation for recommending or performing the abortion illegal; (2) protecting the right of women to sue for wrongful death of the child, malpractice, or violation of their civil right to full disclosure; and (3) requiring that all cases of "therapeutic abortion" be investigated by a grand jury.

## SUMMARY

Pro-lifers must come to grips with the reality of human nature. The punitive force of the law will not deter abortionists, but financial liability will. Liability alone will compel today's abortionists to use proper screening, evaluation, and alternatives counseling, and this process, in turn, will truly help women find better and safer ways of coping with their crises.

This same high standard for civil liability will continue to be important even after a Human Life Amendment is passed. Both proponents of self-abortion and practitioners of illegal abortion will most effectively be deterred not just by criminal sanctions, but also by policies that generously empower women to recover financial compensation for the wrongful death of their children, for physical and psychological injuries, and for endangerment. Furthermore, in a truly pro-life society, women who have illegal abortions should not be subjected to shame, but understood as victims of despair. They should be helped first to find reconciliation and second to seek retribution against those who victimized them. In this way, all women will be protected.

Finally, because the law must always provide for the possibility that there are medical cases in which the lives of both the child and the mother cannot be saved, there will always be allowances for therapeutic abortions, or at least therapeutic treatments which threaten the life or health of either the mother or her child. To prevent the abuse of therapeutic abortion, there should be (1) a ban on compensation for therapeutic abortion, (2) exposure to liability in civil court, and (3) an automatic investigation by a grand jury.

# RISK FACTORS

While present research is unable to accurately establish what percentage of women suffer from any specific symptom of post-abortion trauma, it is clear that post-abortion psychological disorders do occur. Indeed, the published literature demonstrates that serious emotional and psychological complications following an abortion are probably more common than serious physical complications.

The present literature has also successfully identified statistically significant factors which can be used to pre-identify individuals who are most vulnerable to experiencing post-abortion psychological sequelae. Examination of these risk factors suggests that most women seeking abortion have one or more of these high-risk characteristics.

Based on these findings, most of which have been published by researchers who *favor* legalized abortion, it would appear reasonable to expect, and demand, that abortion providers: (1) provide pre-consent information about the types of psychological reactions which have been linked to a negative abortion experience and the risk factors associated with these adverse reactions; (2) provide adequate pre-abortion screening using the criteria outlined above to identify women who are at higher risk of negative post-abortion reactions; (3) provide individualized counseling to high-risk patients which would more fully explain why the patient is at higher risk, along with more detailed information concerning possible post-abortion reactions; and (4) assist women who have pre-identifying high-risk factors in evaluating and choosing lower-risk solutions to their social, economic, and health needs.

Since these high-risk factors have been well-established for a considerable period of time, abortion providers who fail to utilize this information in their screening and counseling procedures may incur greater liability for subsequent injuries when malpractice suits are brought on these grounds.

# RISK FACTORS PREDICTING POST-ABORTION PSYCHOLOGICAL SEQUELAE

## I. CONFLICTED DECISION

A. Difficulty making the decision, ambivalence, unresolved doubts[1,2,11,14,16,17,19,23,27,30,36,39,40]

   1. Moral beliefs against abortion
     a. Religious or conservative values[1,17,27,31,35,36]
     b. Negative attitudes toward abortion[7]
     c. Feelings of shame or social stigma attached to abortion[1]
     d. Strong concerns about secrecy[37]

   2. Conflicting maternal desires[23,27]
     a. Originally wanted or planned pregnancy[11,17,21,23,39]
     b. Abortion of wanted child due to fetal abnormalities[2,5,11,14,15,20,22]
     c. Therapeutic abortion of wanted pregnancy due to maternal health risk[2,11,14,20,32,36]
     d. Strong maternal orientation[27,35]
     e. Being married[6]
     f. Prior children[19,35]
     g. Failure to take contraceptive precautions, which may indicate an ambivalent desire to become pregnant[4]
     h. Preoccupation with fantasies of fetus, including, sex and awareness of due date.[16]

   3. Second or third trimester abortion[20,31,32,36]
   (This generally indicates strong ambivalence or a coerced abortion of a "hidden" pregnancy.)

B. Feels pressured or coerced[11,12,14,27,33,35,39,40]

   1. Feels pressured to have abortion
     a. By husband or boyfriend
     b. By parents
     c. By doctor, counselor, employer, or others

   2. Feels decision is not her own, or is "her only choice"[14]

   3. Feels pressured to choose too quickly[13,18]

C. Decision is made with biased, inaccurate, or inadequate information[13,35,36]

## II. PSYCHOLOGICAL OR DEVELOPMENTAL LIMITATIONS

A. Adolescence[3,9,12,13,23,26,32,35]

(Minors are both more likely to have psychological sequelae and to report symptoms of greater severity.)

B. Prior emotional or psychiatric problems[2,4,11,14,17,19,20,27,32]

1. Poor use of psychological coping mechanisms[1,23,27]

2. Prior low self-image[27,33,35,40]

3. Poor work pattern [4,40]

4. Prior unresolved trauma[35]

5. A history of sexual abuse or sexual assault[17,25,38]

6. Blames pregnancy on her own character flaws, rather than on chance, others, or on correctable mistakes in behavior[23,24,29]

7. Avoidance and denial prior to abortion[10]

C. Lack of social support

1. Few friends[4,40]

2. Made decision alone, without assistance from partner[28]

3. A poor or unstable relationship with male partner[4,19,27,33,39]

4. Lack of support from parents and family, either to have baby or to have abortion[1,7,8,14,23,28,40]

5. Lack of support from male partner, either to have baby or to have abortion[1,4,7,8,14,19,23,27,28,32,34,39,40]

6. Accompanied to abortion by male partner[24]

D.    Prior abortion(s)[11,33,35,40]

# THE ROLE OF THE MALE

The attitude of the male partner toward the pregnancy is an important factor in a woman's abortion decision and is also significantly related to how she will adjust after the abortion. Because numerous studies have found support from the partner to be an important predictor of good post-abortion adjustment, researchers were recently startled by the finding that accompaniment to the abortion by the male partner was actually a predictor of *greater* post-abortion depression.

This finding suggests that an outward show of support, such as accompaniment to the abortion clinic, is not an accurate measure of the emotional support a woman *feels*. Instead, accompaniment by the male partner may actually indicate one or more of the following: (1) greater pre-abortion anxiety, which led the woman to insist on accompaniment; (2) overt or subtle coercion on the part of the male, who is "making sure" she does the "right thing;" or (3) a more intimate relationship exists between the partners and this greater intimacy is being stressed by the abortion. In this third scenario, the unplanned pregnancy may be perceived by the woman as a "test" of her partner's commitment to their relationship. She may privately be willing to have the baby, and seal their mutual commitment, *if* he takes this as an opportunity to demonstrate his commitment. Instead, his lack of enthusiasm for, or hostile reaction to, the pregnancy causes her to doubt the depth and endurance of their relationship.

In short, when a woman is accompanied to an abortion by her male partner, the woman is more likely to be choosing abortion because her partner has manipulated her into doing so, or because he has exposed to her a lack of commitment to their relationship. In neither case does she truly feel supported.

## Sources for Risk Factor Outline

1. Adler, et. al., "Psychological Responses After Abortion," *Science*, 248:41-44 (1990).

2. Ashton, "The Psychosocial Outcome of Induced Abortion," *British Journal of Ob&Gyn.*, 87:1115-1122 (1980).

3. Babikian & Goldman, "A Study in Teen-Age Pregnancy," *Am. J. Psychiatry*, 755 (1971).

4. Belsey, et al., "Predictive Factors in Emotional Response to Abortion: King's Termination Study—IV," *Soc. Sci. & Med.*, 11:71-82 (1977).

5. Blumberg, "The Psychological Sequelae of Abortion Performed for a Genetic Indication," *Am. J. of Obstetrics and Gynecology*, 122(7):799-808 (1975).

6. Bracken, "A Causal Model of Psychosomatic Reactions to Vacuum Aspiration Abortion," *Social Psychiatry*, 13:135-145 (1978).

7. Bracken, et al., "Coping with Pregnancy Resolution Among Women in an Urban Population," *Sociology*, 9, 225-254 (1978).

8. Bracken, et. al., "The Decision to Abort and Psychological Sequelae" *Journal of Nervous and Mental Disease*, 158:154-162 (1974).

9. Campbell, N.B., et. al., "Abortion in Adolescence," *Adolescence*, 23:813-823 (1988).

10. Cohen & Roth, "Coping with Abortion," *Journal of Human Stress* 10:140-145 (1984).

11. Council on Scientific Affairs, American Medical Association, "Induced Termination of Pregnancy Before and After *Roe v. Wade*: Trends in Mortality and Morbidity of Women," *JAMA*, 268(22):3231-3239 (1992).

12. Dunlop, "Counseling of Patients Requesting an Abortion," *The Practitioner*, 220:847-852 (1978).

13. Franz W., and Reardon, D., "Differential Impact of Abortion on Adolescents and Adults," *Adolescence*, 27(105):161-172 (1992).

14. Friedman, C., et. al., "The Decision-Making Process and the Outcome of Therapeutic Abortion," *Am. J. of Psychiatry*, 131(12):1332-1337 (1974).

15. Furlong, "Pregnancy Termination for Genetic Indications: The Impact on Families," *Social Work in Health Care*, 10(1):17 (1984).

16. Gath & Rose, "Psychological Problems & Gynaecological Surgery" in *Psychological Disorders in Obstetrics and Gynaecology* (London: Butterworths, 1985).

17. Hern, *Abortion Practice* (Boulder, CO: Alpenglo Graphics, Inc., 1990).

18. Landy, "Abortion Counseling—A New Component of Medical Care," *Clinics in Obs/Gyn*, 13(1):33-41 (1986).

19. Lask, "Short-term Psychiatric Sequelae to Therapeutic Termination of Pregnancy," *Br J Psychiatry*, 126:173-177 (1975).

20. Lazarus, "Psychiatric Sequelae of Legalized Elective First Trimester Abortion", *Journal of Psychosomatic Ob&Gyn*, 4:141-150 (1985).

21. Lemkau, "Emotional Sequelae of Abortion," *Psychology of Women Quarterly*, 12:461-472 (1988).

22. Lloyd, "Sequelae and Support After Termination of Pregnancy for Fetal Malformation," *British Medical Journal*, 290:907-909 (1985).

23. Major & Cozzarelli, "Psychosocial Predictors of Adjustment to Abortion," *Journal of Social Issues*, 48(3):121-142 (1992).

24. Major, et. al., "Attributions, Expectations and Coping with Abortion," *Journal of Personality and Social Psychology*, 48:585-599 (1985).

25. Makhorn, "Sexual Assault & Pregnancy," *New Perspectives on Human Abortion*, Mall & Watts, eds., (Washington, D.C.: University Publications of America, 1981).

26. Martin, "Psychological Problems of Abortion for Unwed Teenage Girls," *Genetic Psychology Monographs*, 88:23-110 (1973).

27. Miller, "An Empirical Study of the Psychological Antecedents and Consequences of Induced Abortion," *Journal of Social Issues*, 48(3):67-93 (1992).

28. Moseley, et. al., "Psychological Factors That Predict Reaction to Abortion," *J. of Clinical Psychology*, 37:276-279 (1981).

29. Mueller & Major, "Self-Blame, Self-Efficacy and Adjustment to Abortion," *Journal of Personality and Social Psychology*, 57:1059-1068 (1989).

30. Osofsky & Osofsky, "The Psychological Reaction of Patients to Legalized Abortion," *American Journal of Orthopsychiatry*, 42:48-60 (1972).

31. Osofsky, et. al., "Psychological Effects of Abortion: With Emphasis Upon the Immediate Reactions and Followup," in H. J. Osofsky & J.D. Osofsky, eds., *The Abortion Experience* (Hagerstown, MD: Harper & Row, 1973), 189-205.

32. Rosenfeld, "Emotional Responses to Therapeutic Abortion," *American Family Physician*, 45(1):137-140, (1992).

33. Rue & Speckhard, "Informed Consent & Abortion: Issues in Medicine & Counseling," *Medicine & Mind* 7:75-95 (1992).

34. Shusterman, "Predicting the Psychological Consequences of Abortion," *Social Science and Medicine*, 13A:683-689 (1979).

35. Speckhard & Rue, "Postabortion Syndrome: An Emerging Public Health Concern," *Journal of Social Issues*, 48(3):95-119 (1992).

36. Vaughan, *Canonical Variates of Post Abortion Syndrome* (Portsmouth, NH: Institute for Pregnancy Loss, 1990).

37. Wallerstein, "Psychological Sequelae of Therapuetic Abortion in Young Unmarried Women," *Archives of General Psychiatry*, 27:828-832 (1972).

38. Zakus, "Adolescent Abortion Option," *Social Work in Health Care*, 12(4):87 (1987).

39. Zimmerman, "Psychosocial and Emotional Consequences of Elective Abortion: A Literature Review," in Paul Sachdev, ed., *Abortion: Readings and Research* (Toronto: Butterworth, 1981).

40. Zimmerman, *Passage Through Abortion* (New York: Praeger Publishers, 1977).

41. See also: Adler, David, Major, Roth, Russo, & Wyatt, "Psychological Factors in Abortion: A Review" *American Psychologist*, 47(10):1194-1204 (1992).

# APPENDIX B

# PRO-WOMAN/PRO-LIFE SOUND BITES

*The following is an example of how a candidate for public office can address the abortion issue from a pro-woman/pro-life perspective in a way which provides "sound bites" for the press which are difficult to distort.*

Abortion is a divisive issue. But certainly we can all agree to this: no woman should feel forced to undergo an unwanted abortion. Women should be protected from coercion by husbands, boyfriends, parents, or abortion counselors. And every woman who wants to keep her child should have access to the public and private agencies offering her and her child care and compassion. This is pro-life. This is pro-woman. This is pro-choice. And that is the type of candidacy that I am offering you.

My opponent opposes legislation which would protect women from being lied to by greedy abortion clinics. I believe that if a woman is going to have an abortion, she deserves to know about every potential risk and alternative.

My opponent opposes legislation which would hold abortion providers financially liable for the physical and *psychological* aftereffects of abortion. I believe that if abortionists are going to do abortions, they had better be able to guarantee that they are doing safe abortions, or they had better be willing to pay for the consequences of dangerous abortions.

I am pro-life; I am also pro-woman. I am seeking to protect women from being coerced into unwanted and dangerous abortions. I want to guarantee the rights of women to know all the risks about abortion and about realistic alternatives—including thousands of volunteer resources which are available to help a women give birth to an unplanned child, and to care for that child long after it has been born.

My opponent says he is pro-choice, but he refuses to do anything to protect the 55 percent of abortion patients who say they are being pressured into UNWANTED abortions. He says he is pro-choice, but he refuses to guarantee a woman's right to know about the risks of abortion and her right to know about the biology of her unborn child.

He says he is pro-woman, but he has abandoned women to the unscrupulous exploitation of fast-buck abortion clinics.

I am both pro-woman and pro-life. I want to protect both the unborn child and the child's mother. The courts have given women a right to seek a safe abortion. So if a woman does have an abortion, I will do all I can to regulate clinics to ensure that it is absolutely the safest abortion possible, that she has a guaranteed right to receive compensation for any physical or psychological complications which occur, and that she is fully informed of *every* risk and alternative.

## A Sample of Questions and Answers

**Media:** What is your position on abortion?

**Candidate:** I believe we absolutely must protect women from dangerous and *unwanted* abortions which are injuring hundreds of thousands of women every year.

We don't hear about it in the press, but our country is faced with a terrible plague of *unwanted* abortions—cases where mothers would rather carry their pregnancies to term but instead submit to unwanted abortions to satisfy the demands of others.

I oppose allowing abortion to be used as an escape route for unloving and irresponsible boyfriends. I oppose allowing parents to force a daughter into an unwanted abortion without regard for her own desires to keep her child. I oppose making women suffer the pain and aftereffects of abortion alone just so others won't be inconvenienced.

A study of over 250 women who claim that they have suffered from post-abortion trauma found that nearly 60% of these women felt forced to submit to an abortion because of pressure from other people. Eighty-three percent say they would have kept their babies if they had received support to do so from their boyfriends, families, or other important people in their lives.[1]

Is it "pro-choice" to allow women to be forced into unwanted abortions? No. That's abandonment. That's abandonment of women in need to the manipulation and greed of our unregulated abortion industry.

**Media:** Would you support legislation which would limit a woman's right to have an abortion?

**Candidate:** I support regulations which would protect women from being pressured into unwanted abortions. I support laws which would make abortion clinics accountable for failing to protect women from being coerced into *unwanted* abortions. If abortion is to be a decision made between a woman and her doctor, then we should hold the doctor responsible for ensuring that the mother's desire to have an abortion is truly her own, and not a decision being forced on her by her husband, boyfriend, or parents.

If my opponent is truly "pro-choice," and not pro-abortion, I am sure he will work with me in seeking legislation to protect these women from unwanted abortions.

**Media:** Aren't your proposals actually intended to make it more difficult for women to get abortions?

**Candidate:** Not at all. My proposals would simply codify the high professional standards which the Supreme Court itself has already described in *Roe* and the other abortion cases. It is the obligation of the physician to ensure that a woman's choice to abort is fully free and fully informed as to risks and alternatives. Abortion providers have legal responsibilities to their patients, and these responsibilities must be met to safeguard the rights of women.

**Media:** How would you propose to heal the divisions in our country over the abortion issue?

**Candidate:** As I have said, there is plenty of common ground for people who are both truly pro-choice and truly pro-life. First, we need to protect women from feeling forced into unwanted abortions.

Second, I think all people of goodwill can agree that we need to do more to understand when and why some abortions are dangerous. In 1989, Surgeon General Koop reported that there had not yet been enough adequate research on the aftereffects of abortion. Dr. Koop recommended a $100-million-dollar research project to study the effects of this most common of all surgeries in America today.

What was the response from Congress? Nothing. They ignored the Surgeon General's appeal for more research. Why? Because pro-abortion lobbyists have argued against such research because they are afraid that proof of abortion's risks will increase clinics' liability for the damages women suffer.

If abortion is truly safe, why are pro-abortionists so hostile to funding a major study to prove once and for all whether or not abortion is truly as safe as they claim?

If my opponent is truly concerned about the health needs of women, then surely he will help me in pushing for research to measure the health risks of abortion so that women can make more fully informed choices Surely this is an area on which all reasonable people can agree. The only reason to oppose more post-abortion research is if one is more concerned about the health of the abortion industry than one is about the health of women. Does the safety of women come first, or the freedom of an unregulated abortion industry? The women come first, of course. I challenge my opponent to support this necessary research to protect women's health.

**Media:** I don't understand what you mean by "unwanted" abortions. If a woman chooses to have an abortion, that's the choice she wants.

**Candidate:** I can't tell you how many times I have heard women's stories of how they were threatened, badgered, pressured, and even literally dragged to abortion clinics by abusive husbands, angry parents, or selfish boyfriends. These women would rather have had their babies, but the pressures they faced from other people or circumstances made them feel they had no, choice and no one at the clinics offered to help them overcome these pressures.

Another example is found in China's national one-child policy, where couples are brutally forced to undergo unwanted abortions. This points to another important difference between my opponent and myself. My opponent supports government funding to agencies which support *forced* abortions on unwilling women for the purpose of suppressing population growth in less developed countries. Is this what it means to be pro-choice?

Of course not. Yet he is closing his eyes to minority women in developing countries who are being forced into unwanted abortions. He's even willing to help subsidize such programs.

This makes me wonder. Where will he stand on women's rights here in the U.S., if someday he suddenly decides there are too many people in our own country? Will he support reproductive freedom and the right of women to bear as many children as they choose, whether it is 3, 8, or 15 children? Or will he support forced abortions on American women to satisfy the demands of the radical population control lobbyists.

Will he be "pro-choice" then, or will he simply be pro-abortion? This is what I would like to know. This is what I believe all voters have a right to know.

What does his "pro-choice" stand mean? Does it mean defending the welfare of women when they are threatened by unwanted and dangerous abortions? Or does it just mean defending the profit margins of our unregulated abortion industry?

If he and his colleagues in the legislature are truly pro-choice, then let us cooperate and start protecting women from coercion and deceit so their choices are fully free and fully informed.

# MORE LEGISLATIVE INITIATIVES

Chapter Nine described the central features of our pro-woman/pro-life legislation. Here, I would like to take a moment to mention a few additional ideas which would not directly fit into the Freedom of Choice Act but would help to create a more truly pro-life/pro-woman society.

## State Amendments or Referendum

Everyone knows that ideas which are popular with the public may not always be popular with state legislators or governors. Therefore, wherever it is difficult to pass pro-woman statutes like the FOCA described in Chapter Nine, petitions should be circulated to introduce either a binding referendum or an amendment to the state constitution. In the latter case, the amendment would be attached to the rights reserved by the people. Even if such an initiative fails to pass, the educational rewards are immense because once the initiative is on the ballot, a lot of media attention will be given to the issue. At the very least, this is a low-cost public relations campaign which can be launched with just the time of the volunteers who circulate the petition.

The following is an example of an amendment which would appeal to the middle majority—or at least leave them wondering why they should not support it.

Women have a civil right to full disclosure of all risks, alternatives, or other information which a patient might reasonably consider relevant to a decision to accept or refuse a recommendation for abortion. Full disclosure must be given to the woman, or in the case of a minor, to the minor's parents or legal guardian. The State may not limit a woman's right to seek recovery in civil court for any injuries related to induced abortion.

This simple amendment, which is perfectly reasonable to people in the middle majority, would (1) establish that it is a violation of a woman's civil rights to withhold relevant information, and thus provide cause for civil suit other than medical malpractice; (2) establish that the standard for disclosure is the reasonable patient standard; (3) require parental notice and disclosure of risks; (4) strike down any statutes of limitation for time of filing a civil action against abortionists; and (5) eliminate any ceilings which limit the size of judgments against abortionists.

## Fetal Development Education

Pro-abortionists insist that women don't need information about fetal development because they have already learned all about it in school. This is generally not the case because most sexual education courses avoid "too much" on fetal development because it may be upsetting to girls who have already had abortions and, to the course developers, it does not help to promote acceptance of abortion among teens, one of their primary goals.

To ensure that students do receive adequate education on the development of the human fetus, state education laws should be amended to require that all courses in public schools which include discussion of human sexuality must include at least 2 units (2 hours) per year on fetal development from conception through 24 weeks' gestation. There are easily enough films on fetal development to make this task easy.

Furthermore, classroom guests presenting information on sexuality or family planning information should also be required to begin with at least 10 minutes reviewing fetal development. This 10 minutes spent reviewing the biological results of sexual activity will help to offset the sex-is-for-recreation tone of Planned Parenthood-type presentations.

## Post-Abortion Education

In a vein similar to the above proposal, the state has an interest in educating young people about the reality and risks of abortion. In order to encourage thoughtful informed choices, it is best that young women, and men, receive information about risks and alternatives *prior* to becoming pregnant rather than in the midst of a crisis.

To achieve this goal, the state should mandate that all public school courses where there is discussion of human sexuality and/or birth control methods must include at least 2 units (2 hours) per year on the potential physical, psychological, and social risks of abortion and discussion of resources available for supporting unplanned pregnancies.

Once again, classroom guests presenting sexuality or family planning information must include at least ten minutes of time on the risks of abortion and alternatives to abortion. This requirement, too, will help to balance the tone of Planned Parenthood-type presentations.

## An Abortion Tax

Abortion has real social costs. There is sufficient research to lead a state legislature to reach the reasonable conclusion that abortion increases the incidence of substance abuse, suicide attempts, psychological illness, reproductive injuries leading to premature births resulting in newborns' disabilities, and other public health problems. Having reached this finding, it would be reasonable to establish a "use tax" (calling it a "sin tax" would be politically incorrect) on abortion. According to this legislation, a service tax, perhaps in the range of $25, would be levied on each and every abortion. This amount would be earmarked for support of state-funded drug abuse programs, wheel chair access ramps, post-abortion counseling programs, or similar services which the state supplies or subsidizes. The rationale is that women who have abortions, or who have gad children born subsequently who are handicapped due to premature birth, are more likely to need these services and the tax on abortion is appropriate help to pay for these social costs up front.

Obviously, a $25 service tax would not nearly cover all of the social costs of abortion. In addition, the tax is so low that it is not even intended to be a financial deterrent. But such a tax would provide an invaluable educational service, both in the attempt to pass the law and when women were told why they are paying this tax.

## Full Disclosure for Minors Receiving Family Planning Services

Finally, I would like to add that the same approach of expanding patients rights to full disclosure can be used to address the problem of family planning agencies which effectively encourage sexual experimentation among minors by distributing birth control products without adequate counseling. There is no doubt that this practice increases sexual behavior, and because of birth control failures (both method failures and user failures), increases the number of teenage pregnancies and abortions.

Informed consent laws should be passed which would require birth control counselors to accurately disclose all possible health risks associated with each method of birth control, effectiveness rates for preventing the spread of venereal diseases, including AIDS, and the one-year and five-year user failure rates (which includes failures due to user error) specifically for teens (since teens have a higher failure

rate than adults.) Birth control counselors should also be held liable
for failure to adequately inform the patient of safer alternatives with
similar or better rates of effectiveness. These standards should be
applied for both adults and minors, but especially for minors. Lack of
full disclosure and adequate counseling would provide grounds for
a suit against the manufacturer, the family planning agency, and/or
physician. Again, the failure to disclose should be construed as a violation of the patients civil rights. Additional damages could be
sought to any physical or psychological complications associated
with the birth control device.

## Parental Consent for Contraceptive Training

Because all contraceptive technologies involve certain health risks
and the risk of failure leading to unplanned pregnancies, there is
clearly an important parental interest in what their children are taught
and given. In addition, parents and their children have the right to
practice their faith without interference or harassment by the state.

The promotion of birth control technologies clearly violates the
religious freedom of parents and religious communities who are
teaching their children that contraception is immoral. While the
Catholic position against contraception is most widely noticed, this
view is shared by many faiths, including many non-Christian religions and, prior to 1930, all Protestant denominations. This moral
teaching, then, is not some new-fangled doctrine but a longstanding
belief of many religious peoples.

Certainly, the first amendment establishment clause, if it has any
meaning at all, forbids the government from seeking to establish a
moral doctrine which is contrary to the long-held moral theology of
so many established religions. Therefore, schools and family planning agencies should be required to obtain written permission from
parents before they are allowed to promote the use of birth control
technologies to minors, much less distribute to them contraceptive
drugs, plugs, jellies and jams.

State laws should mandate that if any parent withholds written
permission for birth control training in a public school, the course
should be canceled or moved to an optional evening class so that no
student feels embarrassed in front of his or her peers for being
excluded from the course. This provision is in keeping with the same
reasoning used by the Supreme Court when it banned school prayer.
If school prayer must be banned to avoid the embarrassing exclusion
of non-participators, the same standard should be applied to protect

students' rights when their religious faith precludes their participation in contraceptive training.

## Welfare Reform

Welfare reform is a hot political topic and one to which pro-woman/pro-life supporters must pay close attention. For most of us, I believe, the real question behind welfare reform is not whether the indigent need our help (they do), but whether this assistance should principally come from individuals, the Church, or government.

While there are many compelling arguments for getting the government completely out of the welfare business, I strongly believe this goal can be accomplished without targeting first, and most grievously, women and their children—born or unborn. Yet, this is exactly what pro-abortion social engineers are trying to do. Their solution to poverty is to eliminate the poor, or at least the children of the poor.

In short, I believe there are moral ways and immoral ways to dismantle our present welfare system. Specifically, I believe it is unjust and immoral to discriminate against children and their mothers simply because a mother is unwed or an unborn child has been preceded by siblings.

Welfare reform proposals for "family caps" and "child exclusion" are defended on the grounds that increased economic pressures on child-bearing will deter irresponsible behavior. There is some truth to this theory. Loss of the safety net provided by welfare programs will cause some young women will avoid becoming pregnant. But it is also true that there will continue to be unintended pregnancies, and, more importantly, intended pregnancies followed by male abandonment. Social engineers know this, and if they succeed in their effort to cut off welfare support for these pregnant women, they will succeed at increasing the pressure on these women to abort.

Pro-woman and pro-life advocates must oppose this type of anti-life reform. We must find a better solution. While it is not wrong to enforce the financial responsibilities which attach to irresponsible sexual behavior, this must be done in a manner which builds up families rather than encourages abortions. To find the proper solution, it is best to first accurately define the problem.

The problem is not children on welfare. The problem is that their mothers are unwed. More specifically, their fathers are absent. As many conservative critics have argued, the problem is that the present welfare system is destructive of families. It diminishes the financial responsibility of men for their children, and actually discourages marriage, which reduces welfare support, and thereby increases the incidence of co-habitation in pseudo-marriages which are easily abandoned. It is not that single mothers on welfare prefer to be unmarried, or even to be on the dole. The dilemma is that the present system makes this the easiest way for them to have their families, and, for some, perhaps the only way, as long as fathers are allowed to run from their parental responsibilities.

Clearly then, the focus for welfare reform should be on fathers, not the mothers. For what is the welfare state, in these cases, except a surrogate provider? The scandal, then, is not that mothers are being mothers, but that fathers are *not* being fathers.

No Christian should question that there are cases when women legitimately need financial assistance to care for their children. Indeed, care for the widow is one of the Bible's most repeated commands for alms-giving. The death of the child's father is but one example of a woman's rightful claim to receive the community's support. Incapacity, imprisonment, and abandonment are also legitimate claims. However, in the latter case, abandonment, the Christian society also has every right and duty to find the negligent father and to compel him to fulfill his responsibilities as a provider through social rebuke, civil punishment, fines, seizure of his property, and even forced labor.

Since economic factors do affect sexual behavior, these economic forces should be principally directed at fathers who abandon their children to the care of the state. Furthermore, in order to motivate women to cooperate in holding their mates responsible for their children, the rewards of having a father should be greater than the rewards of having a welfare check. With these thoughts in mind, I would suggest that the legitimate goal of reducing families on welfare is more properly sought in the following proposal.

Children and their mothers would be guaranteed some minimum subsistence payment whenever adequate is not being paid by the father. The only qualification is that the woman *must* identify the child's father. This is a key point, and it should also be applied to any government benefits for unmarried mothers, including WIC, guaranteed student loans, etc. If paternity is disputed, DNA tests would be used to confirm paternity.

Once paternity is established, the father would be held responsible for paying support of no less than 150% of the normal welfare support level which would be available if he were deceased. If it is within the means of his income, even higher support payments should be required. The theory which would be applied in determining this additional payment level is that the woman is entitled to both child support and alimony (or separation payments), since their child is evidence of a common law marriage, even if it is a bigamous marriage. Furthermore, such payments should be sufficient to allow the young mother to be a full-time mother and stay at home with her child, if she wishes. After all, society does not want to discourage a mother from being home with her children during their critical formative years. The prospect of receiving 150%, or more, of what she could receive through welfare payments should motivate most women to cooperate with identifying their children's father(s).

To ensure and record collections, support payments could be made through a government or privately licensed agency. Payments would be withheld only if the woman began to deny or obstruct the visitation rights of the father as defined by court order.

If the husband is dead, incapacitated, or imprisoned, the state would provide welfare payments at the 100% level. If the delinquent father's payments are below the 100% subsistence level, the state would pay the balance up to that level. Furthermore, as long as a father pays less than the 150% level, he would be required to participate in a proportionate amount of workfare to make up the difference.

If, on the other hand, a couple is married and maintains a household together, the father would *not* be held liable to provide 150% of the standard set by welfare support. He would simply provide what he could, and the normal levels of welfare support for the family would be available to them as he seeks employment.

Finally, to safeguard women against being pressured into unwanted abortions by men who want to escape financial responsibility for their children, severe criminal penalties would be imposed against those who would coerce women into unwanted abortions. Abortion clinics should be required to screen women for evidence of coercion and report coercing boyfriends to the authorities.

This proposed system acknowledges that economic forces can influence sexual behavior and encourage the formation of family units. It may even be discovered that the act of enforcing the economic responsibilities of parenthood is far more effective at deterring the sexual license of males than females. Best of all, this approach discourages unwed pregnancies, but without penalizing unwed mothers or their children.

# RESEARCH OPPORTUNITIES

The following is a brainstorming tool consisting of check-list items, concrete suggestions, and half-baked concepts which may be useful to others who are looking to develop post-abortion research strategies and tools.

I believe it should be emphasized that a "perfect" study of post-abortion problems is impossible. One of the biggest obstacles to accurate research is the requirement for voluntary participation. Not only may "concealers" refuse to participate, but there may not even be any record of their having had an abortion, because many women give false names at the time of their abortions. In record-based research, studies of breast cancer for example, cancerous women who conceal a history of abortion will be added to the control group (women with no abortion history) and will thereby artificially depress the reported relative risk. Similarly, in psychological studies, because "concealers" are most likely to be experiencing shame and unresolved stress over a past abortion, their refusal to participate will result in a sample which is artificially "packed" with women who are the least disturbed by their experience. All of these distortions will bias studies in one direction—toward underreporting of abortion related complications. Therefore, even a modest elevation of risk should be interpreted as a minimum complication rate.

I.   Control Groups. Compare women who have had legal elective abortions to women who have had the following experiences:

   A. Childbirth of unplanned pregnancy

   B. Miscarriage

   C. Adoption

   D. Neonatal loss (under 6 mos. of age)

   E. Death of a child (over 6 mos. of age)

   F. Death of a spouse

   G. Illegal abortion

H. Childbirth of handicapped child

I. Victim of rape

J. Victim of sexual abuse

II. Possible sources of comprehensive health care data include:

    A. Any nation with socialized medicine, such as Denmark, Canada, Sweden, or Britain.

    B. Insurance company records

    C. Medicare records

    D. Military records

    E. Prison records

III. Detailed analysis of abortion-related data should be done with existing major data sets gathered in government-funded projects such as:

    A. Yearly survey programs administered by the Office of Demographic Programs

    B. National Longitudinal Study of Youth. Suffers from severe underreporting (those admitting abortion represent only 40% of the expected total), but may still show elevated risks for those who do admit abortion.

        1. Scales in NLSY which can be evaluated
          a. Self-Esteem Scale
          b. Mastery Scale
          c. Center for Epidemiologic Studies Depression (CES-D) Scale
          d. Internal-External Locus of Control Scale

        2. Also includes extensive histories on substance abuse

        3. NLSY also includes interviews with the children of NLSY women, which provides a basis for intergenerational analysis.

    C. Other national surveys which have collected information about abortion history which are probably accessible to non-governmental researchers are the National Survey of Family Growth (NSFG), an ongoing project of the National Center for Health Statistics, and the National Surveys of Young Women. As in NLSY there is very significant underreporting of abortions in both these sets, but they may still prove to be useful.

IV. Post-abortion researchers should seek to influence the design of future government-funded surveys so that they include relevant questions regarding reproductive history. We should also check to see if similar demographic research efforts in Canada and other countries might be amenable to gathering abortion related health data.

V. Tap into existing private data bases

A. Ask psychiatric counseling groups (such as large Catholic Charities group in Delaware which employs over 20 counselors), to review records over the last ten years to note trends in rising number of post-abortion- related cases.

B. Specialized counseling centers, such as drug and alcohol rehabilitation centers, eating disorder facilities, suicide treatment programs, juvenile delinquent programs, etc.

C. The Elliot Institute has three data sets available for additional analysis

D. Insurance company data on health care benefits, cross tabulate abortion payments to higher level of claims for general health care, reproductive health problems, mental health care, drug abuse, suicide, accidental injuries, etc. It may be possible to convince insurance companies that this issue has an economic impact on their insurance programs.

VI. Motivating factors to obtain the cooperation of parties with access to comprehensive health records.

A. Health Insurance Providers who fund abortion

1. If abortion injures a woman's overall health, it is very costly. Insurers who fund abortion may be driving up their own expenses.

2. We should try to convince the health insurance industry to analyze long-term health care patterns of women who have requested insurance payments for abortion. Are they more likely to make subsequent claims for mental health or reproductive health? Are they more likely to drop coverage, change jobs, or exhibit other transitory behavior?

3. Insurers could generate a list of women who received payments covering an abortion (and a control group who did not) and then go out and do a study with questionnaires or

field interviews of these women. (Could this include women who are no longer covered?) These follow-up interviews would not have to include any questions regarding the abortion, since this is already known from insurance records, and could therefore be double-blind studies.

B.  Military

Present the military with the question: Does an abortion effect the military readiness of a female (or male) soldier? If an abortion increases self-destructive behavior, or reduces one's sense of self-preservation, this abortion-related dysfunction may place the unit at risk. If an abortion increases drug and alcohol abuse, especially during times of stress, it may place a unit at risk. If an abortion can cause PTSD, the disordered defense mechanisms can place a unit at risk. If an abortion can cause difficulty concentrating, memory loss, increased anxiety and outbursts, and greater difficulty in interpersonal reactions, this reduces a soldier's effectiveness in both peacetime and war.

VII. Strategies for developing our own data bases

A.  Undertake random retrospective surveys of all reproductive experiences of subjects, including pregnancy outcomes, complications of pregnancies, birth control patterns at each pregnancy, satisfaction level with each pregnancy outcome, present state of fertility (i.e., fertile, sterilized, hysterectomy patient, post-menopause), and demographics for each pregnancy. Include psychosocial history, with questions regarding any history of major psychological illnesses, substance abuse, and suicidal ideation with time frame references to start and recovery from said problems for cross reference to pregnancies.

B.  Survey women facing a crisis pregnancy at abortion clinics and crisis pregnancy centers to evaluate beliefs and pressures faced by aborting women using a series of questions related to decision-making and prior attitudes to get a "time slice" of mental state of women in the midst of their crisis, and compare against results of retrospective studies asking the same questions. Use for comparing dropouts ("concealers") to those who agree to a followup interview.

C.  Develop a survey for women who are known to have experienced post-abortion grief which concentrates on identifying and charting the "time delay" of post-abortion reactions among this population of women. This approach would help develop a "time delay standard" by which all past and future studies must be evaluated. Compare curve to post-partum depression reaction time. The following is some data from one of our Elliot Institute surveys relevant to the delayed reaction effect, and the numbers seeking psychiatric counseling.

1. Only 21% experienced the majority or worst of their negative reactions almost immediately, 19% experienced the majority of their negative reactions within the first six months; and 60% did not experience majority of their reactions until a year or more post-abortion.

2. 33% sought help from psychologist/psychiatrist, 24% from a social worker, 35% from clergy.

3. 10% reported being hospitalized for pscychological treatment because of the abortion, and 20% reported suffering a nervous breakdown sometime after their abortion.

4. 55% stated they experienced symptoms too severe to function normally at work or at home.

D. Contact a random sample of ob/gyn's, general practitioners, and mental health providers and request that they survey the reproductive history of their next 20 female patients and do a psycho-social history including CASE and CAPS-1. If the study population is confined to women seeking pre-natal care, concern for their present pregnancies may help to motivate "concealors" to reveal their past abortions and so help to mitigate the research problems caused by high concealment rates.

E. In suits against abortion clinics, especially class action suits, seek a court order requiring the clinic to allow a survey of women coming into the clinic to determine the prevalence of predictive high-risk factors. This would be relevant to establishing a pattern of negligence. It may also be possible to seek a court order to release records of previous patients for a survey of post-abortion reactions to determine if other patients also experienced the post-abortion sequelae at issue.

F. It may be of value to duplicate any or all of the above studies in a culturally foreign country such as Japan, India, or China in order to determine if any negative reactions to abortion are universal.

VIII. Abortion group and control group(s) can be compared according to treatment received or identified behavioral problems, such as:

A. Psychiatric hospitalization or history of psychological counseling

1. Using health care records (like Denmark study by David), generate a weekly breakdown for postpartum and abortion-related psychiatric hospitalization for first 3 months after the event, and a monthly breakdown over 10 years post-event.

2. Same as above, checking for records of psychological counseling.

B. Drug or alcohol dependency or participation in detoxification programs

C. Participation in treatment programs for eating disorders

D. Divorce, marital counseling, or breakdown of other significant relationships

E. Sexual dysfunction

F. Suicidal tendencies

G. Mothering difficulties: inhibited bonding or smothering and separation anxiety

H. Child abuse or neglect

I. Replacement pregnancies or an increased tendency to have subsequent out-of-wedlock births

J. Sleep disorders and nightmares

K. Survivor guilt

L. Major personality changes

M. Psychological numbing

N. Anxiety attacks

O. Pathological grief or complicated mourning

P. Disordered coping skills

Q. Outbursts of uncontrollable rage

R. Hatred of others; homocidal ideation

S.  Fear of decision-making; fear of leaving home; fear of punishment by God; fear of losing children; other fears

T.  Physiological responses to sounds, sights, smells, or touches associated with abortion

U.  Ability to cope with infertility problems or other reproductive losses such as miscarriage

IX.  Intra-population studies. Focus on investigation of factors which are predictive of adverse reactions post-abortion.

A.  Comparing teens who abort to older women who abort.

B.  Comparing women with a history of multiple abortions to those with a single abortion

C.  Look for other demographic characteristics significantly associated with different experiences

D.  Further investigation of high-risk factors predictive of negative post-abortion reaction. Develop model for "concealers" based on high-risk factors identified on intake forms or by demographics.

X.  Specialized studies

A.  Additional studies are necessary to examine the problem of "concealers" and "drop-outs," since the refusal to participate in post-abortion studies may itself be evidence of post-abortion problems.

1. Do demographic comparisons of "concealers" and "drop-outs" compared to study participants

2. Do a double-blind study where "concealers" do not know that researcher leaders already know they have had abortions.

3. Compare dropout rates in abortion studies to dropout rates in other areas where there is some shame involved, such as post-rape studies or post-mastectomy studies. This may indicate that there is more stress and shame associated with abortion than with rape or mastectomy.

B.  General population study to identify awareness of cases where women were pressured into unwanted abortions. How many women will admit a history of abortion in connection with feeling pressured by others? Are most people willing to consider coercive abortion a form of abuse?

C. Check for correlation between abortion (esp. coerced abortions) and domestic violence, both women attacking men and men attacking women.

D. Survey female prison populations, looking for correlation between abortion and domestic violence, child abuse or child homicide, other violent crimes, and substance abuse.

E. Research potential relationship between abortion and egg donors, surrogate motherhood, etc.

F. Investigate possible parallel between post-aborted women and PTSD war veterans who exhibit reaction formation. The former become immersed in pro-abortion activities and the latter becoming immersed in war games, "mercenary" activity, and other militaristic activities.

G. Measure degree of hostility among "defenders" against those who challenge rightness of abortion choice. Is such hostility within a "normal" range? Is there a parallel to the hostility which some PTSD war victims felt toward those who protested against the Vietnam War?

XI. Impact of abortion on siblings

  A. Relationship of abortion to child abuse/neglect

    1. Search clinical experience; expand on case studies

    2. Seek cooperation of state agencies (i.e., Dept. of Children and Family Services) responsible for child neglect cases; investigate pregnancy history of neglector.

    3. Identify and survey women/couples convicted of killing an infant; develop case studies.

  B. Impact on maternal bonding

    1. Identify standard for measuring bonding strength.

    2. Identify influences of previous experiences on bonding patterns.

    3. Investigate bonding differences for women who bore children before an abortion and subsequent to abortion.

  C. Investigate children's reactions to knowledge that their mothers aborted siblings.

# NOTES

## INTRODUCTION

1. David C. Reardon, *Aborted Women, Silent No More*, (Chicago: Loyola University Press, 1987), 11-21. See also, Mary K. Zimmerman, *Passage Through Abortion* (New York: Praeger Publishers, 1977), 62-70.

## CHAPTER ONE: REMAINING TRUE TO OURSELVES

1. John Whitehead and Michael Patrick, "Exclusive Interview: U.S. Surgeon General C. Everett Koop," *The Rutherford Institute*, Spring 1989, 32, 34.

2. Ibid., 31-34.

3. Colman McCarthy, "A Psychological View of Abortion," St. Paul Sunday Pioneer Press, *The Washington Post*, March 7, 1971. Dr. Fogel, who did 20,000 abortions over the subsequent decades, reiterated the same view in a second interview with McCarthy in 1989 in which he disagreed with the Koop's inability to report on the detrimental effects of abortion. "The Real Anguish of Abortions," *The Washington Post*, Feb. 5, 1989.

4. John Paul II, *Crossing the Threshold of Hope* (New York: Alfred A. Knopf, 1994), 207-207.

5. Reardon, *Aborted Women*, 161-218.

6. O.E. Worcester, M.D., "From A Woman Physician: An Open Letter to Dr. W.W. Parker," JAMA, 22:599 (1894) reprinted in "JAMA 100 Years Ago," *JAMA*, 271:15, April 20, 1994.

## CHAPTER TWO: THE MIDDLE MAJORITY

1. Reardon, *Aborted Women*. See especially Chapter 8, "Business Before Medicine," 253-271.

2. John Powell, *Abortion: The Silent Holocaust* (Allen, TX: Argus Communications, 1981), 67.

3. Howard Kurtz, "Poor Choice of Words from Abortion Rights Advocate?" *The Washington Post*, Feb. 7, 1994.

4. According to one major poll, 77% of the public believe abortion is the taking of a human life, with 49% equating it with murder. Only 16% claim to believe that abortion is only "a surgical procedure for removing human tissue." Even one-third of those who describe themselves as strongly pro-choice concede that abortion is the taking of a human life. (Hunter, *Before the Shooting*, 93.) Similarly, another major poll found that 65% of those who favor legalized abortion and 74% of those who have had an abortion, believe abortion is morally wrong. (*Los Angeles Times* Poll, March 19, 1989.)

5. James Davison Hunter, *Before the Shooting Begins: Searching for Democracy in America's Cultural War* (New York: The Free Press, 1994), 108.

6. Ibid., 107-110.

7. Ibid., 123.

8. Ibid., 126.

9. Ibid., 128-129.

10. Ibid., 130.

11. Ibid., 139.

12. Ibid., 140-145.

13. Ibid., 89, footnote 11.

14. Ibid., 88.

15. Ibid., 101.

## Chapter Three: The Political Opportunity

1. Daniel Callahan, "An Ethical Challenge to Prochoice Advocates," *Commonweal*, Nov. 23, 1990, 684. Similarly, a survey of women who subsequently regretted their abortions found that 55% reported feeling "forced" into their abortion by other people, with 61% saying they felt their lives at that time were being controlled by others. Reardon, *Aborted Women*, 11.

## Chapter Four: The Key Is in *Roe*

1. Randall J. Heckman, *Justice for the Unborn* (Ann Arbor, MI: Servant Books, 1984), 103.

2. Bob Woodward and Scott Armstrong, *The Brethren* (New York: Simon and Schuster, 1979), 175, 416; and John T. Noonan, Jr., *A Private Choice* (Toronto: Life Cycle Books, 1979), 45.

3. *Roe v. Wade*, 410 U.S. 113 (1973), 165-166.

4. *Roe*, 153. Also, "The privacy right involved, therefore, cannot be said to be absolute....The Court has refused to recognize an unlimited right of this kind in the past." (*Roe*, 154.) "Even an adult woman's right to an abortion is not unqualified." *H.L. v. Matheson* 450 U.S. 397 (1980), 419 (Powell and Stewart, concurring). Also *Planned Parenthood v. Danforth* 428 U.S. 51 (1975), 60 and *Planned Parenthood v. Casey* 120 L Ed 2d 674 (1992), 709.

5. The Supreme Court has affirmed that the "medical, emotional, and psychological consequences of an abortion are serious and can be lasting...." *Matheson*, 411, also 413. The same view is reiterated in *Danforth*, 67 and *Casey*, 698-699.

6. *Casey*, 698.

7. *Roe*, 163-166. These same principles are reiterated throughout the many abortion cases following *Roe*. Most recently in *Casey*, 709, 711, 715-716, 718.

8. *Roe*, 166. Also, "The [*Roe v. Wade*] decision vindicates the right of the physician to administer medical treatment according to his professional judgment up to the points where important state interests provide compelling justifications for intervention." (*Roe*, 165-166.)

9. The decision whether or not to abort should be made "in light of all circumstances—psychological and emotional as well as physical—that might be relevant to the well-being of the patient." (*Danforth*, 66.) Family size, financial concerns, mental health, and physical health are all issues in making a medical recommendation for abortion. "All these are factors the woman and her responsible physician necessarily will consider in consultation." (*Roe*, 153.) This medical decision is especially weighty, because "Abortion is inherently different from other medical procedures, because no other procedure involves the purposeful termination of potential life." *Harris v. McRaie*, 448 U.S. 297, 325 (1980).

10. *Roe*, 163.

11. *Akron v. Akron Center for Reproductive Health*, 462 U.S. 416 (1983), 448. One can almost hear in the background of these decisions an invoking of the sacred names Dr. Welby and Dr. Kildaire. Indeed, it is precisely because the Court was using the model of an ideal physician that it found cause for excluding the state from "interfering" in the medical practice of these "competent, conscientious, and ethical" physicians. On the other hand, because the Court has created this idealized standard, abortionists can be held more liable for abortion-related injuries when they fail to live up to this ideal.

12. *Doe v. Bolton*, 410 U.S. 179 (1973), 192.

13. Ibid.; also *Colautti v. Franklin*, 439 U.S. 379 (1979), 394.

14. *Roe*, 166.

15. American College of Obstetricians and Gynecologists: Committee on Professional Standards, *Standard for Obstetric-Gynecological Services* (1981). Also, ACOG Executive Board, *Statement of Policy - Further Ethical Considerations in Induced Abortion*, (Washington, DC: ACOG, 1977), p2: "In responding to the patient's expressed wish for termination of her pregnancy, there may be a ten-

dency for the physician to act solely as a technician. Such action denies the physician's traditional role as a counselor and advisor. Physicians have an ethical responsibility to assure quality counseling is provided by them or others."

16. Warren Hern, *Abortion Practice* (Boulder, CO: Alpenglo Graphics, Inc. 1990), 86.

17. *Roe*, 166. Women are free to request abortions, and women are the parties who are intended to benefit from this procedure, but since abortion is a medical procedure the right to abortion is a medical privilege of physicians. "The [*Roe v. Wade*] decision vindicates the right of the physician to administer medical treatment according to his professional judgment up to the points where important state interests provide compelling justifications for intervention." (*Roe*, 165-166.)

18. "[A] woman has at least an equal right to choose to carry her fetus to term as to choose to abort it." *Maher v. Roe*, 432 U.S. 464, 472, n.7.

19. "If the pregnant girl elects to carry her child to term, the *medical* decisions to be made entail few—perhaps none—of the potentially grave emotional and psychological consequences of the decision to abort." (*Matheson*, 412-413.)

20. For a complete discussion of a woman's right to full disclosure under *Roe* and subsequent rulings, see Chapter Eight.

## CHAPTER FIVE: DEVIATIONS FROM THE ROE IDEAL

1. Woodward and Armstrong, *The Brethren*, 236-237.

2. "Doctor's Abortion Business Is Lucrative," *San Diego Union*, Oct. 12, 1980, B1.

3. Hern, *Abortion Practice*, 106, 108, 126-127.

4. Ibid., 185.

5. Ibid., 108.

6. Phillip G. Stubblefield, M.D., Forward to Hern, *Abortion Practice*, vii.

7. *Roe*, 166.

## CHAPTER SIX: PROPER SCREENING OF PATIENTS

1. "An adequate medical and psychological case history is important to the physician." (*Matheson*, 411.)

2. Hern, *Abortion Practice*, 67-74, 166.

3. Wilmoth, "Abortion, Public Health Policy, and Informed Consent Legislation," *Journal of Social Issues*, 48(3):1-17. See also, Anne Baker, "Counselor's Corner," *Hope News* (Granite City, IL: The Hope Clinic for Women, Ltd., December 1994), 2-4.

4. In a review of 11 studies which examined various mid- and long-term negative psychological effects of abortion, the lowest incidence rate reported was six percent and the highest was 32 percent, the average reported rate being 15 percent. (Dagg, "The Psychological Sequelae of Therapeutic Abortion—Denied and Completed," *Am. J. Psychiatry*, 148:5, May 1991, 578-585.) Another major study found that 49% of 360 women surveyed experienced psychological maladjustments post-abortion. (Belsey, et al., "Predictive Factors in Emotional Response to Abortion: King's Termination Study—IV," *Soc. Sci. & Med.*, 11:71-82 (1977).) Still other researchers have reported even higher rates by accounting for women who refuse to participate in follow-up programs precisely because they have had, or continue to experience, psychological stress related to the abortion and do not wish to aggravate this stress by participation in the study.

5. Over 70% of women having abortions are doing so against their conscience, with 74% agreeing with the statement, "I personally feel that abortion is morally wrong, but I also feel that whether or not to have an abortion is a decision that has to be made by every woman for herself." (*Los Angeles Times* Poll, March 19, 1989. See also, Zimmerman, *Passages Through Abortion*, and Reardon, *Aborted Women*.) Thirty to 55% report feeling pressured to abort by others, and a similar percentage express some desire to keep their child (Zimmerman, Reardon). Approximately 45% of abortions are done on women with a prior history of abortion, and over one-fourth are performed on teenagers. In addition, some trauma experts estimate that as many as one in three women have been sexually abused in childhood. (See for example, Judith Lewis Herman, M.D., *Trauma and Recovery* (New York: Basic Books, 1992), 30.) It is likely that the percentage of women having abortions who have a prior history of abuse, trauma, or other psychological problems is as high, or higher, than that for the general population. These statistics, regarding only a few of the known high-risk factors, clearly indicate that the majority of aborting women are at high-risk of suffering post-abortion psychological sequelae.

6. Sylvia Stengle, executive director of the National Abortion Federation, has affirmed in interviews that there are conditions in which an abortionist would be "ethically bound" to refuse a contraindicated abortion. Junda Woo, "Abortion Doctor's Patients Broaden Suits," *Wall Street Journal*, Oct. 28, 1994, B12:1.

7. Hern, *Abortion Practice*, 84, 86-87.

8. Herman, *Trauma and Recovery*, 20-28.

9. Landy, "Abortion Counseling—A New Component of Medical Care," *Clinics in Obs/Gyn*, 13(1):33-41 (1986).

10. Ibid.

11. E. Friedman, et al., eds., *Obstetrical Decision Making*, Second Edition (Philadelphia:B.C. Decker Inc., 1987), especially Borton, "Induced Abortion," 44, and Stewart, "Psychosocial Assessment," 30.

12. Belsey, et al., "Predictive Factors in Emotional Response to Abortion: King's Termination Study—IV," *Soc. Sci. & Med.*, 11:71-82 (1977). See also,

Miller, "An Empirical Study of the Psychological Antecedents and Consequences of Induced Abortion," *Journal of Social Issues*, 48(3):67-93 (1992).

13. "It is common to find that a woman has presented herself for an abortion even though she does not really want one; her partner or her parents want her to have one. In this instance, it is extremely important for the counselor to make it clear to the patient that the decision is hers and that no one can force her to have an abortion." (Hern, *Abortion Practice*, 81.)

14. "It is difficult at times to determine whether subtle coercion is occurring or whether the patient is truly making the decision herself. Under these circumstances, it is especially important that the counselor determine the patient's true attitude and decision as distinguished from how she may feel about the decision." (Hern, *Abortion Practice*, 80.)

## CHAPTER SEVEN: ALTERNATIVES COUNSELING

1. Another collection of testimonies which show how women's needs have been misdiagnosed and wrongly treated with abortion is found in Frederica Mathewes-Green, *Real Choices* (Sisters, OR: Multnomah Books, 1994). These and other testimonies show that while the pregnancy is generally the focal point of attention, there are actually other life problems which need to be resolved and the pregnancy has merely brought these other problems to the fore.

2. "Prior to an abortion, the woman should be counseled on the options for management of an unwanted pregnancy." ACOG, *Standards for Obstetric-Gynecologic Services*, Sixth Edition (Washington, DC: ACOG, 1985), 63.

"The condition under which pregnancy counseling takes place must guarantee that the woman is provided with privacy, confidentiality, adequate information and emotional support, all of which permit her to explore alternatives and gather information to make her own decision about her pregnancy." Saltzman & Policar, *The Complete Guide to Pregnancy Testing and Counseling* (San Francisco: Planned Parenthood of Alameda/San Francisco, 1985), 6.

"[While] decision counseling may or may not be offered on-site, access to such [decision] counseling must be available. If decision counseling is available through referral only, facilities must have documentation of referral sources, and staff must be knowledgeable about counseling referrals." And the purpose of decision counseling is "to assist the woman, as needed, in decision-making by helping her face the task of choosing, encouraging a careful examination of all options...." NAF, *Standards for Abortion Care*, Rev. (Washington, DC: National Abortion Federation, 1987), 3-4.

3. Reardon, *Aborted Women*, 188-218.

4. Life After Assault League, 1336 W. Lindbergh, Appleton, WI, 54914, (414) 739-4489, Kay Zibolsky, President.

5. *Doe v. Bolton*, 192.

6. *Roe*, 165.

7. An example of how general practitioners are expected to be familiar with pre-abortion counseling and screening is found in Rosenfeld, "Emotional Responses to Therapeutic Abortion," *American Family Physician*, 45(1):137-140 (1992).

## Chapter Eight:
## The Woman's Right to Full Disclosure

1. Louisell & Williams, *Medical Malpractice*, Section 8.02 (1985); Stuart, "Abortion and Informed Consent: A Cause of Action," *Ohio Northern University Law Review*, 14(1):1-20 (1987).

2. Schneyer, "Informed Consent and the Danger of Bias in the Formation of Medical Disclosure Practices," *Wis. L. Rev.* (1976), 124; also, Stuart, "Abortion and Informed Consent", 1-20.

3. *Cooper v. Roberts*, 220 Pa. Super. Ct., 260, 267, 286 A.2d 647, 650 (1971). See also, *Wilkinson v. Vesey*, 110 R.I. 606, 624, 295 A.2d 676, 687 (1972).

4. *Canterbury v. Spence*, 464 F.2d 772 (D.C. Cir. 1972), 780.

5. Ibid., 787-88. Also, "A risk is thus material when a reasonable person in what the physician knows or should know to be the patient's position would be likely to attach significance to the risks or clusters of risks in deciding whether or not to forego the proposed therapy." (*Canterbury*, 792.) In short, any risk that could affect the decision must be disclosed.

6. *Canterbury*, op. cit.; *Wilson v. Scoll*, 412 SW.2d 299 (1967).

7. Joseph W. Stuart, "Abortion and Informed Consent: A Cause of Action," *Ohio Northern University Law Review*, 14(1):9-10 (1987).

8. Lewis, "How Adolescents Approach Decisions. Changes Over Grades Seven to Twelve and Policy Implications," *Child Development*, 52:538-544 (1981); Weithorn & Campbell, "The Competency of Children and Adolescents to Make Informed Treatment Decisions," *Child Development*, 53:1589-1598 (1982).

9. Standards of care requiring full disclosure of risks, screening for medical and psycho-social risk factors, exploration of alternatives, and adequate time for consideration are set out in the following: M. Borton, "Induced Abortion," E. Friedman, et al., eds., *Obstetrical Decision Making*, op. cit., and F. Barnes, ed., *Ambulatory Maternal Health Care and Family Planning Services Policies, Principles, Practices*, (Committee on Maternal Health Care and Family Planning, Maternal and Child Health Association, American Public Health Association, Interdisciplinary Books and Periodicals for the Professional and Layman, 1978).

10. For a discussion of pre-abortion screening standards and the risk factors for which patients should be screened, see Reardon, "Identifying High-Risk Abortion Patients," *The Post-Abortion Review*, 1(3):3-6, 1993.

11. *Fogal v. Genesee Hospital,* 41 A.D.2d 468, 473, 344 N.Y.S.2d 552, 559 (1973); and *Bowers v. Talmage,* 159 So.2d 888, 889 (Fla. Dist. Ct. App. 1963).

12. *Canterbury,* 789.

13. "The privilege [to withhold risk information which, in itself would present a threat to the patient's well being] does not accept the paternalistic notion that the physician may remain silent simply because divulgence might prompt the patient to forego therapy the physician feels the patient really needs. That attitude presumes instability or perversity for even the normal patient, and runs counter to the foundation principle that the patient should and ordinarily can make the choice for himself." (*Canterbury,* 789.)

14. Annas, *The Rights of Hospital Patients: The Basic ACLU Guide to a Hospital Patient's Rights* (New York: Discus Books, 1975), 68.

15. Ibid.

16. "The very foundation of the doctrine of informed consent is every man's right to forego treatment or even cure if it entails what for him are intolerable consequences or risks, however warped or perverted his sense of values may be in the eyes of the medical profession, or even of the community, so long as any distortion falls short of what the law regards as competency. Individual freedom here is guaranteed only if people are given the right to make choices which would generally be regarded as foolish." Harper & James, *The Law of Torts* (1968 Supp.), section 17.1, 61.

17. "If the pregnant girl elects to carry her child to term, the medical decisions to be made entail few—perhaps none—of the potentially grave emotional and psychological consequences of the decision to abort." (*Matheson,* 412-413.)

18. *Casey,* 698.

19. *Danforth,* 67. The patient's right to "full knowledge" is repeated in *Akron,* 448. The medical profession has seen in these rulings a trend toward defining the physician's right to determine what information should be disclosed about risks and alternatives "only as an adjunct to the realization of patients' rights, and not as significant in themselves." Kapp, "Abortion and Informed Consent Requirements," *Am. J. Obstetrics and Gynecology,* 144(1):1-4 (1982).

20. *Danforth,* 66.

21. *Casey,* 715.

22. Stuart, "Abortion and Informed Consent," 14, note 92.

23. Ibid., 17, citing *Whalen v. Roe,* 429 U.S. at 604, n.33., and *Canterbury,* 789, and others.

24. *Danforth,* 67; see also, *Casey,* 718.

25. For additional discussion of this principle, see Jipping, "Informed Consent to Abortion: A Refinement," *Case Western Reserve Law Review,* 38:329-386 (1987/88).

26. *Casey*, 718-719; see also the discussion in Stuart, "Abortion and Informed Consent," 18-19.

27. Ibid.

28. Daniel Callahan, "An Ethical Challenge to Prochoice Advocates," *Commonweal*, Nov. 23, 1990, 685, 686.

29. Junda Woo, "Abortion Doctors' Patients Broaden Suits," *The Wall Street Journal*, Oct. 28, 1994, B12.

30. Landy, "Abortion Counseling", op. cit.

31. Zimmerman, *Passage Through Abortion*, 139.

32. For discussions of heightened psychological accessibility of persons in crisis, see Gerald Caplan, *Principles of Preventive Psychiatry* (New York: Basic Books, 1964), and Howard W. Stone, *Crisis Counseling*, (Fortress Press, 1976).

33. Reardon, *Aborted Women*, 15-19.

34. Linda Bird Francke, *The Ambivalence of Abortion* (New York: Random House, 1978), 179.

35. Zimmerman, *Passages Through Abortion*, 139; also, Reardon, *Aborted Women*, 16-18.

36. Kupelian, "Abortion, Inc." *New Dimensions* (October 1991), 14.

37. Bond, "Mother Files $1 Million Lawsuit," *National Right to Life News*, Oct. 23, 1986, 6.

38. Zimmerman, *Passage Through Abortion*, 110-112, 143; Reardon, *Aborted Women*, 11-20.

39. Statistical analysis demonstrates that patient dissatisfaction with abortion counseling is a highly significant predictor ($p < 0.0001$) of severe psychological reactions after an abortion. Franz and Reardon, "Differential Impact of Abortion on Adolescents and Adults," *Adolescence*, 27(105):161-172 (1992); see also, Vaughan, *Canonical Variates of Post-Abortion Syndrome* (Portsmouth, NH: Institute for Pregnancy Loss, 1990); and Steinberg, "Abortion Counseling: To Benefit Maternal Health," *American Journal of Law & Medicine*, 15:4, 483-517 (1989).

40. See Zeckman and Warrick, "Abortion Profiteers," Special Reprint, *Chicago Sun-Times*, 1978; and Carol Everett, *The Scarlet Lady: Confessions of a Successful Abortionist* (Brentwood, TN: Wolgemuth & Hyatt, 1991).

41. Reardon, *Aborted Women*, 251-243.

42. Ibid., 256.

43. "Doctor's Abortion Business Is Lucrative," *San Diego Union*, Oct. 12, 1980, B1:1.

44. Ample documentation of this can be found in the following: J. Kasun, *The War Against Population: The Economics and Ideology of Population Control*, (San Francisco: Ignatius Press, 1988); A. Chase, *The Legacy of Malthus: The Social Costs of the New Scientific Racism* (New York: Alfred A. Knopf, 1977); J.

Simon, *The Ultimate Resource* (Princeton, NJ: Princeton University Press, 1981); G. Greer, *Sex and Destiny* (New York: Harper & Row, 1984).

45. Schwartz, "Bringing the Sexual Revolution Home: Planned Parenthood's 'Five-Year Plan'", *America* 138:6, 18 February 1978, 114-116.

46. Planned Parenthood has frequently supported coercive population control. For example, at the White House Conference on Hunger in 1969, Dr. Alan Guttmacher of Planned Parenthood supported a national plan of (1) mandatory abortion for any unmarried girl found pregnant within the first three months of pregnancy, and (2) mandatory sterilization of any such girl giving birth out of wedlock for a second time. E. Craven, "Abortion, Poverty and Black Genocide: Gifts to the Poor?", Hilgers and Horan, eds., *Abortion and Social Justice* (New York: Sheed and Ward, 1972), 235.

Similarly, Frederick Jaffe, former Vice President of the Planned Parenthood/World Population and head of research for Alan Guttmacher, has argued for government population programs which would require permits for children, compulsory sterilization of all who have two children, compulsory abortion, the addition of fertility control agents in the water supply, and programs to "encourage homosexuality" because it is a non-fertile form of sexual activity. *Family Planning Perspectives*, Special supplement, U.S. Population Growth and Family Planning: A Review of the Literature, vol. 2, no. 4, October 1970, ff. at 24.

Former Planned Parenthood president Faye Whattleton has likewise promoted an us-against-them, rich-versus-poor mentality as motivation for population control at any price (Simon, *The Ultimate Resource*, 327).

47. Kasun, *War Against Population*, 91.

48. Lawrence Lader, *Abortion II: Making the Revolution*, (Boston: Beacon Press, 1973), 218-222.

49. Lawrence Lader, "The China Solution," *Science Digest*, 91:4, April 1983, 78.

50. Transcript of "Oprah Winfrey Show," July 6, 1989.

51. In 1970, Planned Parenthood President Dr. Alan Guttmacher testified before a Senate subcommittee that the health dangers of the Pill are secondary to the social "dangers" of pregnancy and overpopulation. "Expert Decries 'Alarm' on Birth Control Pill," *New York Times*, Feb. 26, 1970, 50:3.

As another example, at a 1962 conference sponsored by the Population Council, the IUD was being promoted as the panacea for controlling the world's "overpopulation." Arguing that the risks of IUD use were acceptable, Dr. J. Robert Willson, of the University of Michigan School of Medicine defended its wide-spread promotion, saying, "If we look at this from an overall, long-range view, perhaps the individual patient is expendable in the general scheme of things, particularly if the infection she acquires is sterilizing but not lethal." Mendelsohn, *Male Practice: How Doctors Manipulate Women* (Chicago: Contemporary Books, 1981), 120.

Similarly, Dr. Ravenholt, head of the U.S. Agency for International Development's population control programs, defended the widespread promotion of Depo-Provera, despite initial negative results, on grounds that the ill-effects could not be fully ascertained until tested on tens of millions of women. Ehrenreich, et.al., "The Charge: Genocide," *Mother Jones*, Nov. 1979, 30.

52. Reardon, *Aborted Women*, 18-20.

53. While the sincerity of population controllers' beliefs is not questioned here, it is noteworthy that the myth of overpopulation has been thoroughly debunked. Indeed, the overwhelming benefits of population growth are only now becoming fully appreciated. (See the exhaustive works of Simon, Kasun, Chase, op. cit.) Notably, even population controllers admit that the evidence against their theories of overpopulation problems is impossible to refute, but they insist that their approach of forced population control is still a safer bet. See for example, Hardin, "The Tragedy of the Commons," *Science*, December, 1968, 1243-1248. Hardin, incidentally, claims to have been the first to develop the rhetoric of a "woman's right to control her own body"; yet, in practice he supports coercive population control programs, especially of "feeble-minded" groups, because "Injustice is preferable to total ruin." *Ibid*.

## CHAPTER NINE: THE LEGISLATIVE OPPORTUNITY

1. David Reardon, "Psychological Reactions Reported After Abortion," *The Post-Abortion Review*, 2(3):4-8, (Fall 1994).

2. *Roe*, 159-162.

3. *Roe*, 163-164.

4. As previously noted, Sylvia Stengle of the National Abortion Federation admits that in such cases the abortionist would be ethically bound to refuse to perform the abortion. Woo, "Abortion Doctor's Patients Broaden Suits", *Wall Street Journal* Oct. 28, 1994, B12.

5. "Mixed feelings and *uncertainty about proceeding* with an abortion seem to be associated with later guilt, preoccupation with fantasies of the fetus, including its sex, awareness of the term delivery date and being upset at seeing other women with babies." Gath & Rose, "Psychological Problems & Gynacological Surgery" in *Psychological Disorders in Obstetrics and Gynaecology* (London: Butterworths, 1985). See the additional citations in Appendix A.

## CHAPTER TEN: A HEALING STRATEGY

1. For examples of their testimonies, see *The Post-Abortion Review*, and *Aborted Women, Silent No More*.

## CHAPTER ELEVEN: CONQUERING DESPAIR

1. See *Aborted Women, Silent No More* for twenty testimonies of women who have had abortions.

2. Mathewes-Green, *Real Choices*, 19. *Real Choices* is another excellent book examining the pressures which push women into unwanted abortions.

3. Zygmunt Bauman, *Modernity and the Holocaust* (Ithaca, NY: Cornell University Press, 1989), 130.

4. This general description of the stance of Christ and Satan before and after sin is drawn from the audio-tape "The Devil" by Archbishop Fulton Sheen and is applied here specifically to the case of abortion.

## CHAPTER TWELVE:
## TRUSTING GOD'S MERCY FOR UNBORN CHILDREN

1. Cyprian, *Letters*, 72[73]:22 (A.D. 255).

2. Tertullian, *On Baptism*, 15:1; 16:1-2 (A.D. 203).

3. This type of *a fortiori* argument, "If Y is true, then how much more likely that Z is true," was frequently used for teaching and theological deduction by Jesus and Paul. See Matt. 7:11, 10:25, 12:12; Luke 11:13, 12:24, 28; Romans 11:12, 24; 1 Cor. 6:3; Heb. 9:14.

4. Jack Hayford, *I'll Hold You In Heaven* (Ventura, CA: Regal Books, 1990), 47.

5. Dr. Kenneth McAll, *Healing the Family Tree*, (London: Sheldon Press, 1986), 27, 33, 34, 48, 52. McAll, a Protestant who was initially resistant to "prayers for the dead," provides a good discussion on the practices of the early Church regarding prayerful committal of the dead and how these accord with Scripture. See pages 88-97.

6. *Catechism of the Catholic Church* (1994), par. 1261.

7. Vatican II documents, reflecting on God's saving will, include the dogmatic statement that "since Christ died for all (Rom. 8:32) . . . we must hold that the Holy Spirit offers to all the possibility of being made partners, in a way known to God, in the paschal mystery" (*Gaudium et Spes*, 22). This statement would seem to weigh against the theory of Limbo. If an unborn child is denied the opportunity of baptism by water, then "the possibility of being made partners" in Christ's redemption must mean that some other means of sanctification is available.

8. John Paul II, *Evangelium Vitae* (1995), par. 99.

## CHAPTER THIRTEEN:
## HEALING, PUBLIC RELATIONS, AND RESEARCH

1. This fear of post-abortion research is exactly why no federal funds have been earmarked for such research even though former Surgeon General Koop's letter to President Reagan stated that more research was needed. Pro-abortionists know that the truth can only hurt them.

## CHAPTER FIFTEEN: THE POLITICAL DYNAMICS

1. Lader, *Abortion II*, 36-40.

2. Feminists for Life of America, 733 15th St. NW, Suite 1100, Washington, DC 20005; phone: (202) 737-3352.

## CHAPTER SIXTEEN: WHAT WE CAN HOPE TO ACHIEVE

1. Reardon, *Aborted Women*, 287-291.

2. Nancy Howell Lee, *The Search for an Abortionist* (Chicago: University of Chicago Press, 1969), 103-113; and Reardon, *Aborted Women*, 291-300. The latter includes a discussion of why the rate of psychological injuries from abortion has gone up since legalization, pointing out that this is principally because the increase in the number of women having abortions has occurred mostly among the group of women who are most at risk of suffering psychological sequelae.

3. For a rundown of efforts to promote self-abortion, especially if *Roe* is overturned, see "Non-medical Abortion—Wave of the Future?" *Data Digest*, Issue 3 (1992), Baptists for Life, Inc., PO Box 3158, Grand Rapids, MI 49501.

4. Charles E. Rice, *No Exception: A Pro-Life Imperative* (Notre Dame, IN: Tyholland Press, 1990), 75. Rice argues that there are only two cases where "abortion" can be permitted to save a mother's life: removal of a cancerous uterus which contains a non-viable human fetus, and removal of a fallopian tube containing an ectopic pregnancy. Moral theologians classify these as "indirect abortions," which are allowed under the principle of the "double effect" where the intention is to save a life (the good effect) by removing a diseased organ. In such cases, the death of the unborn child (the negative effect) is not intended and is not the cause of the good effect. Instead, the good effect, saving the mother's life, is the direct result of removing the diseased organ, not the result of killing the child. Even if there arose some other

case in which a woman's life could only be saved by abortion, Rice argues that it should not be allowed. But even Rice notices that this standard carries with it some ambiguity, for example, in the case of a cancerous uterus, where a judgment must be made as to whether or not the pregnancy can be continued long enough to save the child without the cancer killing the mother first.

5. The risk of deferring moral decisions to "experts" is highlighted by Zygmunt Bauman's reflections on the social dynamics of moral compromise. His analysis of the Holocaust is especially relevant to the problem of deteriorating moral standards present in committee systems. See especially his discussion of Milgram's experiments in Bauman, *Modernity and the Holocaust*, op. cit.


## APPENDIX B: PRO-WOMAN/PRO-LIFE SOUND BITES

1. Reardon, *Aborted Women*, 11-13.

# BIBLIOGRAPHY

## PERIODICALS

*Newsletter*, Association for Interdisciplinary Research in Values and Social Change, 419 7th Street NW, Suite 500, Washington, DC 20004.

*The Post-Abortion Review*, Box 7348, Springfield, IL 62791-7348.

## BOOKS

Loraine Allison, *Finding Peace After Abortion* (St. Meinrad, IN: Abbey Press, 1990).

Linda Bartlett, *From Heartache to Healing: Coping with the Effects of Abortion* (St. Louis, MO: Concordia Publishing House 1992).

Theresa Karminski Burke with Barbara Cullen, *Rachel's Vineyard: A Psychological and Spiritual Journey of Post Abortion Healing* (New York: Alba House 1995).

Linda Cochrane, *Women in Ramah: A Post-Abortion Bible Study* (Falls Church, VA: Christian Action Council, 1987).

Douglas Crawford and Michael Mannion, *Psycho-Spiritual Healing After Abortion* (Kansas City, MO: Sheed & Ward, 1987).

John Dillon, *A Path to Hope: For Parents of Aborted Children and Those Who Minister to Them* (Mineola, NY: Resurrection Press, 1990).

Sheila Fabricant, Matthew Linn, and Dennis Linn, *Healing Relationships with Miscarried, Aborted and Stillborn Babies* (Kansas City, MO: Sheed and Ward, 1985).

Holly Francis, *5 Steps Toward Post-Abortion Healing* (Boston, MA: St. Paul Books & Media, 1992).

Luci Freed and Penny Yvonne Salazar, *A Season to Heal: Help and Hope for Those Working Through Post-Abortion Stress* (Nashville, TN: Thomas Nelson Publishers, 1993).

Debra Jones, *Rainbows in the Night: Bible Study for Individuals or Groups* (Memphis, TN: Post-Abortion Ministries).

Nola Jones, *Post-Abortion Syndrome: A Therapy Model for Crisis Intervention* (Vacaville, CA: Victims of Choice, 1989).

Pat King, *After Abortion: Stories of Healing* (Ligouri, MO: Liguori Publications 1992).

Pam Koerbel, *A Guide to Effective Post-Abortion Support Groups* (Memphis, TN: Post-Abortion Ministries).

Pam Koerbel, *If I Knew Then: A Collection of Post-Abortion Poems* (Memphis, TN: Post-Abortion Ministries).

David Mall and Walter Watts, eds., *The Psychological Aspects of Abortion* (Washington, DC: University Publications of America, 1979).

Michael Mannion, *Abortion and Healing: A Cry to Be Whole* (Kansas City, MO: Sheed & Ward, 1986).

Michael Mannion, ed., *Post-Abortion Aftermath* (Kansas City, MO: Sheed & Ward, 1994).

Frederica Mathewes-Green, *Real Choices* (Sisters, OR: Multnomah Books, 1994).

Kenneth McCall, *Healing the Family Tree* (London: Sheldon Press, 1982).

Nancy Michels, *Helping Women Recover From Abortion* (Minneapolis, MN: Bethany House Publishers, 1988).

Philip Ney and Marie Peeters, *How to Talk With Your Children About Your Abortion: A Practical Guide for Parents* (Victoria, British Columbia).

Philip Ney and Marie Peeters, *Post-Abortion Survivors Syndrome* (Victoria, British Columbia: Pioneer Publishing, 1993).

David Reardon, *Aborted Women, Silent No More* (Chicago: Loyola University Press, 1987).

David Reardon, *Abortion Malpractice* (Denton, TX: Life Dynamics, 1993).

David Reardon, *The Jericho Plan: Breaking Down Walls Which Prevent Post-Abortion Healing* (Springfield, IL: Acorn Books, 1996).

Teri Reisser and Paul Reisser, *Help for the Post-Abortion Woman* (Zondervan Publishing House, 1989).

Vincent M. Rue, *Postabortion Trauma: Controversy, Diagnosis & Defense* (Denton, TX: Life Dynamics 1994).

Terry Selby, *The Mourning After: Help for Post-Abortion Syndrome* (Grand Rapids, MI: Baker Book House, 1990)

Anne Speckhard, *Psycho-Social Stress Following Abortion* (Kansas City, MO: Sheed and Ward, 1987).

Susan Stanford-Rue, *Will I Cry Tomorrow* (Grand Rapids, MI: Fleming H. Revell, 1990).

Thomas Strahan, *Major Articles and Books Concerning the Detrimental Effects of Abortion* (Charlottesville, VA: The Rutherford Institute, 1993).

Leo Thomas and Jan Alkire, *Healing As A Parish Ministry* (Tacoma, WA: Institute for Christian Ministries, 1994).

Holly Trimble, *Healing Post-Abortion Trauma: Help for Women Hurt by Abortion* (Stafford, VA: American Life League, 1988).

Jeannette Vought, *Post-Abortion Trauma: 9 Steps to Recovery* (Grand Rapids, MI: Zondervan Publishing House, 1991).

# INDEX

"This may be the most powerful book ever published on abortion."
—Conservative Book Club

"Quite simply indispensable. From this point on, any feminist who fails to acknowledge...abortion trauma can justly be accused of indifference to women's pain."
—Juli Loesch, Feminists for Life, *Harmony*

## ABORTED WOMEN, SILENT NO MORE
### by David C. Reardon

This is the book that is redefining the abortion debate. A comprehensive review of the aftereffects of abortion, this book documents:
- The physical aftereffects of abortion
- The psychological aftereffects of abortion
- Characteristics of high-risk abortion patients
- Post-abortion conversion and reconciliation patterns
- Complete testimonies of 20 aborted women
- A detailed national survey of 252 aborted women

It is a definitive work. Focus On The Family's *CITIZEN* magazine calls it the "standard reference book on post-abortion problems." *Booklist*, the professional librarian's buying guide, rates it "highly recommended." *Librarian's World* recommends it as "an excellent resource recommended for all libraries." Pro-life reviewers are even less restrained:

"Deeply researched . . . powerful analysis . . . thoroughly readable."
—*Fidelity*

"Moving, thoughtful, and informative."
—Rev. Richard John Neuhaus, author

"An exposé of the unscrupulous abortion merchants."
—Cal Thomas, syndicated columnist

"Cuts through platitudes . . . gives exploited women a voice."
—*National Catholic Reporter*

"Do yourself a favor and buy this book."
—Dr. Wanda Franz, President, National Right to Life

"Well-written, informative, powerful and in the end hopeful."
—*Voices in the Wilderness*

List Price: $15.95.
Available through Acorn Books. Call 1-800-BOOKLOG or 1-217-546-9522.

# THE JERICHO PLAN: BREAKING DOWN THE WALLS WHICH PREVENT POST-ABORTION HEALING

Is your church divided over the abortion issue? Is you pastor hesitant to preach about abortion? If so, your help is needed to implement *The Jericho Plan*.

*The Jericho Plan* is an indispensable tool for clergy who want to preach about abortion in a way that heals divisions in their community. By understanding the minds of women and men who have had abortions, clergy can now preach in a non-divisive way which is faithful to the full truth of (1) the sanctity of human life and (2) the bounty of God's mercy.

*The Jericho Plan* provides clergy with a working knowledge of post-abortion issues, sample sermons, testimonies, and a very specific multi-step process for creating a unifying and healing environment in their own church communities.

The specific steps of *The Jericho Plan* include the following:

1. Increasing the congregation's empathy and compassion for post-aborted women;

2. Reducing the defensiveness of those involved in abortion and stimulating their desire to be understood;

3. Educating the congregation about the many symptoms of post-abortion trauma, including its destructive effects on the lives of women, men, grandparents and siblings;

4. Explaining how and why denial and avoidance behaviors are obstacles to healing which prolong psychological and spiritual suffering;

5. Building up confidence in post-aborted women and men that they will be understood, accepted, and supported by their community;

6. Stimulating their desire for healing; and finally,

7. Encouraging reconciliation with God through acknowledgement of one's personal responsibility for the abortion(s) and inviting participation in post-abortion recovery programs.

Unless hearts are first girded with hope for healing, sermons which only condemn the sin of abortion will do nothing to help the post-aborted. On the other hand, hearing the truth of what abortion does to women and men makes *walls come down because this is what they know*. This is what they have felt and experienced. Plus, the knowledge that one's church community understands us is itself healing.

If your pastor, or other clergy in your community, have not yet read and implemented *The Jericho Plan*, order it as a gift for them today. Your support and encouragement may be all that they need. Together we can turn silent ministers into *vocal* pro-life/pro-healing activists. Our friends and family need to hear this healing message of hope from the pulpit. You can help bring it to them. Please order *The Jericho Plan* today.

List Price: $8.95
Available in March, 1996. Call 1-800-BOOKLOG or 1-217-546-9522.

Stay informed with

# THE POST-ABORTION REVIEW

"Incredibly powerful! If only more people would read it, abortion would end!"

"I'm so excited about your new publication. I've gone through an abortion myself, just two years ago. This is a much needed area of research."

"Once in a while I read something that really makes me feel great, and this just happened to me. The whole newsletter is terrific. Keep up the great work!"

"Your newsletter is *top-notch*. God bless you for your hard work."

Our readers love *The Post-Abortion Review*, and so will you.

Our quarterly publication focuses on the impact of abortion on women, men, siblings and society. In includes summaries of the latest research findings, first hand testimonies, and critiques of pro-abortion propaganda, and the latest development in post-abortion healing and the pro-woman/pro-life effort.

Here are some titles from the information-packed issues you have already missed:

- Abortion and the Feminization of Poverty
- New Study Confirms Link Between Abortion and Substance Abuse
- Rape, Incest, and Abortion: Searching Beyond the Myths
- Two Senseless Deaths: The Long Road to Recovery

*The Post-Abortion Review* is published by the Elliot Institute and edited by David Reardon, Ph.D., author of *Aborted Women, Silent No More* which the Conservative Book Club calls "the most powerful book ever published on abortion."

*The Post-Abortion Review* is available only to financial supporters of the Elliot Institute, a 501(c)3 organization which is entirely dependent on the financial gifts of its supporters. Your tax deductible gift will support our research and education efforts. Together, we can make a difference.

The recommended donation to receive *The Post-Abortion Review* is $20. As a special introductory offer, we will send you *The Post-Abortion Review* for any donation over $15. Donors of $40 or more may request a free copy of *Aborted Women, Silent No More* (a $16 value) in addition to four informative issues of *The Post-Abortion Review*.

Send your donation to:

*The Post-Abortion Review*
PO Box 7348-A
Springfield, IL 62791-7348.